THE PROMISE OF PROSPERITY

VISIONS OF THE FUTURE IN TIMOR-LESTE

THE PROMISE OF PROSPERITY

VISIONS OF THE FUTURE IN TIMOR-LESTE

EDITED BY JUDITH M. BOVENSIEPEN

Australian
National
University

PRESS

PACIFIC SERIES

ANU PRESS

Published by ANU Press
The Australian National University
Acton ACT 2601, Australia
Email: anupress@anu.edu.au

Available to download for free at press.anu.edu.au

ISBN (print): 9781760462529
ISBN (online): 9781760462536

WorldCat (print): 1076557329
WorldCat (online): 1076557499

DOI: 10.22459/PP.2018

Cover design and layout by ANU Press. Cover photograph by Judith M. Bovensiepen.

Contents

Part I: Looking at the future through the past

Part II: State visions of development

List of figures

Acronyms

AAC	*Associação dos Antigos Combatentes* [Association of Former Combatants]
AIC	Asia Investment Company
AMP	*Aliança de Maioria Parlamentar* [Parliamentary Majority Alliance]
ANP	*Autoridade Nacional do Petróleo* [National Petroleum Authority]
AVR	*Associação Veteranos dos Resistência* [Association of Resistance Veterans]
CAVR	*Comissão de Acolhimento, Verdade e Reconciliação de Timor-Leste* [Timor-Leste Commission for Reception, Truth and Reconciliation]
CMATS	Certain Maritime Arrangements in the Timor Sea (treaty)
CPT	*Companhia dos Petróleos de Timor* [Oil Company of Timor]
CSPT	*Companhia Superior dos Petróleos de Timor* [Superior Oil Company of Timor]
CUP	*Companhia Ultramarina dos Petróleos* [Overseas Petroleum Company]
DDR	disarmament, demobilisation and reintegration
FALINTIL	*Forças Armadas da Libertação Nacional de Timor-Leste* [The Armed Forces for the National Liberation of Timor-Leste]
F-FDTL	*FALINTIL - Forças de Defesa de Timor-Leste* [FALINTIL - Timor-Leste Defence Force]
Fretilin	*Frente Revolucionária de Timor-Leste Independente* [Revolutionary Front for an Independent Timor-Leste]

FVF	*Fundação dos Veteranos das FALINTIL* [FALINTIL Veterans Foundation]
GDP	gross domestic product
HIV/AIDS	Human Immunodeficiency Virus/Acquired Immune Deficiency Syndrome
LNG	Liquified Natural Gas
MU	*Ministério do Ultramar* [Ministry of Overseas Territories]
RAEOA	*Região Administrativa Especial de Oé-Cusse-Ambeno* [Special Administrative Region of Oecusse-Ambeno]
RDTL	*República Democrática de Timor-Leste* [Democratic Republico of Timor-Leste]
SEZ	special economic zones
SSGM	State Society and Governance in Melanesia
SVD	*Societas Verbi Divini* [Divine Word Missionaries]
TOC	Timor Oil Company
UDHR	Universal Declaration of Human Rights
UN	United Nations
UNDP	United Nations Development Programme
UNMISET	United Nations Mission of Support in East Timor
UNMIT	United Nations Integrated Mission in East Timor
UNTAET	United Nations Transitional Administration in East Timor
ZEESM	*Zonas Especiais de Economia Social de Mercado de Timor-Leste* [Special Economic Zones for Social Market Economy of Timor-Leste (sometimes referred to as ZEEMS)]

List of contributors

Bernardo Almeida is a development and legal professional, with a special focus on land-related legislation. His main country of work is Timor-Leste, where he lectured on property rights at the National University of East Timor and worked as a legal adviser to the Ministry of Justice for five years, specialising in the land sector. Almeida has also worked in Afghanistan, with the United Nations Development Programme and UN Habitat. Currently, he is preparing his PhD thesis at the Van Vollenhoven Institute of Leiden University Law School (Netherlands), focusing on the development of the formal land tenure system in Timor-Leste.

Susana Barnes received her doctorate in anthropology from Monash University. Her research interests include the anthropology of island Southeast Asia, customary governance and land tenure, intergenerational wellbeing and healing, kinship and exchange, colonial and postcolonial history, and international development. She is currently an Adjunct Professor in Archaeology and Anthropology at the University of Saskatchewan.

Judith M. Bovensiepen is a Senior Lecturer in Social Anthropology at the University of Kent, who has been conducting fieldwork in Timor-Leste since 2005. Her research interests span a variety of topics, including political and religious transformations, development and natural resource management, as well as colonial and postcolonial history. She is the author of *The land of gold: Post-conflict recovery and cultural revival in independent Timor-Leste*, published by Cornell University Press, Southeast Asia Program Publications in 2015. She is also the guest editor of a (2018) special issue of *The Asia Pacific Journal of Anthropology* (with Laura S. Meitzner Yoder), entitled 'Megaprojects and national development models in Timor-Leste'.

Alex Grainger's current research focuses on the political economy of land acquisition and infrastructure in maritime Southeast Asia, especially Indonesia and Timor-Leste. Originally trained as a political scientist at London School of Economics and Political Science, he has also taught politics at the School of Oriental and African Studies, University of London, and most recently has been a postdoctoral Research Associate at the University of Kent.

Douglas Kammen is an Associate Professor in the Department of Southeast Asian Studies at the National University of Singapore. His research focuses on the military, political violence and history in Timor-Leste and Indonesia, and he is the author of *Three centuries of violence in East Timor*, published by Rutgers University Press in 2015.

Andrew McWilliam is Professor of Anthropology at Western Sydney University. He has active research projects in Indonesia and Timor-Leste and has published widely on customary resource tenures, community economies and the anthropology of governance. He is the author of several monographs and edited volumes, including *Land and life in Timor-Leste: Ethnographic essays*, (co-edited with E. G. Traube) (ANU Press, 2011); and *A new era? Timor-Leste after the UN*, (co-edited with S. Ingram and L. Kent) (ANU Press, 2015).

Laura S. Meitzner Yoder is Professor of Environmental Studies and Director of the Human Needs and Global Resources Program, Wheaton College, Illinois, USA. Her work centres on the environmental history and political ecology of Southeast Asia.

Guteriano Neves is an independent policy analyst based in Dili. He earned a Master's degree in public policy from the Crawford School of Public Policy, The Australian National University. Previously, he has worked as an adviser on political economy and regional integration at the Office of the President of the Democratic Republic of Timor-Leste. He has been writing on petroleum-related issues for over 10 years and has contributed several book chapters on petroleum-related issues in Timor-Leste.

Lisa Palmer is an Associate Professor in the School of Geography at the University of Melbourne. Since 2004, she has conducted fieldwork in Timor-Leste and has published widely on the ongoing importance of its customary land and resource management practices and the influence of these processes on nation-building and development. She is author of *Water politics and spiritual ecology: Custom, environmental governance and development*, published by Routledge Explorations in Environmental Studies in 2015.

Kate Roll is a Lecturer in politics at Somerville College, Oxford University, and a Senior Research Fellow at the Saïd Business School, Oxford. She completed her doctorate in politics at Department of Politics and International Relations, Oxford, in 2014, writing her thesis on the reintegration of former guerrillas in Timor-Leste. Her work focuses on the political economy of post-conflict transitions and policymaking.

Chris Shepherd is an independent researcher affiliated with the Department of Anthropology at The Australian National University. He does research on rural development processes in Latin America and Southeast Asia. He is also interested in the history of anthropology. Shepherd has two books on East Timor: *Development and environmental politics unmasked: Authority, participation and equality in East Timor* (Routledge, 2014) and *Haunted houses and ghostly encounters: Ethnography and animism and in East Timor, 1860–1975* (Nias Press, 2019).

Kelly Silva is Associate Professor in social anthropology at Universidade de Brasília and has been carrying out fieldwork in Timor-Leste since 2002. Her main research interests relate to the transposition, subversion and invention of modernity. She has published widely on politics, kinship and religion in Timor-Leste, including a single-authored monograph *As nações desunidas. Práticas da ONU e a estruturação do Estado em Timor-Leste*, published in 2012.

Josh Trindade is a former adviser on Research and Analysis to the Office of the President of the Democratic Republic of Timor-Leste. He has been researching and working on numerous projects relating to national solidarity, youth, nationalism and Timorese culture and has been writing on ritual practice, customary renewal and East Timorese spiritual values.

Susana de Matos Viegas is a tenured Research Fellow at the Institute of Social Sciences of the University of Lisbon. Her research interests include personhood, kinship and place, identity, territorial belonging, indigenous transformations and historicity, both among the Amerindian peoples of lowland South America and, since 2012, also among the Fataluku-speaking people in Timor-Leste.

Introduction: Political and spiritual visions of the future

Judith M. Bovensiepen

This edited volume is based on a symposium that took place at the University of Kent in April 2016, entitled 'Visions of the Future in Timor-Leste'.[1] The aim was to bring together scholars from around the world who have been carrying out research in Timor-Leste for an open and critical discussion of current developments in the country. The enthusiasm and intensity of the debates we had during the symposium (fuelled by Josh Trindade's essential supply of Letefoho coffee) eventually led to the production of this edited volume. Most of the articles were written in 2016 and revised in 2017.

During the final stages of preparing this manuscript for publication, political events in Timor-Leste unravelled at a breathless pace. The 2017 elections were followed by months of uncertainty, after the minority government led by Fretilin failed to get parliament to support its program

1   The symposium was funded by a grant I received from the Economic and Social Research Council (grant no. ES/L010232/1), and by the University of Kent's School of Anthropology and Conservation Small Grant Fund; I would like to thank both institutions for their generous support.

Not all the participants were able to contribute a chapter to this volume, and I would like to thank Mica Baretto Soares, Alberto Fidalgo Castro, Rui Graça Feijó, Henri Myrttinen and Maj Nygaard-Christensen for their participation, their enriching contributions to the discussion and fantastic feedback on everyone's chapters. I would also like to thank Laura Burke, Morten Nygaard-Christensen and Prash Naidu for their participation as chairs and discussants, and for leading the final debate. Their input has been invaluable. Laura Burke deserves a special thank you for helping with organisational matters during the symposium, which enabled a smooth running of events.

I would also like to thank Emma August Welter, Emma Coupland and Beth Battrick for their excellent proofreading, and Douglas Kammen and Michael Leach for their last-minute input. Finally, I would like to express my gratitude to Viola Schreer, who has not just provided invaluable assistance during the preparation of the symposium and when putting together the manuscript, but whose own research on 'visions of the future' in Borneo has provided me with the most stimulating conversations and allowed me to clarify my own ideas and thoughts on the topic.

and 2017 budget. Parliament was dissolved and new elections were held in May 2018, which were won by the AMP (*Aliança de Maioria Parlamentar* [Parliamentary Majority Alliance]), a coalition of three parties, led by Xanana Gusmão (Leach 2018a). Even more relevant for this book were the groundbreaking developments regarding the disputed oil and gas reserves in the Timor Sea. In March 2018, Gusmão successfully negotiated what, until recently, had seemed almost impossible: a permanent maritime boundary between Australia and Timor-Leste along the median line, and a resource-sharing agreement for the as-yet-untapped Greater Sunrise oil and gas fields, estimated to be worth more than US$40 billion. The new maritime boundary places much of Greater Sunrise in East Timorese sovereign waters, which is roughly the equivalent to the country's 70 or 80 per cent revenue share (Leach 2018b).

While the contributions to this edited volume were finalised before these recent events took place, and hence do not discuss them in detail, the book, especially Part II ('State visions of development'), speaks directly to these turbulent political and economic developments. Recent events highlight the central importance of visions of the future, their relevance in informing policy decisions, and their ability to inspire unprecedented political change. Some of the chapters address the different social imaginaries that emerge from and are enabled by Timor-Leste's oil wealth, while others discuss how such grand visions are undercut and juxtaposed by localised techniques to achieve wellbeing and prosperity. At a time when important decisions about the country's future are being made, I hope that this book can act as a timely reminder that a great diversity of visions of prosperity coexist in Timor-Leste.[2]

---

2   A note on terminology: between the start of the fieldwork that formed the groundwork for this book and the time of publication, the terminology used to refer to the administrative subdivisons of Timor-Leste changed. Where previously, the divisions of the nation were referred to as 'districts', further divided into 'subdistricts', the divisions are now termed 'municipalities', divided into 'administrative posts'. The district of Oecusse-Ambeno became a 'special administrative region'. I would like to thank Josh Trindade for drawing my attention to this. For the purposes of clarity and consistency, throughout this text we refer to all administrative divisions of Timor-Leste as 'districts', which are divided into 'subdistricts'.

'From darkness into light'

In April 2015, representatives of Timor-Leste's national oil company, TimorGap, travelled to Zumalai (in the Covalima district), in order to take part in a consultation with the local population about the planned construction of a highway. The 160-kilometre multi-lane all-weather highway is part of a planned mega petroleum infrastructure development scheme along the south coast, the Tasi Mane project, to be completed by 2020. The highway is intended to connect an oil refinery to be built in Betano to a supply base in Suai and a liquefied natural gas plant in Beaço. The charismatic subdistrict administrator (*chefe de posto*), who introduced the guests from the capital city Dili, was full of enthusiasm. The highway, and the Tasi Mane project in general, he argued, would lead Timor-Leste 'out of darkness and into the light' (*husi nakukun, ba naroman*, in Tetum).

Timor-Leste is one of the most oil-dependent countries in the world; in 2017, oil and gas contributed to 91 per cent of state revenues either directly (19 per cent) or via investments in the Petroleum Fund (72 per cent) (La'o Hamutuk 2018).[3] According to the non-governmental organisation La'o Hamutuk (2018), 'only South Sudan, Libya (and [possibly] Equatorial Guinea …) are more dependent on oil and gas exports than Timor-Leste was'. From 1975 until 1999, the former Portuguese colony was occupied by the Indonesian military and was hence unable to govern its own resources. National independence, which was regained in 2002, generated promises of wealth and ambitious plans for national development. New and radical nationalist and hyper-modernist visions have emerged, which include plans for the said mega-development project to turn the entire south coast into a petroleum infrastructure, as well as plans for a special economic zone (ZEESM [*Zonas Especiais de Economia Social de Mercado de Timor-Leste*, or Special Economic Zone of Social Market Economy of Timor-Leste]) in the enclave of Oecusse that is later to be expanded to the island of Ataúro.[4] These schemes draw on familiar notions that the mobilisation of subterranean wealth may usher in radical societal transformation, while raising immense hopes about the change and development that such projects are expected to bring (see also Bovensiepen and Meitzner Yoder 2018). Yet these plans have also raised serious concerns among civil society groups about the social, economic

---

3   US$1,295 million of investments from the Petroleum Fund remained unrealised (La'o Hamutuk 2018).
4   Please note that sometimes people use the term ZEEMS not ZEESM.

3

and environmental problems such mega-development schemes could produce (see also Bovensiepen and Nygaard-Christensen 2018). There are warnings, especially from within civil society circles, that Timor-Leste will be, or already is, subject to the 'resource curse' – an economic concept that was developed to explain why countries rich in resources tend to have slow economic growth, and why they tend to suffer from severe social problems such as corruption, violence and inequality (Auty 1993; Karl 1997; Ross 2011; Sachs and Warner 2001).

This edited volume brings together a diverse range of chapters that discuss national imaginaries inspired and enabled by oil wealth alongside non-state and non-oil–related visions of prosperity and development. The aim is to analyse disparate ideas about the future in Timor-Leste, acknowledging the significance of oil in shaping these visions, while also drawing attention to ways of imagining the future that are not inspired by oil. What kind of imaginaries are enabled by profits from oil wealth? How do the aspirations and hopes people have for the future shape the ways they govern their local and national resources? How are such hopes realised in practice? And how do people deal with conflicting visions of prosperity in times to come? These are just some of the questions that are addressed in this edited volume. Questions about the future are particularly relevant in Timor-Leste, where visions of independence, freedom and self-determination have been crucial in motivating the 24-year struggle for independence from Indonesia (1975–1999). The book sets its main focus on the era since regaining independence, contrasting state-level visions of the future with various religious, customary, ethical, economic and political ways in which the expectations and conceptualisations of the future motivate action in the present. By exploring how assumptions about the future influence the ways people lead their lives in the present, the book will address broader issues of governance, sustainability, customary renewal and human–environment relations.

In Timor-Leste, different temporal spheres and rhythms are frequently described through the idioms of darkness and light. Interestingly, these metaphors are evoked in starkly contrasting, and at times contradictory, ways. In some instances, metaphors of light are evoked to express modernist and teleological understandings of progress, where the dark is associated with a 'primitive' past, and the future is one of 'civilised' lightness and development (see Shepherd, Chapter 11; cf. Sneath 2009). Indonesian occupiers, for example, represented the Portuguese colonial past as one of darkness, and the present and future of their occupation as one of progress and light (see Kammen, Chapter 1). Such modernist metaphors are challenged by narratives like that of the subdistrict administrator I mentioned earlier, who identified darkness not just with a period of Portuguese colonialism, but also included the period of the Indonesian occupation, while casting the era of national independence as one of light (see Bovensiepen, Chapter 6). The teleology of these two visions is inverted in the assumptions implicit in the concept of the 'resource curse', according to which the future is inevitably one of darkness, since oil wealth is seen to stifle progress, as well as produce conflict and authoritarian governance.

Accounts that identify light with progress are complicated by the common East Timorese identification of the world of the ancestors (and other invisible beings) with darkness, and the world of the living with light (Palmer, Chapter 10). According to this particular vision, even though the world of darkness is clearly seen as non-modern, it is not valued negatively, but is seen as a source of secret and invisible power that shapes the world of light (see also Traube 2017: 51). Metaphors of darkness and light are themes that run through several chapters of the book, and they reveal contrasting assumptions implicit in different visions of the future. These shifting ways of invoking darkness and light are expressions of East Timorese 'historicity' (Hirsch and Stewart 2005: 262) – that is, the diverse ways in which people's orientation towards the present is informed by the way they make sense of the past while anticipating a specific future (see also Viegas, Chapter 9).

The book is divided into three parts. The first part, entitled 'Looking at the future through the past', examines historical projections of the future, focusing specifically on how external powers envisaged the future of eastern Timor at various historical junctures. Whereas Kammen (Chapter 1) teases out the disparate visions of progress that motivated Portuguese, Indonesian and United Nations visions for the future and shaped the ways in which these powers legitimated their presence in the country, Grainger (Chapter 2) focuses on the history of the Timor Oil Company (1956–1968), showing how prospects for oil in Portuguese Timor were not necessarily driven by economic, but rather by political concerns.

These critical examinations of how visions of the future are entrenched with particular forms of governance provide an essential background to the second part of the book, which concentrates on 'State visions of development'. Neves (Chapter 3) tackles the issue of oil dependency head-on, illustrating how the independent state's vision of the future cannot be divorced from its rapidly growing dependence on resource rents, and discussing to what extent independent Timor-Leste has become a rentier economy. The implications of this dependency are examined in the chapters by Meitzner Yoder (Chapter 4), Almeida (Chapter 5) and Bovensiepen (Chapter 6), who analyse different social, legal and political challenges of the government's current mega-development projects in the regions of Oecusse and along the south coast of Timor-Leste. In this context, the generous veteran benefits scheme, enabled by money from the Petroleum Fund, and analysed by Roll (Chapter 7), might be interpreted as a first symptom of the resource curse becoming reality.

These national imaginaries of change find both points of connection and disconnection with the localised hopes for prosperity and wellbeing. These are examined in the third part of the book, which focuses on non-state visions of the future and the moral economies in which such visions are embedded. Trindade and Barnes (Chapter 8), Viegas (Chapter 9) and Palmer (Chapter 10) concentrate on how ordinary people living in rural and urban areas of Timor-Leste imagine a prosperous future and good life, exploring the various ritual and social practices that are employed to realise these imaginaries. Both Palmer (Chapter 10) and Shepherd (Chapter 11) illustrate how ideas about progress, development and prosperity can generate conflict and tension between local and national actors, and Shepherd shows how the need to foreground successful development paths can lead to a suppression of less desirable realities. Finally, Silva (Chapter 12) expands our understanding of local desires for life improvement by discussing the crucially important perspective of the Catholic Church, examining diverse understandings by Catholic priests of how improved moral, social and religious conduct can be achieved in the future, by transforming the relationship between culture and religion. The afterword draws out two recurring and overlapping thematic contrasts between (1) regulatory power and ritual authority, and (2) a related distinction around the luminous qualities of lightness and darkness applied to specific knowledge domains and fields of action.

The remainder of this introduction sketches out how the book contributes to several key themes. First, I will briefly discuss the concept of the 'resource curse', and outline how the book both builds on and departs from this particular understanding of how oil dependency can shape a country's future trajectory. Second, I will discuss how the book draws on anthropological approaches to the future, hope and anticipation, focusing particularly on how future visions inform political agency. And the third main theme to be discussed concerns the ways in which the spiritual significance of the environment and of natural resources influence the political relations implicated in their management. This dual emphasis on spiritual and political ecologies runs throughout the book, which draws attention to the intersection of material and immaterial desires and aspirations.

The resource curse and beyond

Speaking to political scientist Terry Karl, the Venezuelan diplomat Juan Pablo Pérez Alfonzo said: 'Ten years from now, twenty years from now, you will see. Oil will bring us ruin' (Karl 1997: xv). This was the starting point of Karl's book, *The paradox of plenty*, which was one of the key works that contributed to developing the economic theory that came to be known as the 'resource curse'. The term was developed to explain why countries rich in natural resources, instead of experiencing prosperity and rapid development, frequently suffered from economic stagnation, violent conflict, corruption and authoritarianism.

Economists first diagnosed the contradictory effects of resource wealth in the form of the 'Dutch disease' – a term that was coined to explain why productivity in some economic sectors declined (in the case of the Netherlands, manufacturing) when large quantities of natural resources were found (Gelb 1998).[5] As Reyna and Behrends (2008: 6) argue, 'Oil is a particular resource, so oil's curse is a specific instance of the Dutch Disease in petroleum-based resource booms'. Whereas Dutch disease describes how natural resource sectors experience a boom at the expense of other economic domains, the resource curse is used to describe not just economic stagnation, but also political conflict, violence and instability that arise (e.g. Klare 2002). The literature on the resource curse is vast (see, for example, Auty 1993; Karl 1997; Ross 2011; Sachs and Warner 2001; Watts 2001), and cannot be summarised here in detail. However, let me briefly outline the explanations provided for the contradictory effects of resource wealth, and the critiques of the 'resource curse' literature that are relevant to this volume.

---

5   Dutch disease results from a large influx of foreign currency, which Timor-Leste managed to avoid by adopting the US dollar as a currency (Scheiner 2015: 9).

According to Reyna and Behrends (2008), two main political science approaches have been influential in explaining the curse of oil: first, rent-seeking, and second, patrimonialism. The issue of rent-seeking was already emphasised by classical economists in the eighteenth and nineteenth century, including Adam Smith, who warned of the 'perils of natural resource rents' (ibid.: 5), because making a profit from natural resources discourages productive activity. In oil economies, rents are royalties that are accrued through oil sales and this is thought to create 'petro-states', where small elites who benefit from these super-profits are the main holders of power. In these economies, profit is made not through trade or productive enterprise, but by manipulating the political and economic environment and rent-seeking (Krueger 1974). This has concrete institutional effects, argues Karl (1997), as it incentivises entrepreneurs to manipulate state officials and intervene in the market in order to accrue oil profits. The effect is that the profits from a country's wealth are channelled to the elites, rather than to 'those engaged in less remunerative but more productive activities' (Karl 1997: 57). As Reyna and Behrends (2008: 6) argue, 'Oil ministries and companies become institutions that distribute oil rents'. Natural resource wealth, according to Karl's (1997: 15) seminal text *The Paradox of Plenty*, creates certain institutional arrangements that encourage public authorities and private interests to engage in rent-seeking; these arrangements then constrain choices later on (see also Neves, Chapter 3).

Patrimonial political structures are another explanation for the resource curse. Following Weber's (1978, cited in Reyna and Behrends 2008: 7) analysis of ancient and medieval politics, we speak of patrimonialism when a kin group treats the state as a form of private property. Neopatrimonialism is a term used to explain the challenges of development in parts of postcolonial Africa (Médard 1991, cited in Reyna and Behrends, 2008: 7), where public authorities and government roles are populated by members of the same ascendancy. Officials in public institutions use public assets in order to 'maintain or create loyalty among their rent-seeking clients, kin or friends. Oil rents are public assets' (Reyna and Behrends 2008: 7). This gives rise to an entirely new scale of corruption, bad public services and the potential for violence and conflict.

Although the concept of the resource curse has also been criticised in its own terms (see Alexeev and Conrad 2009, cited in Rogers 2015: 367), there is also a recognition that resource wealth does not have the same effect in all countries, in other words that 'sometimes economic development is hampered by the curse and sometimes it is not' (Reyna and Behrends

2008: 6). This is one of the arguments made by some anthropologists who have been critical of the 'unilinear teleology of the resource curse theory (and of "development" more generally)' (Gilberthorpe and Rajak 2016: 4). Rogers (2015: 374) argues that anthropological studies of resource economies have shown that the political, economic and environmental effects of oil production and consumption are not predictable.

However, challenging the unilinear trajectory of resource curse theorists does not mean that there are no patterns in the ways that countries are affected by oil wealth. African countries, such as Nigeria, Chad or Sudan, are often seen to be 'more cursed' than, say, Mexico, Brazil or Venezuela, while countries like Norway are widely considered to have escaped the resource curse (Reyna and Behrends 2008: 11). John Gledhill (2008) further explores this point in his comparative analysis of Mexico, Venezuela and Brazil. He argues that Latin American populist politics, which fostered a sense of resource nationalism through the imaginary of 'the people's oil' (ibid.: 59), not only put oil at the centre of popular imaginaries (ibid.: 58), but also managed to keep the privatisation of public assets at bay. This meant that Latin American business elites did not manage to be as influential as they were in, say, East Asia, since privatisers are seen 'as alienating what should be public goods in their personal interest as well as "selling the patrimony of the nation" to foreign interests' (ibid.: 59). Hence, the management of resource wealth must be understood in the specific context of Latin American history that was shaped by popular struggles for greater social justice (see also Bovensiepen, Chapter 6).

Anthropologists and other social scientists studying resource-rich countries have emphasised the vast diversity of historical trajectories. They have criticised political economy approaches that interpret the development of resource-rich countries merely in terms of the resource curse as risking to erase the cultural and historical specificity of a place. As Rogers (2015: 371) has argued:

> One of the most effective critiques of the resource curse strand of scholarship on oil in social science is that is it incapable of seeing oil as anything other than oil money, as state revenues that can be evaluated by outside experts for how prudently they are spent.

This is why, according to Gilberthorpe and Rajak (2016: 8), there is a need to 're-embed' examinations of resource wealth within the social and historical relations that enable resource extraction. Anthropologists have done this, for example, by examining how resource wealth has the ability to reconfigure state–society relations (e.g. Mitchell 2011) and how it can lead to an absent or 'hollowed out' state (Bridge 2010). They have also investigated how resource extraction can produce 'spatial enclaving' (Appel 2012; Ferguson 2005), or how companies can take on roles usually expected to be carried out by the state (Kirsch 2014; Rajak 2011). There has also been an emphasis on the performative effect of the very concept of the 'resource curse'; for example, in Weszkalnys' (2008) examination of how the expectation of disaster through possible future resource dependency has shaped the political and social reality in São Tomé and Príncipe.[6]

In Timor-Leste, arguments about the risks and dangers of resource dependency have also gained traction in recent years. Charles Scheiner (2014, 2015, 2017), who is a researcher at La'o Hamutuk, the Timor-Leste Institute for Development Monitoring and Analysis, has outlined in detail why Timor-Leste is at risk of becoming subject to the resource curse. First of all, oil is a significant part of Timor-Leste's gross domestic product (GDP) (76.4 per cent in 2013), while the non-oil GDP is largely derived from spending oil money on public administration, infrastructure and government goods and services. Between 2007 and 2013, the productive parts of the economy (agriculture and manufacturing) shrank by 13 per cent (Scheiner 2015: 2). Second, Scheiner (2014, 2015) stresses, the state budget is strongly dependent on money from oil and gas. In 2014, oil and gas provided more than 93 per cent of state revenues (either directly or through previous investment). Taxes were reduced in order to attract foreign investment, which means that the country now has 'the third lowest total tax rate in the world' (Scheiner 2015: 4).

The 2016 and 2017 state budgets maintained similar levels of dependency on income from oil and gas, exceeding spending from Timor-Leste's Petroleum Fund that would be considered to be sustainable (La'o Hamutuk 2016). This reliance on income from oil and gas, and the heavy investment in public administration and infrastructure, is problematic because other sectors of the economy, such as agriculture, are not developed in the same way. With different interest groups, such as veterans, making claims to public funds, and investment concentrated on mega infrastructure projects, Scheiner (2014) concludes that there is an urgent need to take action towards more sustainable and equitable development that would

---

6   For overview articles on the resource curse from an anthropological angle, see e.g. Gilberthorpe and Rajak (2016), Reyna and Behrends (2008) and Rogers (2015).

include the increase of food production, the cancellation of wasteful spending and of current megaprojects, as well as investing in education, nutrition and health. Scheiner (2015: 10) argues that geographic and historical factors make Timor-Leste acutely vulnerable to the negative impacts of the resource curse.

Like Scheiner, who worries Timor-Leste's future is one that will be shaped by the curse of oil, James Scambary (2015) has argued that symptoms that typically characterise the resource curse can already be identified in Timor-Leste. He states that funds from petroleum wealth have encouraged and supported the development of neopatrimonialist and clientelist political networks, connected to descent-based social organisation, affiliations from clandestine networks that were established during the resistance against Indonesian occupation, and the remnants of the command-style resistance structure. These political affiliations have been mobilised to sideline due bureaucratic process (despite the existence of Weberian sociolegal institutions), especially with regards to the construction industry. This has given rise to corruption, as well as ineffective infrastructural provisions. Like Scheiner, Scambary maintains that current megaprojects and dwindling oil and gas resources will only exacerbate existing inequalities. In this volume, Neves (Chapter 3) develops this approach by illustrating how the rent-seeking behaviour of East Timorese elites is shaping the state, its structure, policies and institutions.

This volume provides a critical comparative examination of state visions of development in Timor-Leste, including an examination of how the availability of large sums from the Petroleum Fund has given rise to plans for massive infrastructure development. We discuss the legal basis of the government's land acquisition (Almeida, Chapter 5); the ways in which government actors appropriate local and national political narratives in the planning and implementation of the ZEESM (Meitzner Yoder, Chapter 4); how ideas of sovereignty and resistance are mobilised in the implementation of the Tasi Mane project in Suai (Bovensiepen, Chapter 6); how oil money is used to fund a large-scale veteran benefits scheme (Roll, Chapter 7); and how oil rents have shaped the nature of the post-conflict state institutions in Timor-Leste (Neves, Chapter 3).

The use of oil rents for mega-development projects in Timor-Leste has been heavily criticised by civil society groups and researchers in recent years. Cryan (2015) has stressed, among others, the dangers of land loss along the south coast, where the petroleum infrastructure project is to be built. For subsistence farmers, losing land without viable alternatives could lead to impoverishment, social problems, joblessness and social tensions (see also Bovensiepen, Chapter 6). Laura Meitzner Yoder (2015) has criticised the top-down nature of the plans to turn the enclave of Oecusse into a special economic zone (ZEESM), and she interprets the plans along the lines of Scott's (1998) critique of state-initiated, utopian social engineering projects. She argues that ZEESM, with its initial plans for a hotel, an international university and an international hospital, was designed to cater for outsiders, rather than to improve local lives.

Given the critiques of the concept of the resource curse by anthropologists on the one hand, and these critical assessments of the current political and economic situation of Timor-Leste on the other, how useful is it to speak of the 'resource curse' in Timor-Leste? While Rogers (2015: 371) clearly has a point in stressing that an uncritical universal application of the concept of the resource curse risks reducing all aspects of people's lifeworlds to particular economic principles, I would not go as far as saying that there is not an element of predictability in the trajectory of oil-rich nations. Even if resource wealth creates different effects in different countries, there is still overwhelming evidence that oil wealth tends to stifle development, produce political instability, foster corruption and clientelism, and hamper the development of a diversified economy. The effects might be different in different countries, depending on their particular social context or postcolonial histories, and perhaps the longevity of their democratic institutions; however, this is not to say that the resource curse is merely an 'economic discourse' without a concrete social reality.

Nevertheless, this volume seeks to go beyond the vision of the resource curse to examine ideas about the future. It takes the political realities of Timor-Leste's increasing oil dependency and the social problems this produces seriously, while examining this particular analysis alongside a range of other ideas about how future prosperity might be achieved.

Future orientations

Until quite recently, there was relatively little interest in anthropology in studying the future. Persoon and van Est (2000: 7) have contrasted anthropologists' reluctance to study the future with the attitude of environmental scientists and planners who are, as they say, 'obsessed with the future', since 'scenarios and models based on visions of coming times are their primary analytical instruments'. However, the authors have also emphasised that the future has been implicit in many of the topics that anthropologists have examined, such as attempts to manipulate the future through divination and sacrifice or the way people anticipate the future in the maintenance of material culture (Persoon and van Est 2000: 11).

Viegas (Chapter 9) illustrates this in her examination of how a resident of Lautém mobilises the blessing of the ancestors through divination in order to generate a prosperous future for his business venture. Similarly, Trindade and Barnes (Chapter 8) describe a range of metaphors that some East Timorese evoke and practices they initiate to achieve 'good life' and prosperity for themselves and for future generations. Trindade and Barnes draw on Appadurai's (2013: 5) argument that the future is a 'cultural artefact' and his emphasis on the need to 're-orientate anthropological inquiries into understanding how humans construct their cultural futures'. This book makes a specific contribution to this approach. The first two parts of the book (in addition to Shepherd's analysis in Chapter 11) are dominated largely by an examination of more unilinear views of state planners and development practitioners who tend to think about the future in terms of progress, plans, goals and targets (see Appadurai 2013). The third part examines the role of customary practices, and ancestral and religious values in shaping ideas about the future.

Sandra Wallman, one of the first scholars who tried to develop the future as an analytical concept in anthropology, states that anthropologists have neglected the topic of the future because of their hesitation to make 'predictions' (1992: 2). Wallman's argument is that, rather than trying to predict the future, anthropologists should try to interpret how ideas about the future affect what people do in the present. She maintains that images of the future shape the present at least as much as images of the past do (ibid.: 2; cf. Hirsch and Stewart 2005: 262). 'The future has political as well as analytical consequences. Assumptions about it govern the management of resources at every level – domestic, national and global' (Wallman 1992: 3). Wallman's approach to studying 'contemporary futures' (the title of her book) allows her to bridge the widespread opposition between unilinear and non-unilinear understandings of the future. Thinking about the future as a forward-looking orientation in the present has given rise to a whole range of different anthropological studies that examine how practices of anticipating, imagining or dreaming about times to come can shape everyday life (see, for example, Cross 2014; Gardner et al. 2014; Schielke 2015; Weszkalnys 2008, 2014).

Cast as invoking 'an ever-further horizon' (Crapanzano 2004: 104) or as a way of reorienting knowledge (Miyazaki 2004), some consider 'hope' to be a key sentiment that can shape future orientations in the present. Hope for a more prosperous life in the future, a sentiment that connects different temporal spheres, is a theme that runs through this book. Viegas (Chapter 9), for example, explores how hopes for a successful business venture are fuelled by mobilising ties of the past (clandestine networks from the resistance and ancestral connections) in order to produce specific outcomes of prosperity in the future. Paying attention to the ways in which hope expresses a future orientation in the present helps us to avoid interpretations, which posit history as progressing along linear lines with a clear-cut end point (see Miyazaki 2004: 15; Crapanzano 2004: 2). Hope orients knowledge, without closing off future possibilities.

By making visible the diversity of ideas about the future that coexist in different domains of life in Timor-Leste, the chapters in this book, taken together, bring out the indeterminacy of developments in Timor-Leste and defy the idea that things will necessarily progress in a specific direction – either following the course of resource doom or bringing about an *el dorado* of resource abundance. However, as Part II of this book shows, hopes for prosperity may also reinforce teleological visions. In Chapter 11, Shepherd examines how evaluators in the development industry conceal the ambiguities of data they collect during the evaluation process (the 'shadows', as he calls them) in order to highlight the success of the institutions they evaluate. This insight has broader application. Modernist narratives of prosperity might not replace local visions entirely, but the large-scale reach of national development plans may well lead to a back-staging of alternative moral economies of reciprocity, while foregrounding capitalist notions of progress and wellbeing.

Social and economic conditions shape the ways people perceive their own political agency (Sanchez 2018), and, in Timor-Leste, people's historic participation in the resistance struggle against Indonesia and memories of this time influence how they hope for change. It is often when a situation is particularly dire (and hence seems hopeless) that hope is reinvigorated (see also Crapanzano 2004: 114; Pelkmans 2013; Schreer 2016). Part II of the book illustrates that people can be hopeful, even when they do not feel that they have control over the events that shape their livelihoods. This is visible in the responses to current megaprojects by 'affected community' members in Oecusse and Suai, who argue that 'whether they like it or not' they have to accept the government's plans and resettlement programs (see Almeida, Chapter 5; Bovensiepen, Chapter 6).

The passive hope of residents living in megaproject development zones is contrasted by the more active hope implicit in techniques to achieve prosperity through purposeful ethical action.[7] Kelly Silva, in Chapter 12, explores how ideas about future improvement are directed towards the self, by examining how Catholic priests reflect on the appropriate relationship between the Catholic faith and existing cultural practices. Trindade and Barnes (Chapter 8), as well as Viegas (Chapter 9) and Palmer (Chapter 10), describe how people tap into the ancestral realm to realise the promise of prosperity. Unlike evangelical and neoliberal ideologies that evacuate the 'near future' (Guyer 2007: 414), rural communities in Timor-Leste direct hope towards the ancestors (located, one might say, simultaneously in the distant future and in the distant past), in order to gain benefits for themselves and their relatives in the near future.

However, since the ancestors are 'considered the living dead in the present' (Persoon and van Est 2000: 11), locating prosperity in the ancestral realm does not just involve looking 'back', it also involves turning to ancestral manifestations in the inhabited environment. This is why, in many local idioms and practices, looking after the environment is a way of bringing about a prosperous future. Let us explore this in more detail in the last section.

Spiritual and political ecologies

Examining the interface between religion and ecology, Lisa Palmer (2015: 8) has argued (following Sponsel 2010) that in Timor-Leste the relationship between people and their environment might best be understood through the term 'spiritual ecologies'. This term refers to the localised ritual interpretations of the environment and the role of spiritual agents within it, allowing her to examine how such perceptions

---

7   Many studies of hope make a distinction between 'active' and 'passive' hope. According to Zigon (2009: 254), a more meaningful distinction is between hope as 'the background attitude that sustains an already accomplished social life' and 'the temporal orientation of intentional ethical action in … moments of … moral breakdown'.

affect people's engagement with the world and management of resources that surround them. Quite crucially, Palmer uses the term in the plural, showing that there are different, and at times competing, logics at play, and illustrating how there can be frictions between different ways of engaging with the environment. However, rather than merely concentrating on the different ontological assumptions implicit in competing ecologies, Palmer (2015: 21–23) strives to open her analysis up to political implications of these different spiritual ecologies, and to their ongoing transformation. In other words, she draws attention to the way customary practices can be deeply political (see also Bovensiepen 2015).

The approach outlined by Palmer is a good starting point for the diverse chapters in this edited volume, which pay attention to the ways in which future visions are embodied in people's spiritual and political relations with the environment. The significance of the land and its resources in shaping the ways in which different East Timorese groups identify and how they manage relations among themselves cannot be overstated (see, for exmple, Bovensiepen 2015; Friedberg 2007; McWilliam and Traube 2011; Palmer 2015; Palmer and de Carvalho 2008; Shepherd 2013; Trindade 2012).[8] Even though there is great regional diversity, it is possible to identify some characteristic patterns that mark the relationship between people and place in Timor-Leste. First of all, the landscape is widely considered to be inhabited not just by humans, but by a whole range of non-human or invisible beings, such as spirits and ancestors. Second, human beings are often seen as being in debt to this non-human world, and prosperity and wellbeing can only be achieved by continually repaying these obligations. Finally, the inhabited environment in Timor-Leste is closely connected to human perceptions of time. This final point is most significant for this book (especially Part III), since local visions of the future can be discerned in several cases by examining the temporality of the landscape.

First, about the cohabitation of human and non-human beings. One of the recurring themes in many of the accounts about human origins in Timor-Leste is the suggestion that the first human ancestors emerged from a specific site in the landscape, such as a stone, a mountain, a field or a piece of forest. These accounts are often secret and only revealed during specific ritual occasions. There is a subtle awareness that these accounts

---

8   The connection between place and identity is of course also an important theme in the anthropology of Eastern Indonesia (see e.g. Allerton 2009; Fox 2006; Vischer 2009).

could enter into tension with biblical accounts about human origins. These poly-ontological (one might even say totemic) accounts (which posit multiple independent origins of human groups in the landscape) are often hidden and subjugated to mono-ontological accounts (which posit a single origin of humanity, usually at a 'navel' place in Timor-Leste), which are more easily integrated into biblical narratives (cf. Scott 2007).

Places that have an ancestral connection tend to be described as sacred or potent (*lulik*, or its regional variants), and they have to be treated with respect either by being avoided or by being approached in a ritually appropriate manner only. The power of the ancestors is also visible in *lulik* houses (also referred to as customary houses – *uma lisan*), in which objects handed down from the ancestors are stored. These houses stand for entire groups of people and contain multiple smaller houses or subgroups. It is in ancestral *lulik* houses that ancestors maintain a presence that can shape the everyday lives of the people who look after these houses and their broader patrilineal or matrilineal kin group.

In addition to the ancestral presence in the landscape and in the built environment, there are other spiritual agents that inhabit the environment, such as land or water spirits. These spirits are considered to be guardians or 'custodians' (Palmer 2015: 49) of specific sites or places. They tend to appear in uninhabited places and can be seen as threatening to human beings (Bovensiepen 2009). There are accounts of other non-human beings that are considered to inhabit the environment, such as witches, wild, gnome-like beings (*dore fuik*) or kidnapper-thieves, referred to as *ninjas* or *lakahonik* in Tetum (ibid.).

Notions of debt and reciprocity are key to understanding the relationship between humans and the inhabited environment (see Bovensiepen 2015; Hicks 2004; McWilliam 2001; McWilliam et al. 2014; Palmer 2015; McWilliam and Traube 2011). *Lulik* places, such as springs, rocks, hilltops or forests, are often considered to have a life-giving quality and hence require small offerings in order to mobilise this quality. Sometimes *lulik* places are marked out with a small fence around stones and people know to avoid these sites. Several language groups in Timor-Leste have 'totem poles', whose split V-shape points into the sky, connecting humans to the spiritual universe (Trindade 2015). Rituals to produce rain, or to mobilise the life-giving quality of springs or fields, are frequently carried out at these sites. The rituals to mobilise the life-giving properties of the environment echo exchanges between life-giving and life-taking groups, where the 'wife-givers' need to be compensated through a range of different gifts by the 'wife-takers' (in patrilineal areas). There are also small rituals that involve making offerings to ancestral *lulik* places in order to gain good health, fertility and prosperity, and to attain a good and prosperous life (*tempu rai-diak*) (see Trindade and Barnes, Chapter 8; and Palmer, Chapter 10).

War, untimely deaths and social problems (such as infertility or conflict between groups or individuals) are commonly explained through a failure to compensate life-giving entities appropriately or to show due respect. Again, this can involve both human life-givers (wife-givers) or non-human life-givers (sites in the landscape). Whereas many different groups in Timor-Leste have stressed that some of their members used the powers of *lulik* land in order to fight the Indonesian occupiers, conflicts that broke out in 2006 (after independence had been regained) were frequently explained in terms of a failure to thank the subterranean powers of the land appropriately for their help. When a person suffers an untimely death, such 'red' deaths may be explained either as a witchcraft attack or in terms of an ongoing cycle of deaths that was set into motion by a murder that happened decades ago. Absence of rain, infertility of livestock or bad harvests are also frequently seen as resulting from a lack of gratefulness that is shown to the giving environment; such problems are remedied through a number of rituals in which the land is repaid and debts are resolved. Attitudes towards government officials can be structured in similar ways. In Betano, for example, a number of farmers told me that they were happy to give the land to the government, since this act would indebt the government in such a way that government officials would be obliged to repay them and look after them in the future (cf. Miyazaki 2004).

The notion of reciprocity, which is key in the way many rural East Timorese relate to their environment, is significant not just for anthropological discussions of exchange, but connects past, present and future, bringing out the 'temporality of the landscape' (Ingold 1993: 157). Past gifts need to be repaid continuously in the present, and very specific practices are anticipated in the future in response to exchanges that take place in the present moment. The landscape is a source of knowledge that informs such anticipations and imaginations. Ingold's (ibid.: 155) suggestion that meaning is 'gathered from' the landscape, not 'attached to' it, is useful for understanding this dynamic. Conspicuous sites in the landscape are often interpreted to be signs of ancestral significance, and it is through these sites in the landscape that house groups in Timor-Leste talk about their local histories by recounting the journeys of the ancestors. Narratives about the autochthonous origins of human beings are evoked to make arguments about the spiritual significance of a particular place and the descendants of these first ancestors. Such accounts can be complemented with narratives about how the original populations passed on political power to newcomers, while the autochthones maintained certain ritual responsibilities. This enabled the integration of colonial powers into narratives about ancestral origins (Traube 1986).

However, sites in the landscape are not just evidence for past events, they are also seen to contain signs that reveal something about the future. Everyone who has spent some time living in Timor-Leste probably knows multiple examples of this way of making sense of the present and the future by interpreting the lived environment. This can include the sighting of a large black bird as a sign that ominous events are near, or the suggestion that heavy rains in 1975 signified the impending occupation by Indonesia (Carolina Boldoni, pers. comm.). When water rose inside the newly built electric power plant in Betano more recently (in the Manufahi district), this was interpreted as a sign that the ancestors were unhappy with the construction work and special ritual precautions had to be taken in order to ward off disaster in the future.

The landscape is mined for signs to be interpreted, yet certain individuals are thought to be able to communicate with and even control the environment and hence are able to influence the future. These 'masters of words' (*lia-nain*) – ritual speakers – can try to change the outcome of events set in motion, and every customary house has at least one *lia-nain* to speak on its behalf. At times, government officials draw on the aura of such traditional authorities in order to present their own future visions. For example, a story often told is how Xanana Gusmão stopped the rain during a community consultation in Suai. Local residents were so impressed by his powers to 'control nature' (*manda natureza*) that they agreed to give up 1,113 hectares of land for the Tasi Mane project to the government.

In this account, the opposition between state versus non-state visions collapses as a state official is seen to draw on localised animist practices – integrating them into a national oil-fuelled vision of modern times to come. Along these lines, the three parts of this book should not be taken as entirely distinct, but as coexisting in a field of connection, friction and, at times, opposition.

References

Alexeev, M. and Conrad, R. (2009) 'The elusive curse of oil', *The Review of Economics and Statistics*, vol. 91, no. 3, pp. 586–598. doi.org/10.1162/rest. 91.3.586.

Allerton, C. (2009) 'Introduction: Spiritual landscapes of Southeast Asia', *Anthropological Forum*, vol. 19, no. 3, pp. 235–251. doi.org/10.1080/00664 670903278387.

Appadurai, A. (2013) *The future as a cultural artefact: Essays on the global condition*, London and New York: Verso.

Appel, H. C. (2012) 'Walls and white elephants: Oil extraction, responsibility, and infrastructural violence in Equatorial Guinea', *Ethnography*, vol. 13, no. 4, pp. 439–465. doi.org/10.1177/1466138111435741.

Auty, R. (1993) *Sustaining development in mineral economies: The resource curse thesis*, London: Routledge.

Bovensiepen, J. (2009) 'Landscapes of life and death in the central highlands of East Timor', in Allerton, C. (ed.) *Spiritual landscapes in Southeast Asia: Changing geographies of potency and the sacred*, Special issue of *Anthropological Forum*, vol. 19, no. 3, pp. 323–338. doi.org/10.1080/00664670903278437.

Bovensiepen, J. (2015) *The land of gold: Cultural revival and post-conflict reconstruction in independent Timor-Leste*, Ithaca, NY: Cornell University Press, Southeast Asia Program Publications (SEAP).

Bovensiepen, J. and Meitzner Yoder, L. (2018) 'Introduction: Political dynamics and social effects of megaproject development' in Bovensiepen, J. and Meitzner Yoder, L. (guest eds), *Megaprojects and national development models in Timor-Leste*, Special issue of *The Asia Pacific Journal of Anthropology* , vol. 19, no. 3, pp. 381–394. doi.org/10.1080/14442213.2018.1513553.

Bovensiepen, J. and Nygaard-Christensen, M. (2018) 'Petroleum planning as state building in Timor-Leste' in Bovensiepen, J. and Meitzner Yoder, L. (guest eds), *Megaprojects and national development models in Timor-Leste*, Special issue of *The Asia Pacific Journal of Anthropology*, vol. 19, no. 3, pp. 412–431. doi.org/10.1080/14442213.2018.1513553.

Bridge, G. (2010) 'Geographies of peak oil: The other carbon problem', *Geoforum*, vol. 41, no. 4, pp. 523–530. doi.org/10.1016/j.geoforum.2010.06.002.

Crapanzano, V. (2004) *Imaginative horizons: An essay in literary-philosophical anthropology*, Chicago and London: The University of Chicago Press.

Cross, J. (2014) *Dream zones: Anticipating capitalism and development in India*, London: Pluto Press.

Cryan, M. (2015) *Dispossession and impoverishment in Timor-Leste: Potential impacts of the Suai supply base*, SSGM Discussion Paper 2015/15, Canberra: State, Society & Governance in Melanesia, The Australian National University. Available at: ssgm.bellschool.anu.edu.au/sites/default/files/publications/attachments/2016-07/dp_2015_15-cryan.pdf.

Ferguson, J. (2005) 'Seeing like an oil company: space, security, and global capital in neoliberal Africa', *American Anthropologist*, vol. 107, no. 3, pp. 377–382. doi.org/10.1525/aa.2005.107.3.377.

Fox, J. J. (2006 [1997]) *Poetic power of place: Comparative perspectives on Austronesian ideas of locality*, Canberra: ANU E Press.

Friedberg, C. (2007) 'Par-delà visible' [Beyond the visible], *Natures Sciences Sociétés*, vol. 15, no. 2, pp. 167–176. doi.org/10.1051/nss:2007044.

Gardner, K., Ahmed, Z., Rana, M. M. and Bashar, F. (2014) 'Field of dreams: imagining development and un-development at a gas field in Sylhet', *South Asia Multidisciplinary Academic Journal*, vol. 9. Available at: samaj.revues.org/3741.

Gelb, A. (1988) *Oil windfalls: Blessing or curse?* Oxford: Oxford University Press.

Gilberthorpe, E. and Rajak, D. (2016) 'The anthropology of extraction: Critical perspectives on the resource curse', *The Journal of Development Studies*, vol. 53, no. 2, pp. 1–19. doi.org/10.1080/00220388.2016.1160064.

Gledhill, J. (2008) '"The people's oil": Nationalism, globalization, and the possibility of another country in Brazil, Mexico, and Venezuela', *Focaal: Journal of Global and Historical Anthropology*, vol. 52, pp. 57–74. doi.org/10.3167/fcl.2008.520104.

Guyer, J. I. (2007) 'Prophecy and the near future: Thoughts on macroeconomic, evangelical, and punctuated time', *American Ethnologist*, vol. 34, no. 3, pp. 409–421. doi.org/10.1525/ae.2007.34.3.409.

Hicks, D. (2004 [1976]) *Tetum ghosts and kin: Fertility and gender in East Timor*, 2nd ed., Long Grove: Waveland.

Hirsch, E. and Stewart, C. (2005) 'Introduction: Ethnographies of historicity', *History and Anthropology*, vol. 16, no. 3, pp. 61–274. doi.org/10.1080/02757200500219289.

Ingold, T. (1993) 'The temporality of the landscape', *World Archaeology*, vol. 25, no. 2, pp. 152–174. doi.org/10.1080/00438243.1993.9980235.

Karl, T. L. (1997) *The paradox of plenty: Oil booms and petro-states*, Berkeley and Los Angeles: University of California Press.

Kirsch, S. (2014) *Mining capitalism: The relationship between corporations and their critics*, Berkeley: Stanford University.

Klare, M. (2002) *Resource wars*, New York: Owl Books.

Krueger, A. O. (1974) 'The political economy of the rent-seeking society', *The American Economic Review*, vol. 64, no. 3, pp. 291–303.

La'o Hamutuk (2016) 'General state budget 2016', La'o Hamutuk – Timor-Leste Institute for Development Monitoring and Analysis. Available at: www.laohamutuk.org/econ/OGE16/15OGE16.htm.

La'o Hamutuk (2018) 'Rights and sustainability in Timor-Leste's development', La'o Hamutuk – Timor-Leste Institute for Development Monitoring and Analysis. Available at: www.laohamutuk.org/econ/briefing/RightSustainCurrentEn.pps [accessed 23 June 2018].

Leach, M. (2018a) 'In Timor-Leste, a vote for certainty', *Inside Story*, 14 May 2018. Available at: insidestory.org.au/in-timor-leste-a-vote-for-certainty/ [accessed 29 May 2018].

Leach, M. (2018b) 'A bold move has turned into a breakthrough for the young nation', *Inside Story*, 8 March. Available at: insidestory.org.au/timor-leste-architect-of-its-own-sunrise/ [accessed 29 May 2018].

McWilliam, A. (2001) 'Prospects for the sacred grove: Valuing *lulic* forests on Timor', *The Asia Pacific Journal of Anthropology*, vol. 2, no. 2, pp. 89–113. doi.org/10.1080/14442210110001706125.

McWilliam, A., Palmer, L. and Shepherd, C. (2014) 'Lulik encounters and cultural frictions in East Timor: Past and present', *The Australian Journal of Anthropology*, vol. 25, no. 3, pp. 304–320. doi.org/10.1111/taja.12101.

McWilliam, A. and Traube, E. G. (2011) *Land and life in Timor-Leste: Ethnographic essays*, Canberra: ANU E Press. doi.org/10.22459/LLTL.12.2011.

Médard, J.-F. (1991) *Etats d'Afrique Noir: Formation, mécanismes et crise* [States of Black Africa: Formation, mechanisms, crises], Paris: Karthala.

Meitzner Yoder, L. S. (2015) 'The development eraser: fantastical schemes, aspirational distractions and high modern mega-events in the Oecusse enclave, Timor-Leste', *Journal of Political Ecology*, vol. 22, pp. 299–321. doi.org/10.2458/v22i1.21110.

Mitchell, T. (2011) *Carbon democracy: Political power in the age of oil*, London and New York: Verso Books.

Miyazaki, H. (2004) *The method of hope: Anthropology, philosophy and Fijian knowledge*, Stanford: Stanford University Press.

Palmer, L. (2015) *Water politics and spiritual ecology: Custom, environmental governance and development*, London: Routledge. doi.org/10.4324/97813 15883250.

Palmer, L. and de Carvalho, D. do A. (2008) 'Nation building and resource management: The politics of "Nature" in Timor-Leste', *Geoforum*, vol. 39, issue 3, pp. 1321–1332. doi.org/10.1016/j.geoforum.2007.09.007.

Pelkmans, M. (2013) 'Ruins of hope in a Kyrgyz post-industrial wasteland', *Anthropology Today*, vol. 29, no. 5, pp. 17–21. doi.org/10.1111/1467-8322. 12060.

Persoon, G. A. and van Est, D. M. (2000) 'The study of the future in anthropology in relation to the sustainability debate', *Focaal: Journal of Global and Historical Anthropology*, vol. 35, pp. 7–28.

Rajak, D. (2011) *In good company. An anatomy of corporate social responsibility*, Palo Alto, CA: Stanford University Press.

Reyna, S. and Behrends, A. (2008) 'The crazy curse and crude domination: Toward an anthropology of oil', *Focaal: Journal of Global and Historical Anthropology*, vol. 52, pp. 3–17. doi.org/10.3167/fcl.2008.520101.

Rogers, D. (2015) 'Oil and anthropology', *Annual Review of Anthropology*, vol. 44, pp. 365–380. doi.org/10.1146/annurev-anthro-102214-014136.

Ross, M. L. (2011) 'The political economy of the resource curse', *World Politics*, vol. 51, pp. 297–322. doi.org/10.1017/S0043887100008200.

Sachs, J. D. and Warner, A. M. (2001) 'The curse of natural resources', *European Economic Review*, vol. 45, no. 4, pp. 827–838. doi.org/10.1016/S0014-2921 (01)00125-8.

Sanchez, A. (2018) 'Relative precarity: Decline, hope and the politics of work', in Hann, C. and Parry, J. P. (eds) *Industrial labour on the margins of capitalism: Precarity, class and the neoliberal subject*, London: Berghahn, pp. 297–331.

Scambary, J. (2015) 'In search of white elephants: The political economy of resource income expenditure in East Timor', *Critical Asian Studies*, vol. 47, no. 2, pp. 283–308. doi.org/10.1080/14672715.2015.1041281.

Scheiner, C. (2014) *The 'resource curse' in Timor-Leste*, SSGM In Brief 2014/29, Canberra: State, Society & Governance in Melanesia, The Australian National University. Available at: www.laohamutuk.org/econ/exor/IB-2014-29-Scheiner.pdf.

Scheiner, C. (2015) 'Can the Petroleum Fund exorcise the resource curse from Timor-Leste?', La'o Hamutuk – Timor-Leste Institute for Development Monitoring and Analysis. Available at: www.laohamutuk.org/econ/exor/ScheinerFundExorciseCurseJun2015en.pdf [accessed 23 June 2018].

Scheiner, C. (2017) 'As Bayu-Undan dries up: Challenges and opportunities', Paper presented at the 2017 Conference of the Timor-Leste Studies Association. Available at: www.laohamutuk.org/misc/TLSA2017/Scheiner TLSABayuDriesEn.pdf [accessed 23 June 2018].

Schielke, S. (2015) *Egypt in the future tense: Hope, frustration, and ambivalence before and after 2011*, Bloomington: Indiana University Press.

Schreer, V. (2016) 'Longing for prosperity in Indonesian Borneo', unpublished PhD thesis, University of Kent.

Scott, J. (1998) *Seeing like a state: How certain schemes to improve the human condition have failed*, New Haven: Yale University Press.

Scott, M. W. (2007) *The severed snake: Matrilineages, making place, and a Melanesian Christianity in Southeast Solomon Islands*, Durham: Carolina Academic Press.

Shepherd, C. J. (2013) *Development and environmental politics unmasked: Authority, participation and equity in East Timor*, London: Routledge.

Sneath, D. (2009) 'Reading the signs by Lenin's light: Development, divination and metonymic fields in Mongolia', *Ethnos*, vol. 74, no. 1, pp. 72–90. doi.org/10.1080/00141840902751204.

Sponsel, L. (2010) 'Religion and environment: Exploring spiritual ecology', *Religion and Society: Advances in Research,* vol. 1, pp. 131–145. doi.org/10.3167/arrs.2010.010109.

Traube, E. G. (1986) *Cosmology and social life: Ritual exchange among the Mambai of East Timor*, Chicago and London: University of Chicago Press.

Traube, E. G. (2017) 'Returning to origins in an expanding world: Customary ritual in independent Timor Leste', in Viegas, S. M. and Feijó, R. G. (eds) *Transformations in independent Timor-Leste: Dynamics of social and cultural cohabitations*, London: Routledge, pp. 45–60.

Trindade, J. (2012) 'Lulik: Valor Fundamental Timoroan Nian [Lulik: the core of Timorese values]', in M. Leach, N.C. Mendes, A.B. da Silva, B. Boughton & A. da Costa Ximenes (eds) *Peskiza foun kona ba / Novas investigações sobre / New Research on / Penelitian Baru mengenai Timor-Leste*, Hawthorn: Swinburne University Press, pp. 16–29.

Trindade, J. (2015) 'Relational dimensions within Timor-Leste customary society', in Smith, S., Mendes, N. C., da Silva, A. B., Ximenes, A. da Costa and Fernandes, C. (eds) *Timor-Leste: The local, the regional, the global. Proceedings from the Timor-Leste Studies Association Conference*, Melbourne: Swinburne University Press, pp. 85–89.

Vischer, M. P. (2009) *Precedence: Social differentiation in the Austronesian world*, Canberra: ANU E Press. doi.org/10.22459/P.05.2009.

Wallman, S. (1992) 'Introduction: Contemporary futures', in Wallman, S. (ed.) *Contemporary futures: Perspectives from social anthropology*, London and New York: Routledge, pp. 1–20. doi.org/10.1017/CBO9780511611858.001.

Watts, M. (2001) 'Petro-violence: Community, extraction, and political ecology of a mythic commodity', in Peluso, N. L. and Watts, M. (eds) *Violent environments*, Ithaca and London: Cornell University Press, pp. 189–212.

Weber, M. ([1925] 1978) *Economy and society: An outline of interpretive sociology*, Roth, G. and Wittich, C. (eds), Berkeley: University of California Press.

Weszkalnys, G. (2008) 'Hope & oil: Expectations in São Tomé e Príncipe', *Review of African Political Economy*, vol. 35, no. 117, pp. 473–482. doi.org/10.1080/03056240802411156.

Weszkalnys, G. (2014) 'Anticipating oil: The temporal politics of a disaster yet to come', *The Sociological Review*, vol. 62, S1, pp. 211–235. doi.org/10.1111/1467-954X.12130.

Zigon, J. (2009) 'Hope dies last: Two aspects of hope in contemporary Moscow', *Anthropological Theory*, vol. 9, no. 3, pp. 253–271. doi.org/10.1177/1463499609346986.

Part I: Looking at the future through the past

1

Progress and propaganda in Timor-Leste: Visions of the future in comparative historical perspective

Douglas Kammen

It has now been just over a decade since revenue from Timor-Leste's offshore oil and gas fields began to accrue in the country's Petroleum Fund, making possible vast increases in the size of the annual state budget and public spending. This set the stage for the Government of Timor-Leste to formulate plans for a number of megaprojects intended to fuel rapid economic development. Politicians and planners envisioned a petroleum corridor on the south coast: a pipeline and divided highway would connect a supply base, a petrochemical refinery, a liquefied natural gas plant, and entirely new planned cities. In Dili, plans were drawn up for a glittering new port facility in Tibar and a complete overhaul of the national airport, including a runway spanning the sandy Comoro River. Down the coast, new legislation designated Oecusse to be a Special Zone for Social Market Economy, where a proposed US$4.1 billion in combined state and private investment promised to create a shining new city with high-tech manufacturing, a major port facility and a world-class university. Public debate in Timor-Leste over these major infrastructure projects quickly became polarised, with critics charging that the allocation of funds for these projects was naïve, reckless and irrational, while government officials countered with accusations that critics were misinformed about project aims, alarmist about outcomes and unsympathetic to the legitimate desires of the Timorese people.

It is perhaps useful to recall that visions of future prosperity are by no means new in Timor. In the sixteenth and seventeenth centuries, representatives of the Portuguese crown speculated about the presence of vast mineral wealth in Timor. In the mid-nineteenth century, Portuguese governors discussed the possibility of replicating the cultivation system in Dutch-held Java to produce an agricultural bounty. But neither minerals nor agriculture ever produced a surplus for the state, and the colony entered the twentieth century little changed from the 'most miserable place' encountered by Alfred Russel Wallace (1869: 197) in 1861 and the 'abominable town' Joseph Conrad (2004: 57) visited two decades later.

This chapter examines visions of Timor-Leste's future that emerged following three critical junctures in the territory's modern history – the 1910 republican revolution in Lisbon, the 1975 Indonesian invasion and subsequent annexation of Portuguese Timor, and the 1999 referendum on independence. Following each of these upheavals, external powers formulated and propagated ideas about the fundamental transformation of Timor and Timorese peoples. Comparative sketches of these visions and the means proposed for their achievement may provide a helpful framework for thinking about contemporary dreams of the future in Timor-Leste.

The fountain of life

The 1910 republican revolution in Portugal marked a critical juncture in the history of the overseas empire. The new Republican Government promised administrative reforms that would drag Portugal and its empire into the twentieth century. In the colonies, however, the message promoted by Portuguese officials, many of whom were staunch monarchists, was one of benevolent metropolitan tutelage and colonial loyalty. This attitude is nicely illustrated by the first public speech by beleaguered Governor Soveral Martins in Dili on 5 November 1910:

> A telegraph brought us news of the revolt that gave Portugal a new regime, satisfying the ideals of its people and its future by opening a new era of happiness and progress for all. Loyal daughter, the colony of Timor could not but follow, with loving enthusiasm, the mother country, embracing the new ideas with faith in the future and enduring belief in a greater Portugal. (Quoted in Oliveira 2004: 43)

This was wishful thinking, for a year later the imminent threat posed by republicanism to indigenous rulers (both *regulos* and village-level *chefes de suco*) and a sharp increase in the head tax contributed to a major armed uprising in Manufahi district that was taken up in a number of other regions in the colony.

If the republican revolution of 1910 marked a key juncture, the content of the new Portuguese vision of progress only took shape gradually over the following two decades. It was driven by the interplay of two related processes, the origins of which were fundamentally external to Timor. The first of these was the adoption of emerging international techniques of governmentality. In 1905, Portugal promoted new international standards for the modern census in its colonial possessions. This quickly – and for the first time – led to the collection of systematic population data and facilitated far more efficient taxation. The second dynamic involved passage of a series of juridical codes and legislative decrees regarding the place of the indigenous colonial peoples within the Portuguese nation. Borrowing practices most fully developed in the Netherlands Indies and French colonies in Africa, the Portuguese state began to codify customary practices into a separate legal system applicable to the indigenous population (Clarence-Smith 1985: 138; Newitt 1995: 449). These initiatives marked the transition from the old 'monarchical' model, in which Timorese villagers were viewed as subjects of particular kingdoms-cum-administrative units, to a new imperial model in which indigeneity implied non-civilised status.

Racially based colonial legislation was counterbalanced by new promises of inclusion. Laws on assimilation were passed in the African colonies in the late 1910s and replicated in Timor via Decree-Law 7/151 of 1920. This opened up the possibility for cultural advancement – from non-civilised to civilised status – for those who could demonstrate that they were Christian, spoke Portuguese, were monogamous and dressed in European fashion. Colony-specific legislation was superseded in 1930 by promulgation of an empire-wide organic statute. Article 2 of this statute stated:

> It belongs to the organic character of the Portuguese nation to fulfil its historical mission: to possess and colonise overseas territories and to civilise the indigenous population living in them, thus at the same time exerting the moral influence to which it is committed by the Padroado over the Orient. (Ferreira 1964: 54)

The new slogan was 'One state, one race, one faith, and one civilisation'. This was, in short, a radically new vision of a future in which, at least in theory, Timorese could and would become Portuguese.

The reality, however, was that the requirements for assimilation were so stringent, and bureaucratic intransigence so strong, that assimilated status lay out of reach for the vast majority of the indigenous population. In Angola and Mozambique, less than 1 per cent of the population achieved this status in the 1930s. The number of *assimilados* in Portuguese Timor was not reported in the colonial censuses in the 1930s, but we can be certain that only a tiny number of individuals successfully achieved this status. One reason, no doubt, was that the arrival of significant numbers of deportees (political *deportados* as well as social *degredados*) had a profound impact on status consciousness and the hardening of a 'colour' bar in the colony. In 1951, the only year for which figures are available for Portuguese Timor (Felgas 1956: 329), there were only 1,541 Timorese who had formally been granted *assimilado* status.[1]

While Prime Minister António Salazar's *Estado Novo* (New State) promoted the idea of Portugal's historic mission to civilise colonial subjects and promised that these subjects (or, more accurately, their descendants) could become full members of the Portuguese nation, few officials believed that this would in fact ever occur. This scepticism was stated most directly by Colonial Minister Armindo Monteiro in 1935:

> We do not believe that a rapid passage from their African superstitions to our civilization is possible. For us to have arrived where we are presently, hundreds of generations before us fought, suffered and learned, minute by minute, the intimate secrets in the fountain of life. It is impossible for them [African and other colonial subjects] to traverse this distance of centuries in a single jump. (Quoted in Isaacman and Isaacman 1983: 40)

In official circles in the Ministry of Overseas Affairs and in Portuguese Timor, the view was that the indigenous population was indolent – accepting of bare subsistence livelihoods – and economically wasteful, squandering livestock and other hard-earned resources for ceremonial rather than economically 'rational' purposes. These officials thus concluded

---

1   In response to the colonial wars in Africa, the legal statute specifying the categories 'civilised' and 'non-civilised' was abolished in 1961 and all colonial subjects were henceforth declared Portuguese citizens (Ferreira 1964: 37).

that the solution lay in forcing Timorese peoples to engage in productive labour, which would not only monetise the economy and benefit state coffers, but also transform the indigenous population.

The three strands of the Portuguese vision – Timorese loyalty, civilisational advancement and the need for the disciplinary power of labour – were put on display in the colonial exposition held in the town of Liquiçá in 1937. The exposition was accompanied by an extensive photographic effort between 1937 and 1940 to document the indigenous population and the civilising mission of the colonial state (Salema 2003). These photographs are divided into three sections. The first section, titled 'Types of Secondary Characteristics and Languages' (*Tipos característicos segundo as línguas*), includes hundreds of photographs of bare-chested couples – some old, some young – as well as images of loyal traditional rulers, individuals in traditional dress and Catholicised women. The second section, called 'Forms of Work' (*Formas de Trabalho*), is divided into subsections that cover industry, commerce, rural arts, indigenous crafts and musical instruments. A final section, titled 'Civilising and Colonising Actions' (*Acção Civilisadora e Colonisadora*), documents public works projects, sanitation, schools, missionary activities and administration.

The irony, of course, is that in their two centuries in Timor, the Portuguese themselves had demonstrated little in the way of initiative, discipline or labour. In the 1930s, roads beyond Dili were still dirt tracks, buildings were dilapidated and there was virtually no manufacturing. The official promise of progress and the 'vision' of future civilisation and citizenship was, in short, a chimera. Furthermore, it was a product of the African colonies that, once imported into Portuguese Timor, became more fantasy than reality. Nonetheless, insofar as the vision was premised on a comparison of the Portuguese and the indigenous subjects, it included the Timorese people as not only objects, but also willing agents of their own subjugation.

Mother's lap

General Suharto's New Order regime justified the invasion of Portuguese Timor in December 1975 on the grounds that it was acting to prevent the emergence of a communist foothold in island Southeast Asia and end what they presented as a 'civil war' between the nascent East Timorese political parties. At a deeper historical level, Indonesia rationalised the invasion and integration of East Timor in terms of two assumptions about the past. The first of these is the wholly anachronistic notion that East Timor was part of great pre-colonial empires, to which Indonesian ideologues traced the country's political ancestry. A book produced by the Department of Foreign Affairs (1977: 12), for example, claimed: 'Prior to the arrival of the colonial powers, Timor had been part of the Sriwijaya and Mojopahit Empires, which successfully dominated much of Southeast Asia for nearly one thousand years'. In this view, European colonialism had separated the East Timorese people (conceived in the singular!) from 'mother' Indonesia (also anachronistically conceived as pre-existing). The introduction to a 1976 volume on the 'integration' of East Timor into the Republic of Indonesia could thus explain:

> Although the actual physical struggle only lasted for two years, the aspiration for 'integration with Indonesia' that motivated that struggle had, in truth, existed and remained alive in the hearts of the East Timorese people for decades, even centuries. It was already there before the people of East Timor were separated from the big family of the Indonesian people by the colonial powers. Indeed, the aspiration for 'integration with Indonesia' repeatedly motivated rebellions by the East Timorese people against the colonial government in 19 [sic], 1945–1949, and 1959. (Soekanto 1976: preface)

The second feature of Indonesian thinking was that over the course of four centuries, Portugal had failed to develop the territory of East Timor and its people. Drawing on imagery prominent in early Indonesian nationalist discourse, Indonesian officials depicted 'the period of Portuguese rule as an age of "darkness" and the Indonesian period as an age of "light"' (Mubyarto et al. 1991: 59). To support this charge, Indonesian statements and publications drew on a wide array of statistical data that the Salazar–Caetano dictatorship had made pains to present to the world in English. This line of thinking is nicely captured in a 1984 article in the Jakarta press:

> The Indonesian government placed great emphasis on Portuguese neglect of its colony, citing figures on how few roads had been paved, limited access to education, and the lack of basic health care outside of Dili. After 400 years of colonial rule, Portugal had only established 70 primary schools; after 8 years Indonesia had established 436 primary schools. (Achiruddin 1984)

Based on these twin assumptions about the past, Indonesian propaganda presented integration as a family reunion. In his 1976 independence day address, president Suharto directly addressed the East Timorese people, stating, 'We view you as siblings now returning to the big family of the Indonesian nation'. Government publications repeatedly celebrated East Timor's 'return to the lap of mother Indonesia' (Soekanto 1976). Certain of the righteousness of their cause, Indonesian officials believed the invasion of Portuguese Timor would be easy, integration of the territory into the Republic of Indonesia uncontested, and the benefits of returning to 'mother Indonesia' welcomed by the population.

If in 1976 Indonesian officials could present choreographed voting as self-determination and waving crowds as evidence of popular approval, then what vision did Indonesian officials have of the future of the new province? Certainly not the ensuing two years of frontal warfare, the devastating loss of life from hunger and disease in 'relocation camps', or the heroic survival of Fretilin's armed resistance. Rather, the official Indonesian vision of East Timor's future replicated New Order propaganda at home: technical know-how and political order would lead to development (*pembangunan*), which could be measured in quantifiable units of roads and bridges, irrigation canals and rice production, schools and clinics, and even the ever-growing number of letters posted and increasing attendance at the movie theatre. On 16 October 1984, the *Jakarta Post* reflected official views of the province's tremendous potential:

> Vast resources remain untapped in E. Timor. If all funds and forces in East Timor are mobilised by dint of advanced technology, the province is bound to become the richest in the country.

This vision is depicted most clearly in the volumes published on a near-annual basis by the Indonesian Government. These show, in sequential order, images of the backward state of the territory resulting from four centuries of Portuguese rule, development projects funded by Jakarta and officials in modern uniforms happily encouraging development. Most importantly, the movement from backwardness to modernity is captured in an array of bar charts, pie charts, graphs and tables – proof of good intentions and the promise of future prosperity.

Most international observers rightly dismissed the official Indonesian claims about physical and social development in the territory as propaganda intended to gloss over the terrible abuses of fundamental rights perpetrated in the territory. The most revealing critique of official reporting came not from abroad, but rather from a research team, headed by Professor Mubyarto, from the Gadjah Mada University Research Centre for Village and Regional Development. The research was commissioned by the Bank of Indonesia to assess why the East Timorese people were 'uncooperative, apathetic and constantly suspicious' (Mubyarto et al. 1991: viii). The researchers visited the territory in 1981, the year of the massive 'fence of legs' operation against the armed resistance, with a second visit in 1989, just as the province was being 'opened' to Indonesian as well as foreign visitors. The final report includes chapters on 'Village Life and Economy', 'Social, Political and Religious Systems', 'Problems of Village Development', and a concluding chapter entitled 'Towards Peace and Prosperity'. The report concluded:

> [while] the integration of East Timor into Indonesia has brought physical progress to the island, it has not yet been able to eliminate social, economic and political problems resulting from an integration process which has cost too many human lives. (ibid.: 4)

The authors identified two fundamental reasons for East Timorese alienation: first, military rule over the territory; and second, the exclusion of key groups, including 'traditional community leaders', educated youth and the Catholic Church, from meaningful participation in social and political life. Together, military rule and political exclusion resulted in 'trauma' and 'culture shock'. The report, in short, laid bare the hollowness of Indonesian propaganda about progress.

The English-language version of the Gadjah Mada report was made public in December 1991, a mere month after the tragic Santa Cruz massacre, in which more than 250 young Timorese were massacred during a peaceful funeral procession. This marked a turning point not only in the resistance, but also in how Indonesian officials discussed the East Timor problem, with increasingly open laments about how 'ungrateful' the East Timorese were for the development that Indonesia had brought.

The answer to the East Timor problem, of course, was more propaganda. While the Indonesian military scrambled to respond to the Santa Cruz massacre, still others sought to shore up the vision of a happy and prosperous future in Indonesia's 27th province. Although produced before Santa Cruz, one of the most telling propaganda efforts was the 1990 film *Langit Kembali Biru*, about two young lovers wrenched apart by the political conflict of 1975. Manuel is a Fretilin supporter who becomes a guerrilla fighter in the jungle, while his girlfriend Ana (played by Governor Carrascalão's daughter Sonia) is from a family that supported integration with Indonesia. In the end, of course, love wins out: Manuel comes over to the pro-integration side and marries Ana to live happily ever after in the bounty bestowed by Indonesia's Father of Development.

A world of norms

In some respects, the United Nations' vision for East Timor was set from the time of the 5 May 1999 agreement to hold a referendum on the future of the territory. This did not mean that the long-suffering people of East Timor (which later became Timor-Leste) would immediately join the ranks of independent nation-states (the personal views of UN officials notwithstanding), but rather that basic human rights would be protected and the right to self-determination upheld. The violence perpetrated by the Indonesian military and the pro-Jakarta militias in the lead-up to the referendum served to harden this basic perspective on the UN role. When the results of the referendum were announced on 4 September 1999, the Indonesian military and its proxies engaged in a final spree of violence, destroying infrastructure and forcing hundreds of thousands of East Timorese into Indonesian West Timor, presumably to demonstrate that the population was 'voting with their feet' in favour of Indonesia.

It was under these circumstances that the UN scrambled to assemble an international peacekeeping force, eventually led by Australia, and, with a decision by the Indonesian Parliament to formally relinquish the territory, to establish the United Nations Transitional Administration in East Timor (UNTAET). The UNTAET mandate was clear: 'to provide security and maintain law and order throughout the territory', 'to establish an effective administration' leading to independence, and 'to establish the conditions for sustainable development' (UNSC 1999: 2–3).

Over the next decade there was a huge outpouring of writing on Timor-Leste, of which more than half focused squarely on the UN. The two themes that dominate this literature are peace-building and state-building, often conflated. Many of the most reflective authors exhibit a sense of unease, as if something that doesn't quite fit – or perhaps fits too well (Chopra 2002; Hasegawa 2013). For this reason, it is perhaps useful to step back from these concerns, which were more about the UN itself than Timor-Leste, by considering the distinction between state-building, which involves extending the geographic reach of the state and the strength of its institutions, and regime-building, which involves setting the rules within which political activity is conducted and teaching these rules to the population at large. Viewed in these terms, we can better untangle the mandates of the various UN missions that operated in Timor-Leste between 1999 and 2010, as well as how the highest-ranking UN officials viewed their task and the future of the territory.

The UNTAET mission, which was in charge of the political transition from 1999 until the restoration of independence in May 2002, quickly came face to face with the problem of reconciling the aims set out in its mandate. UNTAET, Anthony Goldstone (2004: 85) writes, placed 'a premium on achieving short-term humanitarian and administrative goals at the expense of longer-term capacity- and institution-building goals'. Alongside this, the United Nations Development Programme (UNDP) and the World Bank were both intent on introducing a variety of neoliberal norms and practices. The precise details of these arrangements are beyond the concern of this article. For present purposes, the key point is that greater stress was placed on establishing the rules of the game than on building institutions that would support the new state when independence was restored in May 2002.

The United Nations Mission of Support in East Timor (UNMISET), mandated to provide assistance to the new government of Timor-Leste, was in place from 2002 until 2005. UNMISET retained responsibility for security for several years, leading a number of commentators to question just how sovereign the new state of Timor-Leste really was. Beyond this technical consideration, and clearly with an eye to allowing the new government to stand on its own two feet, UNMISET adopted a largely consensual approach, seeking to provide assistance without dictating the formation of institutions or their mandates. Meanwhile, UN emphasis shifted even more strongly in the direction of promoting international norms. This meant encouraging the Government of Timor-Leste to become signatory to a variety of human rights instruments, encouraging Timor-Leste to meet standards for female political representation, and assisting Timor-Leste in joining international associations. In short, the UN vision was one in which Timor-Leste was entering a world of rules.

The 2006 crisis may have shaken international faith in the work of the previous six years, but it also resulted in a rapid decision to deploy yet another mission, the United Nations Integrated Mission in East Timor (UNMIT), which, in the context of the political conflict, publicly declared its neutrality while clearly siding with Xanana Gusmão and the emerging coalition of parties that came to power in 2007 as the Parliamentary Majority Alliance. From the time of the crisis until the mission's end in 2012, the emphasis shifted back to peacekeeping, with support for state-building largely hived off to UNDP and the World Bank.

What, then, was the UN vision of Timor-Leste's future? The short answer to this question is that the UN and its international development partners were eager to usher Timor-Leste into a world of international norms, including a host of human rights instruments, procedural democracy and a market economy with a limited role for the state. A more detailed answer emerges when we consider the three-volume set of photographs released by UNMIT (2012) at the end of the mission. *Securing the Future* highlights the role of UN peacekeepers and police in maintaining security and training the new East Timorese security forces. A second volume, entitled *Building on Stability*, highlights the role of the UN in state-building, with photographs showing national elections, the installation of elected officials, judges and the Dili District Court, and meetings of the East Timor Development Partners. The third volume, *Capturing the Moment*, contains stereotypical photographs of beautiful scenery, smiling children, agriculture and fishing, traditional crafts and plenty of elders.

The effect of these volumes was to announce that – under the guidance of the UN, its missions and international development partners – a democratically elected government, a competent civil service and committed security forces would govern 'traditional' Timorese in rural settings, and urban youth receiving modern education would still proudly dress in colourful double-woven cloth for special occasions. The UN vision was, to borrow a phrase from Rudolf Mrazek (2002), one of itself as 'engineers of happy land'.

Conclusion

This brief history of the future in Timor-Leste has several useful implications for how we think about the present schemes being peddled for a petroleum corridor, planned cities, a special economic zone with high-tech manufacturing, and prestige projects planned for Dili.

First is the matter of state power. The three cases described here all involve visions formulated by foreign powers. By contrast, the current visions are, for the first time in Timor's history, being formulated by East Timorese themselves. However, I think it is misleading to view the 1999–2002 period as marking a complete rupture and to focus on the 'indigenous' sources of these visions. Rather, we should see the administrations of Xanana Gusmão (2007–2015) and his handpicked successor Rui Maria de Araújo (2015–2017) first and foremost as holders of state power, and as such we should ask in which ways they may be replicating perspectives and assumptions characteristic of prior regimes.

The second point concerns the core aspects of the visions promoted by each state. From the time of the 1910 republican revolution, the centrepiece of the Portuguese vision was one of civilisational progress made possible through *labour*. Following the 1975 invasion, the core of the Indonesian vision was one of quantifiable development achieved thanks to the *know-how* of the 'wise parent'. After the 1999 referendum, the core vision of the UN missions was one of a new member state adopting and adhering to *international best practices and norms*, while any deviation would risk damnation in the ranks of failed states. The long-term vision peddled by the current government of Timor-Leste is most closely akin to the Indonesian fetishisation of development, though with one critical difference: whereas the Indonesian vision of physical and economic development always subordinated Timor to a larger, more advanced 'centre', the current vision involves leapfrogging, in the short span of two decades, from a subsistence economy to one characterised by high-tech production and advanced services. Yet the current schemes say very little about labour, know-how or comparative lessons. Instead, current visions of progress are premised solely on capital derived from finite oil and gas reserves.

Third, what place was there for Timorese in each of these visions? In the 1920s and '30s, the indigenous were not simply objects of colonial rule; instead, like Shakespeare's Caliban, they were to be subjects of their own subjugation. The colonial regime would provide the structures for long-term cultural assimilation, but it was up to individuals to make themselves something other than *indigena*s. During the Indonesian occupation, by contrast, East Timorese were to be the passive recipients of development, but at least they were acknowledged as part of the equation. For all its good intentions, the UN vision of international norms, democratic institutions and security is a vision of increasingly pronounced differentiation between elected officials and those recruited to work in the modern state, on the one hand, and grateful peasants living traditional lives, on the other. When we turn to visual representations of the petroleum corridor, the Special Zone for Social Market Economy (ZEESM [*Zonas Especiais de Economia Social de Mercado de Timor-Leste*]) in Oecusse, and other proposed megaprojects, however, one cannot help but notice that Timorese are almost entirely absent. These are plans without people – or at least without recognisably East Timorese people.

References

Achiruddin (1984) 'Bagaimana Timor Timur pada Saat Tinggal Landas?' [How is East Timor at the time of take-off?], Merdeka, 4 June.

Chopra, J. (2002) 'Building state failure in East Timor', *Development and Change*, vol. 33, no. 5, pp. 979–1000. doi.org/10.1111/1467-7660.t01-1-00257.

Clarence-Smith, W. G. (1985) *The third Portuguese empire, 1825–1975: A study in economic imperialism*, Manchester: Manchester University Press.

Conrad, J. (2004 [1915]) *Victory: An island tale*, Oxford and New York: Oxford University Press.

Department of Foreign Affairs (Republic of Indonesia) (1977) *Decolonization in East Timor*, Jakarta: Department of Information, Republic of Indonesia.

Felgas, H. (1956) *Timor Português*, Lisbon: Agência Geral do Ultramar.

Ferreira, E. da Sousa (1964) *Portuguese colonialism in Africa: The end of an era*, Paris: The UNESCO Press.

Goldstone, A. (2004) 'UNTAET with hindsight: The peculiarities of politics in an incomplete state', *Global Governance*, vol. 10, pp. 83–98.

Hasegawa, S. (2013) *Primordial leadership: Peacebuilding and national ownership in Timor-Leste*, Tokyo: United Nations University Press.

Isaacman, A. and Isaacman, B. (1983) *Mozambique: From colonialism to revolution, 1900–1982*, Boulder: Westview Press.

Mrazek, R. (2002) *Engineers of happy land: Technology and nationalism in a colony*, Princeton and Oxford: Princeton University Press.

Mubyarto, L. S., Hudiyanto, E. D., Setiawati, I. and Mawarni, A. (1991) *East Timor: The impact of integration*, Australia: Gadjah Mada University Research Centre for Village and Regional Development and Indonesian Resources and Information Program.

Newitt, M. (1995) *A history of Mozambique*, Bloomington and Indianapolis: Indiana University Press.

Oliveira, L. de (2004) *Timor na história de Portugal* [Timor in the History of Portugal], vol. 3, Lisbon: Agência Geral do Ultramar.

Salema, I. (2003) 'Álbum de Timor colonial dos annos 30 doado a Xanana Gusmão' [Colonial Timor's album of the 30s donated to Xanana Gusmão], *Publico*, 5 March.

Soekanto (ed.) (1976) *Integrasi: Kebulatan Tekad Rakyat Timor Timur* [Integration: Determination of the people of East Timor], Jakarta: Yayasan Parikesit.

UNMIT (United Nations Mission in East Timor) (2012) *Building on stability, securing the future, and capturing the momentum*, 3 vols, UNMIT.

UNSC (United Nations Security Council) (1999) Resolution 1272, 25 October 1999. Available at: dag.un.org/bitstream/handle/11176/36759/S_RES_1272%281999%29-EN.pdf.

Wallace, A.R. (1869) *The Malay Archipelago: The land of the orang-utan, and the bird of paradise*, New York: Harper and Brothers Publisher.

2

The Timor Oil Company's network, 1956–1968: Interacting internal and external infrastructures

Alex Grainger

Since the signing of the bilateral Certain Maritime Arrangements in the Timor Sea (CMATS) Treaty with Australia in January 2006, US$16.69 billion has been deposited in Timor-Leste's sovereign wealth fund (Petroleum Fund of Timor-Leste 2017), albeit with production declining by a half over a period of 10 years since 2006 (EIA 2015). Since the introduction of an 'Infrastructure Fund' in the state budget in 2011, an average of 44 per cent has been budgeted on infrastructure expenditures, with a high-water mark of 53 per cent of expenditures in 2012 (La'o Hamutuk 2018). This includes the planned development of refining and processing facilities on the country's south coast, envisaged as receiving supplies of oil and gas both from the Timor Sea and onshore deposits, as well as attracting oil and gas for refining from other countries. It is therefore unsurprising that the state, and many citizens, view the very heart of Timor-Leste's development as located in the Timor Sea, the site of oil and gas exploration since the mid-1960s. However, state and oil company interest in onshore areas predated offshore exploration.

This chapter examines onshore oil exploration on the south coast of Portuguese Timor in the mid-twentieth century. It begins by showing how perceptions of oil wealth on the part of foreign oil companies and governments shaped the fate of the territory before World War Two. This formative period was characterised by Britain and Australia acting in concert to build transport and trade infrastructure in rivalry with Japan. These foreign governments tried to build networks that would lead to control over the territory's rumoured deposits of oil. This resulted in a concession being secured on behalf of the British and Australian governments by private investors in the face of Japanese competition. Section two describes how, following World War Two, the same (prewar) driving forces initiated exploration again in the 1950s. Their company, the Timor Oil Company (TOC),[1] used labour and material technologies to carry out exploration to try to overcome the challenges of bad weather and navigating Portuguese Timor's terrain. Section three shows that the TOC faced another formidable obstacle in the 1960s when investors reacted to perceived threats to Portuguese Timor by Indonesia by withdrawing investment. Drawing on archival documents, this last section offers an alternative to an existing explanation for the TOC's slowdown, which has previously explained it in terms of either a 1959 rebellion in Viqueque district, or a lack of aptitude in oil exploration on the part of TOC's foreign workforce.

Part of this alternative explanation highlights the role of financial infrastructure in determining TOC's operations from outside the territory. Financial capital was significant in the case of TOC (as in the oil industry more generally) because without investors' large initial outlays, sometimes before oil is even discovered, exploration could not proceed. In other words, the mere promise of the discovery of oil was often enough to stimulate investment, which could in turn lead to interest from larger oil companies thus providing much-needed capital and knowledge, the kind of arrangement eventually solicited by TOC after 1962 (cf. Adelman 1993: 22; Penrose 1965: 253). That the TOC continued to operate after a drop in the level of investment is due to the political connections of its founders with the Portuguese state. While these individuals' political networks trumped market considerations such as a desultory share price (cf. Sabin 2004), the chapter highlights the effects – before 1962 and after – of a different kind of political network of the TOC, consisting of financial infrastructure, labour (in particular the colonial authorities' role in organising access to a pool of workers) and materials used on the ground. The mutual dependence of these infrastructural elements

---

1   The Timor Oil Company was known in official documents as Timor Oil Ltd. I have referred to it throughout the text as the Timor Oil Company.

demonstrate, I argue, the inherent strengths and vulnerabilities of the TOC's network to both domestic (internal) and international (external) events. It is the impact of these international events that are examined in the next section.

External networks: The establishment of the TOC

In 1956, when the public announcement was made that the operator of the sole concession to exploit Timor's oil had been awarded to an Australian company, the TOC, the origins of TOC's concession were already two decades old. This section traces its antecedents back to the 1930s, when it was secured by British government capital. This period saw a struggle between the British and Japanese governments in their attempts to incorporate Portuguese Timor into rival international transport and trade networks to facilitate access to the territory and its oil.

The Japanese state assumed powers to acquire petroleum from overseas in 1934 (Samuels 1987: 177). Throughout the 1930s, the military required access to natural resources in pursuit of its strategic adjectives, which made securing Southeast Asia's petroleum a priority. By the beginning of the 1940s, the military was refining half of Japan's oil (ibid.: 226). By the same period, the extension of submarine and overland telegram and telephone cables supplied a crucial layer of infrastructure that opened up an expanding empire in Asia (Yang 2011: 285–292). Creating this network also involved attempts to connect Japan to Portuguese Timor via an air route that passed through Micronesia (Peattie 1988: 149–150).

Between 1935 and 1940, Britain and Australia became increasingly concerned about Japan's investment in Portuguese Timor's natural resources, including agricultural concessions. Japanese agricultural concessions became largely viewed in the Foreign Office as a 'stepping stone' to the territory's oil concession.[2] Thus, while the British Government initially declined an oil concession that had lapsed in 1935 because studies had indicated that the prospect of commercial quantities of oil being found was doubtful, this view changed in 1939.[3] It was suggested that Belgian financier Serge Wittouck, of the Allied Mining Corporation, the person

---

2   National Archives of the United Kingdom, FO 371/23541/179, Selby: 2 November 1939.
3   National Archives of the United Kingdom, DO 35/372/6, Say: 28 August 1935.

then holding the concession that the government had earlier declined, was acting with the Japanese Government.[4] An Australian, Alec Dodson, made the suggestion by implanting this rumour at the Foreign Office in London at the right moment. Despite Wittouck expressing willingness to sell Asia Investment Company (AIC) for £70,000, some British civil servants thought it credible that Wittouck could be conspiring with the Japanese Government, just six weeks after Britain's declaration of war against Germany in September 1939.[5]

The Japanese Government was also attempting to gain access to Portuguese Timor by opening up air routes to the capital, Dili, in 1940 (Goto 2003: 28). The British, Australian and Netherlands East Indies governments proposed two alternative routes. One connected to an existing route between Macassar and Koepang in Dutch Timor, and another from Australia via Dili, Jakarta and Singapore.[6] These were clear moves to increase access to and influence over the territory. In a countermove, the Japanese military attempted to restrict access via land routes into the Portuguese territory of Macao (the surrounding Chinese territory was, after 1937, under Japanese control) by deliberately blockading transport routes and massing troops on Macao's borders 'to bring pressure on [the] Portuguese over [the] Timor [oil] concession'.[7]

Faced with continuing Japanese pressure on the Portuguese Government in Macao, Lisbon and Timor itself to cede control of the territory's oil concession, in August 1940 the British Government took the decision to supply £12,000 to finance the *Companhia Ultramarina dos Petróleos* (CUP [Overseas Petroleum Company]) to acquire the concession from AIC.[8] Details of the CUP and other concessions can be seen in Table 2.1. The CUP was owned by private investors, including Alec Dodson and his Portuguese business partner, engineer Jose Veiga Lima, and the sum paid for the concession was well below the figure sought by AIC.[9] However, the concession was essentially rendered invalid as the Japanese military occupied Portuguese Timor in February 1942 in response to an Australian and Dutch presence that violated the terms of Portuguese neutrality.

---

4   National Archives of the United Kingdom, FO 371/23541/179, 'Oil Concessions': 26 May 1939.
5   National Archives of the United Kingdom, FO 371/23541/179, Fitzmaurice: 13 March 1939.
6   National Archives of the United Kingdom, FO 371/23541/179, Fitzmaurice: 14 April 1939.
7   National Archives of the United Kingdom, FO 371/24705/7, 'Oil Concessions …': 19 March 1940.
8   National Archives of the United Kingdom, FO 371/24705/7, Henniker-Major: 8 March 1940.
9   National Archives of Australia, NAA A989, 1944/735/854, 'Handbook …': 1944.

After World War Two, during which extreme hardship resulted in many deaths among the Timorese population, Portuguese Timor was initially virtually isolated due to a lack of transport links. Air routes and communications with Australia, which had been considered vital to resist Japanese encroachment on the territory before 1942, were not negotiated throughout 1946.[10] It has been suggested that this situation may have resulted from the Australian Government continuing to begrudge Portuguese wartime neutrality (Gunn 1988: 11).[11] Before the end of the war, Australia proposed that its forces should occupy Portuguese Timor. This proposal was rejected by the British as it would antagonise Portugal, and it had agreed to ensure the sovereignty of Portuguese colonies after the war in exchange for use of the Azores as an allied military base in 1943 (Farram 2017: 25).

In terms of road travel, government officials travelled between Portuguese and Dutch Timor (Farram 2017: 45) – the latter unilaterally declared to be part of the Indonesian Republic's territory in 1945. In 1950, the Portuguese authorities reported that Indonesian troops, having marched to the border area, threatened to invade and expel Europeans from Portuguese Timor.[12] Throughout the 1950s and early 1960s, Indonesia's leaders displayed increasing antipathy towards colonial regimes, including Portuguese Timor; this relationship will be examined in more detail below.

Table 2.1. Concessions awarded for exploration in Portuguese Timor, 1926–1966.

Concession holder	Extent	Financial backer	Concession period
John Arthur Staughton	Full territory of Portuguese Timor	Private Australian capital	1926–1936
Allied Mining Corporation (AMC) (Serge Wittouck)	Full territory (until 1939, then west until 1940)	Asia Investment Company (AIC)	1936–1940

---

10   National Archives of the United Kingdom, DO 35/1721, 'Australian hopes for early negotiations with Portugal ...', Stirling: 13 August 1946.
11   Farram notes several contradictions in this Australian position, chiefly that the Australian–Dutch invasion of Dili in late 1941 'may have been responsible for the subsequent Japanese invasion' (Farram 2017: 25).
12   Arquivo Nacional Torre do Tombo, ANTT UL-10A, Ruas: 15 June 1949.

Concession holder	Extent	Financial backer	Concession period
Oil Concessions and Oil Search Ltd; Oil Search pulled out in March 1939 because did not agree to terms of contract, especially that a Portuguese company must be created for the purpose of holding concession	Eastern half, separated at meridian long. 125°50'E, so to incorporate presumed oil deposits of Pualaca	Private Australian capital	November 1939
Companhia Ultramarina dos Petróleos (CUP [Overseas Petroleum Company]); awarded initially to AIC, then transferred to CUP with compensation	Eastern half	Anglo-Iranian, Standard-Vacuum and Royal Dutch Shell, which acquire shares in CUP to the value of £12,000; supplied by British Government	August 1940–1949
Companhia Superior de Petróleos de Timor (CSPT [Superior Oil Company of Timor])	Western half	Jointly-held Portuguese Government and private investment	1948 – May 1949
Companhia dos Petróleos de Timor (CPT [Oil Company of Timor]); operator: Timor Oil Company, a separate entity from CUP	Full territory	One-third owned by Portuguese Government (CPT); two-thirds private capital (TOC), including Australian subsidiaries of 'major' oil companies	1956–1966 (initial three-year contract signed October 1954)

Source: Author's summary.

In 1949, the CUP concession was abandoned; *Companhia Superior de Petróleos de Timor* (CSPT [Superior Oil Company of Timor]), founded in 1948, was briefly awarded a concession before being dissolved in 1949. Consistent with prewar studies by the 'majors', a study by the French Institute of Petroleum in 1953 found no hard evidence of commercially exploitable oil deposits.[13] Thus, when Dodson and Veiga Lima again approached the Portuguese Government in 1954 to restart their monopoly concession with a new company, the *Companhia dos Petróleos de Timor* (CPT [Oil Company of Timor]), the *Ministerio do Ultramar* (MU [Ministry of Overseas Territories]), believed it had 'nothing to lose', awarding a three-year concession to Dodson and Lima's CPT beginning

---

13 Arquivo Nacional Torre do Tombo, ANTT UL-10A cx. 766, pt. 17, Arquivo Salazar, *'Pesquisa de Petróleo* [oil search]': 3 December 1956; see also Teixeira (1956).

October 1954.[14] But the MU's belief that it had nothing to lose did not exclude from its calculations the possibility that, on the contrary, something could be gained from awarding CPT the concession. Moreover, Dodson and Veiga Lima's prewar connections with the Portuguese state had played an important role in ensuring that the CPT would be in a prime position to be awarded the concession.

I have attempted to show the complex historical and international relations that provide the background to the 10-year monopoly exploration licence to search for oil in Portuguese Timor granted to TOC in 1956. The TOC became the contractor and operator of a concession awarded by CPT. This 1950s concession was a 'revival' of the earlier CUP arrangement between two of the TOC's directors and the Portuguese Government, which dated back to the 1930s. The initial concession was provided not because there were indications of economically viable oil and gas resources, but because, in the run-up to World War Two, the British and Australian governments were concerned about Japan's increasing power in the region.

Whereas this section has provided an overview of how international or 'external' networks sowed the seeds for the development of Portuguese Timor's oil infrastructure, the next section will examine the development of internal transport and communications infrastructure, which was designed to expand TOC's network in the areas of oil and gas exploration.

Internal networks: Materials and labour

In common with other prospecting ventures, TOC relied on the promise of the discovery of oil and the ability to communicate within and between internal (terrestrial) and external (non-terrestrial) networks. For these reasons, TOC spent much of its first five years, from 1956 to 1961, trying to establish and consolidate infrastructure, such as roads, ports, airstrips and radio transmitters, to ensure a smooth transmission of information, people and materials. Foreign oil explorers, mainly from Australia, but also from the US and Europe, also relied on communications beyond this immediate network, primarily in order to relay reports of work and raise further revenue for costly exploration. Transmitting information within this

---

14   Arquivo Nacional Torre do Tombo, ANTT UL-10A cx. 766, pt. 17, Arquivo Salazar, '*Pesquisa de Petróleo* [oil search]': 3 December 1956.

network relied on foreigners with specialised engineering and geological knowledge. These individuals, regularly brought to the territory to observe and sent out to report on their work activities and on furlough, relied on a continuous supply of local labour, secured through the intercession of the Portuguese and their subordinate indigenous authorities.

Between 1956 and 1961, TOC established several bases on the south coast: in Viqueque, Beaço, Suai, Uatulari and Aliambata (see Figure 2.1). The choice of locations was based on geological studies that had identified a formation in the east: the 'Viqueque basin'. Such studies had initially been guided by the existence of surface oil seepages, which locals used in oil lamps and government officials used in their vehicles. These seepages had also been found in the central mountainous areas, but because they were difficult to access, the south coast plains became default sites of exploration.[15] However, the extended wet season on the south coast made it difficult to traverse the road network from north to south or along the lateral south coast road.[16]

When the rains made land impassable, the prospectors dealt with this setback by using the coast as an entry point for all heavy equipment transported on barges from Darwin in Northern Australia. For example, a drilling rig was transported to a landing site on the coast near Viqueque town in 1956. A test hole named Ossulari 1, to the south of Viqueque town, became inaccessible due to blocked tubes, produced no oil or gas, and eventually had to be abandoned in August 1959. Another hole, Ossulari 1A, to which the company built a road from Ossulari 1 in 1957, was of interest, but needed to be researched more thoroughly. Furthermore, the company had already identified new sites in Suai; one such site was indicated by the Nabuc and Ranuc rivers, which bookended an anticline believed to have 'acted as a trap', to where oil migrated from 'deeper parts of the basin'.[17] This explained seepages found at the surface in Suai, near Matai and Ranuc.[18]

---

15   Arquivo Histórico Ultramarino, AHU IGM MU 50,2, 'Relatorio [Report] … Annex': 22 June 1960.
16   Arquivo Histórico Ultramarino, AHU IGM MU 50,2, 'Relatorio [Report] … Annex': 22 June 1960.
17   Arquivo Histórico Ultramarino, AHU IGM MU 50,2, 'Relatorio [Report] … Annex': 22 June 1960.
18   Arquivo Histórico Ultramarino, AHU IGM MU 50,2, 'Relatorio [Report] … Annex': 31 December 1960. TOC was advised by an American consultant, Schneeberger, to turn their attentions to Aliambata, farther to the east, which did not have Ossulari's thick clay or Viqueque's problems of accessibility.

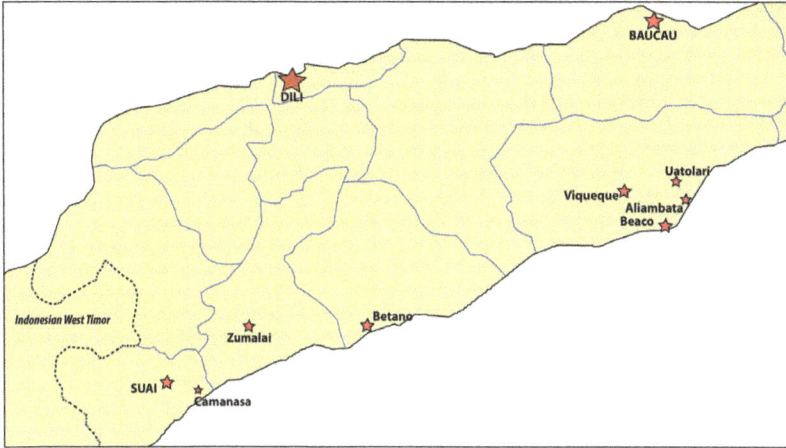

Figure 2.1. TOC exploration sites on the south coast of Portuguese Timor, 1956–1966.

Source: Author's summary.

The results in Suai were from a combination of surveys by TOC's US partner company, Tradewinds, which had first entered into a contract with TOC in November 1958. Tradewinds' research suggested that Matai had good prospects, and the company fitfully began a migration of equipment and people to the west.[19] Under a revised agreement of May 1960, Tradewinds was allowed to choose the drilling site and would receive half of any revenue in Suai, as long as they transported the drilling rig 100 miles from Ossulari to Matai. After delays due to heavy rainfall in May 1960, a barge was used to transport the equipment to Beaço, from where it would be transported by land to Suai at the end of August 1960. On the second and final journey, the barge began to flood and had to land at Luca, to the east of Suai. All the equipment was damaged due to immersion in salt water. An improvised 'beach head' was constructed at Suai, and from there a road was built that also forked towards Zumalai.

By early December, three months after the first consignment was shipped to Beaço, all the equipment had arrived at Suai, with drilling beginning at the new site, Matai 1, early in the same month. Company employees stayed at the house of the *chefe de suco* (head of the village), Lopes, at Camanasa, which was also used as a geologist's office. By the end of

---

19   Arquivo Histórico Ultramarino, AHU IGM MU 50,2, '*Relatorio* [Report] … Annex': 22 June 1960. These results were derived from core drilling, geological surveys and gravimetric surveys by Tradewinds.

1960, TOC had installed three radio transmitters at Beaço, Suai and on a landing barge, and were using six Land Rover vehicles to travel between Viqueque and Suai in the dry season and to transport mail between Suai and Baucau. A chartered Dove aircraft travelled regularly between Suai and Viqueque, and was also used to transport foreign personnel from Suai to Baucau, Dili and Darwin. A British geologist, Michael Audley-Charles, was commissioned to carry out a full geological survey of the territory utilising aerial maps, test drilling and micropaleontology, with samples from the latter process sent to London to determine their geological age. Furthermore, gravity measurements were taken through 380 gravimeter stations that had been established in the 1950s with the support of the state (Botelho 1978).

Labour was also an important component of the network since, without it, exploration could not take place. As noted above, this labour was sourced by the colonial authorities in the locales where TOC worked. TOC was the only enterprise operating in Viqueque in the 1950s that was, at least in theory, semi-autonomous from the state. Its workers earned wages with which colonial taxes could be paid. The exact wages that TOC paid are not known, but adult males in general on whom the head tax[20] was levied were usually unable to pay it and were, therefore, compelled to discharge their obligations by working on state projects. 'Free' labour was also employed on state projects. As we will see in the next section, however, by working for TOC, workers were not necessarily free of the colonial state's oversight.

This section has shown that TOC's activities relied on consolidating its existing sites, expanding to new sites and pushing exploration to ever-greater depths, as part of the 'task of eliminating less promising sites first'.[21] Each of these movements, downwards and outwards, had the potential to be compromised by Portuguese Timor's terrain or climatic conditions, especially seasonal precipitation. While these factors posed serious difficulties for the network, I have tried to show that it was also facilitated by people – the local labour force that, along with materials and equipment, comprised the network's terrestrial elements. The next section

20 The '*imposto indígena*' or indigenous tax. By the 1960s a head tax called the '*imposto domiciliario*' (household tax) replaced the *imposto indígena*, but was still calculated per head.
21 Arquivo Histórico Ultramarino, AHU IGM MU 50,2, '*Relatorio* [Report] … Annex': 22 June 1960.

examines how this internal terrestrial infrastructure interacted with an external financial infrastructure demonstrating how far these elements worked in concert.

Financial infrastructure: International short-circuiting

While labour and transportation and communication equipment supported exploration in Portuguese Timor, the network was also dependent on financial capital from non-territorial sources, outside Portuguese Timor, which had the potential to compromise its operations. Below, I will address the relationship between those financial elements and a decrease in exploration activities during the 1960s.

The period of TOC's move west between 1959 and 1960 coincided with the only known rebellion in the final 30 years of Portuguese rule – in Viqueque in 1959 – with which TOC had at least an indirect connection. As explained by Janet Gunter (2007: 30), the instigators of the abortive rebellion were angry at the corrupt practices of the acting head of Uatulari subdistrict who, they alleged, had taken a majority of wages intended for TOC workers at an exploration site in Aliambata. Despite initial protests, the labourers were forced to continue working for TOC without payment. This grievance – combined with other corrupt practices, encouragement from Indonesians exiled in Portuguese Timor who had been involved in the Permesta rebellion[22] and disaffected elements in Dili – culminated in a rebellion, hastily begun in June 1959 and quashed equally promptly by the authorities.

George Aditjondro has argued that this rebellion subsequently caused a 'lull' in TOC's activities between 1959 and 1968 (Aditjondro 1998: 10). It is true that there was a general slowdown in TOC activities in 1962; however, Carvalho, the Portuguese Government's 'delegate' who reported on TOC activities, attributed this to the Indonesian military landings on West Irian (also known as West New Guinea and today called West Papua), a reference to which is made below. As he wrote:

---

22 The rebellion started on the Indonesian island of Sulawesi in 1957 and became a wider secessionist movement involving Sumatra, before finally ending in 1961.

[T]he effects of the geopolitical situation with Indonesia were felt with great acuity, with its ambitions on New Guinea [creating] reflex effects on companies that expend their capital in that area … [The slowing of work] must be, naturally, the result of *the retreat of capital, afraid of the consequences of Indonesian actions.*[23]

Other circumstances Carvalho reported support the argument that 'the retreat of capital' slowed TOC's work. First, TOC continued drilling at the Viqueque sites, abandoning the dry Ossulari 1 borehole some two months after the rebellion had been put down. Second, Carvalho's reports neither mention the 1959 rebellion nor why TOC's base in Uatulari – the centre of the rebellion, which was staffed by six 'natives' and no foreigners in 1957 – was not mentioned again after this date. It is of course possible that, in addition to Tradewinds' advice to drill in Suai, the rebellion helped to dissuade oil explorers from further activity in the area. But without more evidence such inferences are difficult to sustain. Third, as seen above, 1960 marked the year in which TOC began to concentrate its operations in Suai. In early 1961, Carvalho reported that the Matai 1 borehole had an 'auspicious' emission of oil and gas, giving a sense of 'euphoria' to TOC's explorers.[24] Fourth, TOC deployed labour in different sites according to the opportunities that it perceived for finding oil. It can be seen from Figure 2.2 that in the first quarter of 1961, more indigenous labour was employed in Suai than in Beaço. However, this situation was reversed by the end of the year, probably because of a failure to make further significant discoveries in the Matai area. Therefore, geological and logistical reasons, and external events, rather than the Viqueque rebellion, may explain why TOC's work experienced a slowdown, especially since this occurred more than two years after the rebellion had taken place.

A brief outline of external events related to what was known as West Irian can throw light on how they impacted TOC's operations, including the particular way in which investment decreased, consequently weakening exploration efforts (Aden 1988: 17–242; Nasution 1964: 27).[25] In 1957, the United Nations voted against Indonesia and in favour of continuing Dutch 'stewardship' of West Irian, and agreed upon at Indonesian

---

23 Arquivo Histórico Ultramarino, AHU IGM MU 50,2, '*Informação* [Information] no. 31': 12 May 1962.
24 Arquivo Histórico Ultramarino, AHU IGM MU 50,2, '*Relatório* [Report] No. 24': 12 March 1961.
25 Nasution, the Indonesian Minister of Defence and Security in the period of the West Irian takeover in 1962, claimed that Indonesian proclamations about 'liberating' West Irian had also paralysed European mining operations in the territory.

independence for an indeterminate period of time. The Indonesian Government, having failed three times to force negotiations with the Dutch through a United Nations vote, had in the same period suspended parliamentary democracy and embarked on a path of 'Guided Democracy' under the leadership of president Soekarno. In 1957, it nationalised Dutch property and severed its diplomatic relations with the Netherlands.

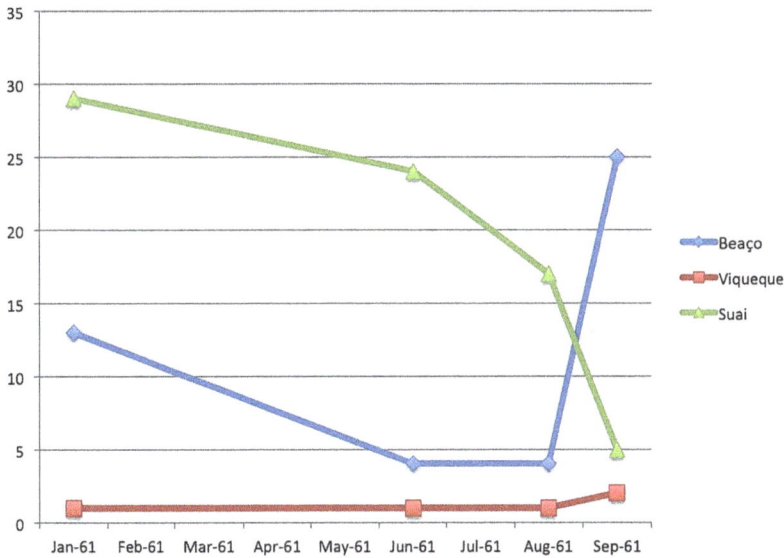

Figure 2.2. Indigenous labour at three TOC sites during 1961.
Source: Arquivo Histórico Ultramarino, AHU Reports 23-27, 1961. Suai figures include labourers employed by Tradewinds.

In the same period, Japan had been converting its domestic energy sources from coal to oil and had also reached an agreement on war reparations with Indonesia, smoothing the way for greater trade between the two countries (Nishihara 1976: 117–122). At this time, Japanese custom for Indonesian products and bestowals of aid amounted to 10 per cent of Indonesia's national budget, in effect obviating the need to rely heavily on western aid. Subsequently, the Japanese market for Indonesian oil precipitated a weakening of the power of three British and US 'major' oil companies that operated an oil oligopoly (Shell, Stanvac and Caltex) by providing an alternative outlet for Indonesian oil.[26]

---

26   These companies threatened to withdraw if their new contracts were not ratified by the Indonesian parliament within 60 days, raising the prospect that the Indonesian Government would seize their assets.

In the four years that followed, Soekarno pursued a policy of 'retaking' West Irian, enlisting Chaerul Saleh – a relatively radical politician from the generation of Indonesian leaders that led the country to independence – as Minister of Basic Industries and Mining in 1959 (Aden 1988: 199; Moon 2009: 262–263).[27] The 'resolution' of the West Irian issue in August 1962 took place in a settlement with the Dutch whereby a plebiscite would be held in the territory no later than 1969. According to Jean Bush Aden (1988: 228), the West Irian agreement was a catalyst that 'pushed [oil] negotiations towards completion' and, by brokering a deal on behalf of US oil companies, the Kennedy administration acted to ensure that the USSR's aid influence would not become ascendant in Indonesia. Although a broader exploration of these circumstances is outside the scope of this article, West Irian was thus deeply intermeshed in the politics of the Cold War and had a profound effect in the region (Defert 1996: 201–236).

Combining an understanding of the regional import of these events, on the one hand, and knowledge of the means through which TOC raised revenues from investors, on the other, affords a greater perspective on how both contexts affected its operations. For while TOC's low share price has been explained as a result of poor 'performance' in the field (Dunn 1996: 42), the reverse may be more accurate: diminished activities were also the result of a low share price. It remains moot as to whether TOC did not find oil because of inadequate research and exploration techniques, or whether there was simply not commercially exploitable oil. In any case, this is a different question to how the company was able to maintain operations. Part of the answer is that TOC, as noted above, did not necessarily require the discovery of oil to continue work. Its sustenance came from investment: the *promise* of hydrocarbon discoveries, through regular reports to stock markets that provided detailed accounts of drilling and from which investors would deduce that oil would imminently be discovered – or not. These reports generated a continuous source of capital for the company. In short, in addition to the investments made by CPT, TOC's fortunes were tied to its shareholders, who regularly changed according to the perceived fortunes of the company.

---

27   When Indonesia invaded West Irian in 1962, Saleh inaugurated a Soviet-funded steel mill that, Moon (2009) tells us, Soekarno named after the operation to take the territory by force.

Although there was a degree of uncertainty about the impact of Indonesian claims to West Irian, investors could also return to finance the company. This is illustrated by the upswing in investment shortly before an agreement on West Irian was reached in August 1962:

> [Exploration] continued below par, although [it was] favourably affected by a small ascensional oscillation after the Indonesian government's statements that disavowed any ambitions on Timor.[28]

Concerns over Indonesian territorial ambitions confirm that the perceived risk of an Indonesian invasion of Portuguese Timor and expropriation of TOC oil assets weighed more heavily in the company's calculations of the early 1960s than the prospect of finding oil. Indeed, effects from the region's events continued to be felt for several years. Financial limitations compelled TOC to scale back its operations and concentrate instead on 'seismic surveying followed by drilling' in Betano throughout 1963, an area it first entered in 1961. It sold the unwieldy 'Brewster' drill kept in Suai and completed negotiations with 'a strong overseas group that has completed its research in Timor and seems to be favourably impressed'.[29] TOC applied for a renewal of its contract in 1966, which was approved in 1968.[30] In part, this explains the 'lull' in TOC activities until that time. Already in 1966, TOC had become interested in offshore exploration, although it later restarted a program of onshore drilling. By 1968, prompted by an international dispute with Australia over the issuing of offshore licences, the attentions of the Portuguese Government had also turned towards Timor's maritime areas.

Conclusion

This chapter has examined the various kinds of internal and external infrastructure that comprised TOC's network, the different elements of which – human, material and financial – necessarily interacted with each other. As this chapter started off by showing, rival powers contested access to Portuguese Timor's oil and its strategic position by attempting to incorporate the territory into external international transport and trade networks. That the British, Australian and Japanese governments were

---

28 Arquivo Histórico Ultramarino, AHU 50,2, '*Informação* [Information] no. 33': 6 August 1962: 5.
29 Arquivo Histórico Ultramarino, AHU 50,2, '*Informação* [Information] no. 33': 6 August 1962: 6.
30 Arquivo Histórico Ultramarino, AHU 50,2, '*Relatório do Administrador por parte do estado* [Administrator Report by the State]…': 22 May 1969.

willing to plan such infrastructure served as an early reminder of the potential for external actors and events to exert influence on the course of the territory's future.

Difficulties in navigating terrain and changing geological appraisals affected the feasibility of conducting oil exploration. In combination with these factors, external events, including the perceived threat of an Indonesian invasion, resulted in a decrease in investor funding. However, this disinvestment did not prove to be fatal for TOC's fortunes and its continuation was testimony to the strength of its political connections with the Portuguese state. Without a larger exploration partner to absorb such an impact, TOC remained vigilant to the perceived threat of an Indonesian invasion until the end of its contract in 1966. The experience of TOC in attracting larger companies to concessions also highlights how smaller companies attempted to sustain themselves and, more broadly, that companies often carried out exploration without discovering viable deposits of oil or making profits.

Archival sources

Arquivo Histórico Ultramarino (AHU), Lisbon, Portugal: AHU IGM MU caixa 50,2 'Companhia de Petróleo de Timor. Relatorios Semestrais e outros assuntos respeitantes á actividade técnica' [Timor Oil Company. Semestral Reports and other issues concerning technical activity].

Arquivo Nacional Torre do Tombo (ANTT), Lisbon, Portugal: ANTT UL-10A caixa 766, Archivo Salazar.

National Archives of Australia (NAA), NAA A989, 1944/735/854. Available at: www.naa.gov.au [accessed 25 September 2016].

National Archives of the United Kingdom, Kew, UK: DO 35/372/6; DO 35/1721; FO 371/23541/179; FO 371/24705/7.

References

Adelman, M. A. (1993) The economics of petroleum supply, Cambridge, MA: MIT Press.

Aden, J. B. (1988) 'Oil and politics in Indonesia, 1945 to 1980', PhD thesis, Cornell University.

Aditjondro, G. (1998) *Is oil thicker than blood? A study of oil companies' interests and western complicity in Indonesia's annexation of East Timor*, Commack: Nova Science Publishers.

Botelho, F. T. (1978) *A gravimetria no Timor Português* [*The gravity meter in Portuguese Timor*], Lisboa: Junta de Investigações do Ultramar, Missão Geográfica de Timor.

Defert, G. (1996) *L'Indonésie et la Nouvelle-Guinée-Occidentale: Maintien des frontières coloniales ou respect des identités communautaires* [Indonesia and West New Guinea: Preservation of colonial borders or respect for community identities], Paris: L'Harmattan.

Dunn, J. (1996) *Timor: A people betrayed*, Sydney: ABC Books.

EIA (US Energy Information Administration) (2015) *International energy statistics: Total petroleum and other liquids production 2015*. Available at: www.eia.gov/beta/international/rankings/index.cfm#?iso=TLS&cy=2015.

Farram, S. (2017) 'Colonial neighbours in an era of change: Portugal and the Netherlands in Timor, 1945–1949', *Bijdragen tot de Taal-, Land- en Volkenkunde*, vol. 173, pp. 23–52. doi.org/10.1163/22134379-17301001.

Goto, K. (ed.) (2003) *Tensions of empire: Japan and Southeast Asia in the colonial and postcolonial world*, Singapore: NUS Press.

Gunn, G. (1988) *Wartime Portuguese Timor: The Azores connection*, Clayton, Australia: Centre of Southeast Asian Studies, Monash University.

Gunter, J. (2007) 'Communal conflict in Viqueque and the "charged" history of '59', *The Asia Pacific Journal of Anthropology* vol. 8, no. 1, pp. 27–41. doi.org/10.1080/14442210601177977.

La'o Hamutuk (2018) 'Resources and websites: Reference archive from La'o Hamutuk', La'o Hamutuk, updated March 2018. Available at: www.laohamutuk.org/DVD/DVDIndexEn.htm#OJE [accessed 18 March 2018].

Moon, S. (2009) 'Justice, geography, and steel: Technology and national identity in Indonesian industrialization', *Osiris* vol. 24, no. 1, pp. 253–277. doi.org/10.1086/605978.

Nasution, A. H. (1964) *Towards a people's army*, Djakarta: C. V. Delegasi.

Nishihara, M. (1976) *The Japanese and Sukarno's Indonesia: Tokyo–Jakarta relations 1951–1966*, Kyoto: University of Hawai'i Press/Center for Southeast Asian Studies.

Peattie, M. R. (1988) *Nan'yō: The rise and fall of the Japanese in Micronesia, 1885–1945*, Honolulu: University of Hawai'i Press.

Penrose, E. (1965) 'Vertical integration with joint control of raw-material production – crude oil in the Middle East', *Journal of Development Studies*, vol. 1, no. 3, pp. 251–268. doi.org/10.1080/00220386508421157.

Petroleum Fund of Timor-Leste (2017) *Quarterly report*, vol. 13, issue XXXIX, La'o Hamutuk. Available at: www.laohamutuk.org/Oil/PetFund/Reports/PFQR17q4en.pdf [accessed 9 March 2018].

Sabin, P. (2004) *Crude politics: The California oil market, 1900–1940*, Berkeley, London and Los Angeles: California University Press. doi.org/10.1525/california/9780520241985.001.0001.

Samuels, R. J. (1987) *The business of the Japanese state: Energy markets in comparative and historical perspective*, Ithaca: Cornell University Press.

Teixeira, J. E. (1956) *Relatório: Missao geológica do instituto francesa do petróleo a Timor* [*Report: Geological mission of the French Institute of Petroleum to Timor*], Junta de investigações científicas do Ultramar.

Yang, D. (2011) *Technology of empire: Telecommunications and Japanese expansion in Asia, 1883–1945*, Cambridge, MA: Harvard University Press.

Part II: State visions of development

3

Political and economic challenges of petroleum dependency in Timor-Leste

Guteriano Neves

One cannot discuss Timor-Leste's development over the last 10 years without mentioning oil as part of the equation. Oil is part of the collective Timorese memory of occupation's dark history; it shapes the path of national development and will continue to shape the country's future with the hopes, dreams and even fantasies that it provides. It shapes the state's structure, policies and democratic institutions, elites' attitudes and behaviour, resource distribution, and the interactions between the state and its citizens. Numerous scholars focusing on Timor-Leste have been highlighting the issues associated with oil dependency since 2002. Although many politicians are aware of these problems, and many policies are in place to mitigate the negative effects of oil dependency, the temptation posed by easy money has proved to be far greater than the willingness to avoid its perils. Warnings about the problems of oil wealth include arguments that Timor-Leste is already subject to the 'resource curse', a term used to refer to 'the negative impacts of non-renewable resource wealth' on people in many poorer countries which rely on external revenue, primarily from petroleum (Scheiner 2015b: 73; see also the Introduction to this volume). The curse of oil is said to manifest itself in unsustainable spending, import dependency and the policies for national development promoted by the government (Neves 2011; Scheiner 2015a). This is a consequence of easy access to petroleum rent in order to meet short-term desires, rather than strategic long-term development (Scheiner 2015a).

One aspect of the 'resource curse' is the 'rentier state', a term coined by Hossein Mahdavy (1970: 428) to characterise Middle Eastern countries that have received a significant amount of revenue from external sources. In the Timorese context, the state has become a rentier state because the government is the primary recipient of petroleum revenues (Beblawi 1987: 385). The rentier state theory situates the state as the unit of analysis by explaining how petroleum dependency shapes the state's relations with society and its role in economic development. Furthermore, it describes the political institutions that are generated and sustained by rent, and examines the social and economic structures of it.

This chapter discusses one element of this literature on oil dependency by assessing the extent to which petroleum dependency has shaped the new state of Timor-Leste into a rentier state and affected its political economy dynamics. This chapter combines academic literature on rentier states with my first-hand experience working with a non-governmental organisation (NGO) and the Office of the President in Timor-Leste. It examines the impact of Timor-Leste's oil dependency over the last 10 years (2007–2017), a period in which the state rapidly expanded, by focusing on three areas affected by oil rent: political institutions, bureaucracy and economic structures.

Rentier development?

Although petroleum revenues have enabled the state to expand over the last 10 years, these revenues function as rent for the domestic economy because the petroleum industry is independent from the domestic economy; domestic inputs are not required in the production process. When the state's revenues are mainly derived from petroleum, the state becomes a rentier state. Hazem Beblawi (1987: 384–85) has identified three characteristics of the rentier state: rent dominates the economy; rent is externally derived; and only a few are engaged in the rent generation, whereas rent distribution impacts the majority. When the government is the principal recipient and distributor of the rent, the state becomes what Giacomo Luciani has termed an 'allocation state' (Luciani 1987: 69).

These realities have been observed in Venezuela (Karl 1997) and Middle Eastern states (Kamrava 2005: 259; Mahdavy 1970: 432; Owen 2004). Writing on Venezuela's case, Terry Lynn Karl (1997: 64) observes that petro-states are 'institutionally too weak to resist further petrolization' and are 'permeated by interests vested in maintaining an oil-based model of accumulation'. Based on Venezuela's experiences, Fernando Coronil (1997: 2) quotes Venezuelan writer José Ignacio Cabrujas, who stated, 'Oil is fantastic and induces fantasies'. According to Coronil (1997), oil money has endowed the Venezuelan state with the 'magical power to remake the nation'; '[i]ts power to awaken fantasies enables state leaders to fashion political life into a dazzling spectacle of national progress through "tricks of prestidigitation"' (ibid.: 2). It does so by expanding bureaucracy, initiating state-led industrialisation, providing social security schemes and expanding social services. Although state-led development gained popularity during the 1950s, in Middle Eastern countries oil indeed facilitates state expansion (Owen 2004: 23) without facing the balance of payment problems (Mahdavy 1970: 432; Owen 2004: 25).

Since the early period of independence, oil has been part of national imaginations of Timor's future. Oil provides easy money that enables politicians to dream up fantastic plans for the country's future; it is a source of hope for modernity and a better life. These imageries of modernity have informed economic policies in Timor-Leste since 2002. The 2011–2030 strategic development plan, which envisions Timor-Leste to be a 'middle-income country' by 2030, places oil at the centre of this vision. According to the introduction (GoTL 2011: 9), having 'one of the world's most vital commodities, petroleum' can help Timor-Leste to secure the foundation of a sustainable and vibrant economy. Petroleum revenue will be 'invested in education and health services … in helping farmers to increase their productivity', funding infrastructure, diversifying the economy and transforming the 'country into a modern nation' (ibid.). This has enabled the state to expand in various sectors over the last 10 years (Neves 2016). The availability of petroleum revenues eventually shapes the state's revenues and expenditure pattern. In 2015 alone, 89 per cent of the state's budget was transferred from the Petroleum Fund (MoF 2015: 6). Between 2011 and 2015, Timor-Leste would have suffered budget deficits of more than US$1 billion every year if not for oil money (MoF 2015: 6). Between 2008 and 2012, the annual budget vastly increased, making Timor-Leste one of the world's leading countries in terms of budget growth (La'o Hamutuk 2011: 7).

The state's expansion can be observed in the state's bureaucracy, state-financed infrastructure projects, the existing insecure social security regime and social services, which have expanded rapidly in number and cost since 2008 (Neves 2013). As the country has only a nascent private sector, the role that business plays in economic development is non-existent. Thus, it is a pragmatic decision for the public sector to be the engine driving economic development. Xanana Gusmão, politician and former guerrilla leader, set in motion the government's infrastructure-focused program, which includes roads, public buildings and electricity (see also Almeida, Chapter 5; Bovensiepen, Chapter 6; and Meitzner Yoder, Chapter 4). Government allocations for infrastructure account for 30 to 40 per cent of the total budget. They reached nearly 50 per cent of the total budget and non-oil gross domestic product (GDP) in 2011 and, in 2016, infrastructure-related spending alone accounted for more than 43 per cent of the total state budget. According to the World Bank, this is 'one of the highest rates of infrastructure spending in the world' (World Bank and Ministry of Finance 2015: ix). The government has also established cash transfer schemes for groups, such as veterans (participants in Timor-Leste's 24-year resistance to Indonesian occupation), the elderly and single-parent households (see also Roll, Chapter 7). According to the World Bank (2013: 1), Timor-Leste's social spending is 'one of the highest budget outlay ratios in the world', higher than all other countries 'with similar population size, poverty headcount, level of mineral resource wealth and fragile state status'. The biggest portion of social security spending goes to veterans, accounting for 60 per cent of the total Ministry of Social Solidarity social assistance budget (ibid.: 3).

Overall, according to the Asian Development Bank (ADB 2015: 1), although revenue from the Joint Petroleum Development Area is modest by international standards, on average, it contributed 80 per cent to Timor's GDP from 2006 to 2012. In 2014, oil accounted for 66.4 per cent of Timor's GDP, with the non-oil sector at 33.6 per cent (NSD 2015: x). Even for the non-oil economy, to a large extent, petro-dollar is recycled through the state budget. Charles Scheiner, from the NGO La'o Hamutuk Timor-Leste Institute for Development Monitoring and Analysis, described this situation as 'oil swamping the entire economy of Timor-Leste' (2015a: 74).

Rent and political institutions

One aspect of rentier state theory concerns the political institutions that rent generates and sustains. Scholars like Ross (2012a), Auty (2012) and Karl (1997) have identified different political institutions in petroleum-dependent countries, examining how rent affects democratic institutions. Ross (2012a) has pointed out that dependency on externally derived revenues undermines democratisation. From a fiscal standpoint, as oil provides easy money, the state operates independent of the domestic economy and does not extract revenue from society through tax (Ross 2012a). This enables the state to be independent from societal structure (Schwarz 2008: 602). It is argued that this fiscal independency undermines public pressure on public officeholders to be accountable to their constituents (Ross 2012a). From the expenditure side, having access to oil enables politicians to coopt different social forces, thus undermining political pressure for democratic reforms (Owen 2004: 122; Ross 2012a). In the Middle East, although oil facilitates state expansion, it also increases the chances for family-type political regimes (Kamrava 2005; Owen 2004).

Patronage politics is another problem associated with rent dependency (Auty 2012; Karl 1997; Dunning 2008). Although this is not an issue unique to oil-dependent countries, the fact that petroleum revenues are concentrated on the executive branch of government makes it more pervasive. According to Karl (1997), oil creates conditions for the centralisation of power in the hands of the executive; the chief of the executive has the final decision over revenue allocation. This drives elites' competition to control rent (Auty 2012). In guaranteeing their survival, political elites make compromises in order to maintain the representation of the dominant class while limiting the scope of representation of the wider political spectrum (Karl 1997). Meanwhile, patron–client relationships, rent-seeking and the distribution of petro-dollars become mechanisms to contain political resentment and ensure regime survival (Karl 1997).

In *The Bottom Billion* (2007), Paul Collier argues that rent generates patronage politics because voters are bribed with public money. Similarly, examining rentier state dynamics in East Asia and the Pacific, Barma states that political authority is individualised, 'resting on … cronyism', 'public resources are … exploited for private gain', and rent distribution is 'dominated by a concentrated elite' (Barma 2014: 260). Furthermore, '[p]olitical competition takes place ... on the basis of extended patron–client networks', and 'public goods are provided to ... mobilise (political) supporters' (ibid.). This clientelism can take various forms, including electoral politics and political parties. 'Political parties' in this context refers to the institutionalisation of clientelist politics, which facilitates the distribution of benefits among party members (Hopkin 2006). As the state expands its societal role in terms of regulations, financial benefits and public service provision, this network expands as well (ibid.). Voters exchange their votes for various benefits through state institutions (ibid.).

How is this relevant for Timor-Leste? Timor-Leste is generally regarded as a democratic country, despite some issues in upholding the rule of law and freedom of the press (Feijó 2015: 59). Freedom House (2016) categorised Timor-Leste as 'partly free', with a score of 65 out of 100 (0 being 'least free' and 100 being 'most free'). Its score for political and civil rights was 3 in a range from 1 to 7 (1 represents the 'most free' and 7 represents the 'least free'). Since 2007, Timor-Leste has also enjoyed political stability. In 2017, its third election was held since the restoration of independence; this was viewed as a free and fair election.

However, the country faces the challenge of growing patron–client relations that are increasingly shaping the political system. This issue has been discussed by scholars such as Rui Feijó (2015), James Scambary (2015) and Naazneen H. Barma (2014), and acknowledged by the former commissioner of Timor-Leste's Anti-Corruption Commission, Aderito de Jesus Soares (2015). Critically examining resource income expenditure in Timor-Leste, James Scambary (2015: 285) argues that 'the convergence of a range of historical, political and cultural factors, and resource wealth has laid the foundations for a clientelist and neo-patrimonial state'. One aspect of clientelism, according to Barma (2014: 266), is that most of the spending goes towards 'enriching the elite'. Both terms – clientelism and patrimonialism – refer to 'politically targeted modes of distribution of state funds' (Scambary 2015: 287). The former entails the distribution of favours or goods between individuals with unequal economic and social status, a relationship that might be mediated by 'brokers' (ibid.). 'The term neo-patrimonialism denotes a lack of distinction between office and office holder masked behind discourses, juridical norms, and institutions that nourish the illusion of a legal-bureaucratic logic' (ibid.: 288).

Led by Dr Rui Maria de Araújo, the Sixth Constitutional Government in 2015 was seen as a new phase in Timor-Leste's political process. Official narratives presented the current government plans as 'Timor-Leste's model' to strengthen democracy, peace and stability based on national consensus – it is not coincidental that the sixth government of Timor-Leste describes itself as a 'Government of National Unity'. However, the opposing argument holds that this national consensus is a mechanism to serve elites' – rather than national – interests, as indicated by the Centre of Studies for Peace and Development (CEPAD 2015: 42). Such observations are pertinent considering Timor-Leste's political developments since 2012. The vast, ambitious ZEESM (*Zonas Especiais de Economia Social de Mercado de Timor-Leste*, or Special Economic Zone of Social Market Economy of Timor-Leste) project in Oecusse is the direct result of elites' consensus to distribute the oil money.[1] An ad hoc committee (*Komisaun Eventual*) was established in December 2015 to discuss the annual state budget behind closed doors, which has aroused suspicion that it is a strategy to protect the interests of the elites (La'o Hamutuk 2015). In February 2016, then president Taur Matan Ruak expressed many of these concerns in a speech to parliament: 'Do not count on the president of the republic to build a society based on power and privileges' (Ruak 2016).

Like Scambary, Barma (2014: 263) argues that clientelism is an emerging trend in Timor-Leste and is recognised among some observers in Timor. The trend manifests itself in the ability of political parties to distribute public resources (ibid.: 266) and in the increasing concentration of power in the hands of the executive (ibid.: 263). Rui Feijó outlined two alternatives to the challenge of how Timor-Leste might manage its wealth: either following 'clearly defined procedures, institutionally framed, and validated through the rule of law', or one that involves 'ad hoc policies, and individual negotiations between the state and private agents, privileging personal ties over individual norms' (Feijó 2015: 64). If such a course of action became a dominant trend, according to Feijó (ibid.), it could 'generate dependency on social and economic actors' with regards to powerholders; furthermore, it could strengthen clientelist networks. A case used as the basis for this claim is the verification process to become officially considered a veteran, which is 'rumoured to be prone to abuses

---

1   According to Laura Meitzner Yoder (2015: 300), the public project is 'a fantastical development scheme for the geographically and politically peripheral' Oecusse district.

and manipulation' owing to the lack of 'a clearly defined set of upheld legal procedures' (ibid.). The allegation of political patronage seems to have played a role in the contract distribution for the 2009 *Pakote Referendum* (Referendum Package), the government's US$70 million investment in (mainly rural) infrastructure projects (Barma 2014: 265; Feijó 2015: 65).

Soares has reinforced Feijó's critical observation with regards to the way the government has contracted the private sector for infrastructure development, observing that 'the fetishising of the private sector in development can result in favouritism towards certain businesses, bypassing laws and procedures, and lead to corruption' (Soares 2015: 210). One example of this practice is the government's decision to award infrastructure projects to *Consorcio Nacional Timorense* (Timorese National Consortium), made up of a 'small group of national contractors' through a 'single source mechanism' (Barma 2014: 265; Soares 2015: 210). This is only one of many instances where the government used a single source process to award contracts to individual businesses, which then 'created the perception of corruption' (Soares 2015: 210). Meanwhile, the practice of brokering foreign contractors' access to 'the state's recent multimillion-dollar project tenders' also creates patron–client relationships in the Timorese economy (ibid.: 210–211).

These growing clientelist networks, I would argue, put the democratic process under threat, as democratic institutions are increasingly rendered to protect patron–client relationships. This is a threat to overall development in Timor-Leste, as it favours certain individuals who are part of clientelistic networks and undermines efforts for collective good (Hopkin 2006). Furthermore, these networks are unjust and inefficient, since the people who are part of them receive a disproportionate amount of benefits compared to the rest of Timor-Leste's citizens (ibid.). Additionally, sustaining political institutions through rent is an inefficient and unhealthy action for economic development; since it is based on elites' ability to control (and hence benefit from) oil rents, it leads to unpredictability for the private sector. These challenges to the country's peace will inevitably arise once the financial benefits from oil have been depleted. If efforts to reform pose a threat to the vested interests of dominant political actors, the growing clientelistic network will inevitably inhibit any such movements.

Bureaucratic expansion and efficiency

The expansion of bureaucracy is an important part of the current development process. Since 2008, state bureaucracy has expanded rapidly, a process that has been facilitated by oil revenue. In 2015, Timor-Leste's state spending on wages and salaries was US$177.5 million, or 11.6 per cent of the total annual budget, and its expenditure on goods and services was US$515.8 million, or 32.8 per cent of total annual spending (MoF 2015: 13). The expansion of state bureaucracy in Timor-Leste follows the pattern of other oil-dependent countries; according to Nazib Ayubi (1990: 131), this is a common consequence of oil wealth. As revenue goes directly into the state's coffers, bureaucratic expansion is part of the state's distributive and allocative roles in society (Ayubi 1990: 136). Michael Ross writes that the government structure of rentier states was, on average, 45 per cent larger than those of their neighbours without oil (Ross 2012b: 28). The peak of Timor-Leste's expansion in state bureaucracy took place between 2012 and 2014, when there were 55 government ministers, vice-ministers and secretaries of state in a country with just 1.1 million people: '[I]t was the largest government in the Asia Pacific' (Horta 2014).

Patron–client relations are part and parcel of Timor-Leste's public institutions, which is a typical symptom of clientelism. This manifests in recruitment and promotion according to political party loyalties in an increasingly politicised public administration. This can be seen in popular expressions about the need to have 'someone inside' (*ema laran*), a 'godfather' or 'guardian' (*Aman Sarani*), or 'one of our own' (*ema ita nian*). The Timorese capital is rife with allegations and rumours that the promotion process is based on political alignment and family affiliation, which tends to undermine creativity and innovation in the public sector. It also undermines meritocracy, as political or family connections are a shortcut to recruitment and promotion for higher positions.

Easy money from oil also enables the state to establish a variety of different institutions tasked with tackling the very same problems. However, rather than solving these problems, having different institutions with similar mandates leads to overlapping roles. Soares has coined the term 'institutional ritualism' to characterise this trend, in which policymakers view the *creation* of institutions as the solution instead of focusing on the problems themselves (Soares 2013: 93). The case he discusses concerns corruption, which is addressed by the ombudsman, the public prosecutor, the audit court, the Criminal Investigation Police and the Anti-Corruption Commission (ibid.: 91–94). Another example of doubling up on roles concerns the oversight of the state's numerous construction projects, which involve the Ministry of Public Works and the National Development Agency. This has even created conflict between the two institutions regarding which is responsible for ensuring quality control in construction projects. Moreover, when the state spends a large amount of money in a context where administrative capacity is weak, it leads to inefficient spending and misuse of public resources.

Allegations and perceptions of corruption are on the rise, which I have observed in public discussions that I have attended, in newspapers, on television and from private conversations I have had with colleagues and friends. Such perceptions can also be observed through common expressions referred to in Soares' analysis of corruption: '*Kasih-uang habis perkara*', an expression left over from the Indonesian occupation, which means 'The matter is finished once you have given the money'; the Tetum expressions '*Keta haluha ami nian serveiza*' ('Don't forget our beer'); '*Nia ita nian ema rasik sa*' ('He [or she] is one of our own people'); and '*bui-hois*' and '*mau-hois*' (terms for a corrupt female and corrupt male public officer, respectively) (Soares 2013: 88). Another reference to the ways in which one requires a guardian or patron to get employment is the notion of the 'big brother' (*maun bo'ot*), which has lead Soares to conclude that there is a 'Maun Bo'ot culture' in Timor-Leste. A *maun bo'ot* is a senior person who 'has strong leverage because of past experience as a former resistance leader or a former clandestine leader' (ibid.: 89) and therefore manages to act as a 'broker' to mediate exchanges between the 'big people' and the 'little man' (see also Scambary 2015: 287).

As the rentier state literature discussed earlier has highlighted, the bureaucracy and policies of a rentier state are affected by oil revenue because the state itself is responsible for allocating these revenues and distributing them to the rest of society. The availability of large quantities of money through oil rents incentivises politicians to spend this money quickly through public employment schemes, subsidies, labour market regulations and short-term and emergency projects. Petroleum money can lead to 'bureaucratic overstretch', which occurs when a government's revenues expand more quickly than its capacity to efficiently manage them (Ross 2012a: 3), leading to misuse of public resources. In the influential book *The Paradox of Plenty*, Karl (1997: 57) argued that oil revenues diminish the state's authority by causing 'rentier psychology', which disproportionately admires and rewards those who can "milk the cow" without effort rather than those engaged in less remunerative but more productive activities'.

The economy and society

From the perspective of common economic sense, one could expect that revenues extracted from natural resources like petroleum could be used to finance the investment necessary for the development of a country. However, since the late 1990s, scholars have found that instead of promoting economic growth, dependence on natural resources inhibits economic growth (Ross 2012a; Auty 2012).

If economic growth per se is an indicator of successful economic development, Timor-Leste should be considered exemplary. Over the last 10 years, the country's non-oil gross domestic product (GDP) has been growing, facilitated nevertheless by petroleum money. Non-oil–related growth has led to general improvement in quality of life, as observed in Timor-Leste's declining poverty rate based on the consumption-based measurement (NSD 2017). According to the report published by the National Statistics Directorate (NSD 2017), the percentage of those living in poverty decreased from 50.4 to 41.8 per cent between 2007 and 2014 (ibid.). Other improvements include the Human Development Index, which has increased by 27 per cent from 0.468 in 2000 to 0.595 in 2015 (OECD 2017: 11). Other notable improvements can be seen in amount of schooling, means of schooling and life expectancy (ibid.).

Nonetheless, it is more important to look at the structure of this growth and how it affects people's daily lives. There is a consensus among policymakers and observers that economic growth is primarily driven by public expenditure, which recycles the rent through state spending (ADB 2015; Inder and Cornwell 2016). For example, construction and public administration, which are the drivers of economic growth, are both directly linked to petroleum money, circulated through annual state spending, and located primarily in Dili (Scheiner 2014: 8). The trend of private sector investment remains flat; it, too, tends to concentrate in Dili and is directly linked to government spending (ADB 2015: 3). On the other hand, agriculture – the source of livelihood for approximately 70 per cent of the population – has declined (ADB 2015; Inder and Cornwell 2016).

Furthermore, the rent-based economic structure has created a distinct middle class that is concentrated in urban areas, primarily Dili. For the most part, they are the main beneficiaries of recycled oil rent. This has widened the gap between those in Dili and the rest of the country. Although the national poverty line decreased between 2007 and 2014, the rural poverty rate is 19.8 per cent higher than its urban counterpart (NSD 2017: 6). Dili stands to be an outlier, with a poverty rate of 29.1 per cent, while the national poverty rate is 41 per cent (NSD 2016: 25). As various studies have pointed out, private sector activities in Timor-Leste also tend to be centralised in Dili (ADB 2015). In 2016 alone, it was estimated that almost 80 per cent of employment in the private sector was concentrated in Dili (NSD 2017: 3). Differences in quality of life are also reflected in the 2016 Public Perception Survey, conducted by The Asia Foundation (2017). The survey revealed that respondents in Dili were more satisfied in terms of public services such as health, education, water and sanitation (The Asia Foundation 2017: 6). Some observers were already issuing warnings in 2011 about the path of development that the country was taking. In the report of her visit to Timor-Leste in November 2011, Magdalena Sepúlveda Carmona, the United Nations Special Rapporteur on extreme poverty and human rights highlighted that despite 'rapid economic growth', 'most Timorese continue to experience poverty, deprivation and insecure employment' (Carmona 2012: 4).

Although a rent-based economy can grow, not much new employment will be generated. Most of the employment in the formal sector is concentrated in the public sector and the nation's capital. According to the 2013 Labour Force Survey, out of a working-age population of 696,200, the labour force participation rate was only 30.6 per cent (NSD 2013: 5). In the same survey, 483,000 were categorised as 'inactive population', out of which 37 per cent were involved in subsistence foodstuff production (ibid.). In 2010, the total amount of those employed in the private sector was 46,700 (NSD 2012: 3); in 2016, this number was estimated to be 58,200 (NSD 2017: 3). This shows that a limited amount of jobs were created in the formal sector during the period when the government's spending was high, but the domestic economy – measured by the non-oil GDP – grew significantly.

As more people enter the job market, the limited employment opportunities generated by the economy have put pressure on the government to respond to such high demand for jobs. The challenge, as recognised by the government (GoTL 2017a: 7), is how to generate employment given that a high proportion of those of productive age live outside of the formal sector, yet 200,000 people will reach working age in the next 10 years (ibid.). Additionally, limited and concentrated employment opportunities drive another social problem: high internal migration to urban areas, primarily Dili. Between 2004 and 2015, the proportion of Timor-Leste's urban population grew from 25 per cent to 33 per cent (Nguyen et al. 2017: 4). During the same period, the population grew from 158,000 to 255,000 in Dili alone – an increase of 62 per cent (ibid.). The evidence suggests that the difference in quality of life is the major factor in this influx of urban migration (ibid.).

Realising the challenges that the country is – and will be – facing, particularly in a context of declining petroleum revenue, 'economic diversification' has become a common expression in policy debate and discussion in Dili (Inder and Cornwell 2016: 6). The previous government, led by Rui Maria Araujo, has provided guidance for 'reform and economic growth' (GoTL 2017b: 134). Alongside the oil sector, the government also prioritises the agriculture, tourism, fisheries and manufacturing industries as the potential sectors for Timor-Leste's development. The government's approach focused on the 'enabling environment' by investing in infrastructure such as electricity and roads, revising legal frameworks such as land, property and private investment law, taking part in the One-Stop Shop SERVE trade investment, and other interventions (GoTL 2017b).

While these are issues faced by people on the technical level, one cannot neglect the political and institutional issues – namely, the economic institutions sustained by the rent and the incentives that exist for them. Economically, rent is the result of earning high profits from economic activities that require a disproportionately low level of productivity (Kamrava 2005: 267). Petroleum revenue is rent because 'the economic return to natural extraction … exceeds production and transport costs and some "normal" return to capital', even when all the production factors are at their optimum capacity (Dunning 2008: 39). This is made more difficult by the fact that petroleum is non-renewable, volatile, capital-intensive and high-technology (Karl 2007: 3; Ross 2012a). When a country depends excessively on its petroleum revenues, it creates a rentier economy in which rent can 'sustain the economy without a strong domestic productive sector' (Beblawi 1987: 385). This shapes the mentality of the elites who control the state in various ways; there is a tendency for elites to ignore the developing non-oil economy, since the state's income is not derived from the domestic economy (Luciani 1987: 69).

This trend can be observed in the overall development path that Timor-Leste is taking, as well as its budget allocation (Scheiner 2015a). Access to rent diverts decision-makers' attention from investment in sectors that are more sustainable (ibid.). Rent makes it easier to buy education and healthcare services from outside the country than to invest locally; easier to import rice than to plant it; and easier to import technical advisers than to build domestic institutions (ibid.). Although government officials frequently state that agriculture is a development priority, this sector receives only 2 per cent of the state's annual budget. There is a strong perception that the younger generations do not want to be involved in agriculture anymore and that people are 'spoiled' by different state subsidies. This attitude was frequently expressed by people during my visits to Laleia, Suai, Balibo and other parts of the country.

The effect of rent dependency has also been transferred to the structure of society. Some groups do not participate in economic production, but share a big portion of the economic gain (Beblawi 1987: 49). In this economic structure, only a few people are involved in rent generation, whereas the majority play a role in either wealth 'distribution or utilisation' (ibid.). The state 'ends up by performing the role of allocating' the externally gained revenue throughout the economy (Luciani 1987: 69). Although most people's incomes increase 'in the short run', the rich and 'powerful benefit disproportionately' from oil revenue, which deepens social inequality (Karl 1997: 65, citing Lewis 1982). Most citizens want a piece of 'oil pie' without having to work hard (ibid.). Citizens growing up in these conditions are accustomed to these subsidies, expecting them to continue without recognising that oil will be depleted (ibid.).

Coined by *The Economist,* the term 'Dutch disease' refers to a situation in which the boom in the natural resources sector produces a decline in the manufacturing and agriculture sectors (Ross 2012a: 21; see also the Introduction to this volume). When a resource boom occurs, it takes away labour and capital from the agriculture and manufacturing sectors, which raises the cost of production. Additionally, when revenues from these resources enter the market, the real exchange rate increases. This makes it cheaper to import agricultural and manufactured goods than to produce them locally. The price will remain the same for the products that are imported, given that it is determined by the international market. Therefore, both sectors lose their share of the domestic market (ibid.). Signs of this phenomenon can be observed in Timor-Leste. My engagement with the local communities in Maliana, Balibo, Suai and Laleia has shown that a high level of subsidies disincentivises local communities from engaging in productive sectors.

Timor-Leste faces an even larger challenge, however. It lacks the basic infrastructure to assist in the emergence of a modern private sector, and the public sector's institutional capacity to support one is weak. Numerous existing policies tend to undermine the government's efforts to strengthen the private sector, including those related to rice import, the high proportion of cash transfer programs, and a low allocation of budget funds for productive sectors. As observed by Beblawi (1987: 385), domestic production suffers from high levels of importation, combined with a rentier mentality, which 'embodies a break in the work-reward' relationship.

Envisioning Timor-Leste's future

When Rui Araújo came to power in 2015, he promised to bring efficiency to the government. He then launched several reform agendas – namely, Civil Service Reform, Economic Reform, Legal Reform and Fiscal Reform. It was argued that these reforms were part of Timor-Leste's efforts to carry out its strategic development plan and meet sustainable development goals. My observation is that these reforms address some of the technical issues that are faced in modern-day Timor-Leste. However, they do not address the political economic aspects of development, which are influenced by petroleum rent and the reality of Timor-Leste as a post-conflict society.

While the country's strategic development plan provides a vision of modernity based on oil, this chapter lays out some of the present and future challenges posed by the centrality of oil in Timor-Leste's economy. First is the challenge for the democratic system, which is visible in the way patron–client relations have begun to shape democratic institutions. If this trend continues, the political system will become more oriented towards the protection of the elites' interests, while the majority of people will be excluded from the political process. Elections can still be a democratic means for people to participate, but they can also be a mechanism for the elites to expand their client networks and legitimise their position through the electoral framework. If patron–client relations come to penetrate institutions more pervasively, it will erode the legitimacy of democratic institutions.

The second issue concerns sustainable and equitable development. The discussion on sustainable development in Timor-Leste seems to have a narrow focus on financial aspects. This is due to public anxiety regarding oil prices, as well as declining oil reserves. The discussion then leads us to another question: How long will petroleum sustain Timor-Leste's development? However, as this chapter has outlined, there are many other compelling reasons to rethink sustainability and development in Timor-Leste beyond oil. Oil-based development is unsustainable not only because oil is running out, but because the development outcomes that oil rent promotes are highly problematic and socially harmful. Oil dependency creates social, political and economic structures that exclude the majority of people from the development process and empowers the urban elites who control the state. It benefits the capital city over rural areas where the majority of people live. A vision of the future of Timor-Leste based on oil is a vision that will decidedly benefit the elites. If we are to envision a future that includes and benefits everyone, it will have to be one without oil.

References

ADB (Asian Development Bank) (2015) *Growing the non-oil economy: A private sector assessment for Timor-Leste*. Available at: www.adb.org/sites/default/files/institutional-document/161516/tim-growing-non-oil-economy.pdf.

Auty, M. A. (2012) 'Introduction and overview', in Auty, R. M. (ed.) *Resource abundance and economic development*, Oxford: Oxford University Press, pp. 3–16.

Ayubi, N. (1990) 'Arab bureaucracies: Expanding size, changing roles', in Luciani, G. (ed.) *The Arab state*, Berkeley: University of California Press, pp. 129–149.

Barma, N. H. (2014) 'The rentier state at work: Comparative experiences of the resource curse in East Asia and the Pacific', *Asia and the Pacific Policy Studies* vol. 1, no. 2, pp. 257–272. doi.org/10.1002/app5.26.

Beblawi, H. (1987) 'The rentier state in the Arab world', *Arab Studies Quarterly*, vol. 9, no. 4, pp. 383–398.

Carmona, M. S. (2012) *Annex: Report of the Special Rapporteur on extreme poverty and human rights on her mission to Timor-Leste (13–18 November 2011)*, Report A/HRC/20/25/Add.1, General Assembly, Human Rights Council, 20th Session. Available at: www.ohchr.org/Documents/HRBodies/HRCouncil/RegularSession/Session20/A.HRC.20.25.Add.1_En.PDF.

CEPAD (Centre for Study, Peace and Development) (2015) *Rezilensia husi Perspektiva Lokal: Mekanismu atu Kompriende Reziliensia. Timor-Leste Relatoriu Nasional* [Resilience from a local perspective. Mechanisms for understanding resilience. Timor-Leste National Report], Dili: CEPAD/Interpeace. Available at: www.interpeace.org/wp-content/uploads/2015/05/2015_05_19_FAR_Relatoriu_Nasional_TET.pdf.

Collier, P. (2007) *The bottom billion: Why the poorest countries are failing and what can be done about it*, Oxford: Oxford University Press.

Coronil, F. (1997) *The magical state: Nature, money, and modernity in Venezuela*, Chicago: University of Chicago Press.

Dunning, T. (2008) *Crude democracy: Natural resource wealth and political regimes*, New York: Cambridge University Press. doi.org/10.1017/CBO9780511510052.

Feijó, R. G. (2015) 'Challenges to the consolidation of democracy', in Ingram, S., Kent, L., and McWilliam, A. (eds) *A new era? Timor-Leste after the UN*, Canberra: ANU Press, pp. 59–70. doi.org/10.22459/NE.09.2015.05.

Freedom House (2016) *Timor-Leste: Freedom in the world 2016*. Available at: freedomhouse.org/report/freedom-world/2016/timor-leste.

GoTL (Government of Timor-Leste) (2011) *Timor-Leste strategic development plan 2011–2030*. Available at: sustainabledevelopment.un.org/content/documents/1506Timor-Leste-Strategic-Plan-2011-20301.pdf.

GoTL (2017a) *National employment strategy 2017–2030: Productive employment shall be a central means of national building and wealth creation*. Available at: timor-leste.gov.tl/wp-content/uploads/2017/07/National-Employment-Strategy-2017-20301.pdf.

GoTL (2017b) *Snapshot of sixth constitutional government mandate (2015–2017)*. Available at: timor-leste.gov.tl/wp-content/uploads/2017/08/Low_EN_Texto_VI-GOVERNO-CONSTITUCIONAL1.pdf.

Hopkin, J. (2006) 'Clientelism and party politics', in Katz, R. S. and Crotty, W. (eds) *Handbook of party politics*, London: SAGE Publications Ltd, pp. 406–412. doi.org/10.4135/9781848608047.n35.

Horta, L. (2014) 'Timor-Leste: Lessons from a failing state?' *Yale Global Online*, 22 May. Available at: yaleglobal.yale.edu/content/timor-leste-lessons-failing-state.

Inder, B. and Cornwell, K. (2016) *Private sector-driven development in an infant economy*. Monash Centre for Development Economics and Sustainability Research, Research Paper Series on Timor-Leste. RP-TL4-English. Available at: www.laohamutuk.org/econ/invest/RP-TL4-English.pdf.

Kamrava, M. (2005) *The modern Middle East: A political history since the First World War*, Oakland: University of California Press.

Karl, T. L. (1997) *The paradox of plenty: Oil booms and petro-states*, Oakland: University of California Press.

Karl, T. L. (2007) *Oil-led development: Social, political, and economic consequences*, Working Paper No. 80, Stanford: Center on Democracy, Development and the Rule of Law, Stanford University.

La'o Hamutuk (2011) *Submission to Committee C: Economy, finances and anti-corruption, National Parliament, Democratic Republic of Timor-Leste: regarding the proposed General State Budget for 2012*, La'o Hamutuk – The Timor-Leste Institute for Development Monitoring and Analysis. Available at: laohamutuk.org/econ/OGE12/LHSubComCPNOJE2012En.pdf.

La'o Hamutuk (2015) *Submission to Timor-Leste National Parliament on the proposed General State Budget for 2016*, La'o Hamutuk – The Timor-Leste Institute for Development Monitoring and Analysis. Available at: www.laoha mutuk.org/econ/OGE16/LHSubPNOGE16-18Nov2015en.pdf.

Lewis, S. R. (1982) *Development problems of the mineral-rich countries*, Center for Development Economics, Research Memo 74, Williamstown: Williams College.

Luciani, G. (1987) 'Allocation vs. production states: A theoretical framework', in Beblawi, H. and Luciani, G. (eds) *The rentier state (Nation, state and integration in the Arab world, vol. 2)*, London: Croom Helm, pp. 63–82.

Mahdavy, H. (1970) 'The patterns and problems of economic development in rentier states: the case of Iran', in Cook, M. A. (ed.) *Studies in the economic history of the Middle East: From the rise of Islam to the present day*, London: Oxford University Press, pp. 428–467.

Meitzner Yoder, L. S. (2015) 'The development eraser: Fantastical schemes, aspirational distractions and high modern mega-events in the Oecusse enclave, Timor-Leste', *Journal of Political Ecology*, vol. 22, pp. 299–321. doi.org/10.2458/v22i1.21110.

MoF (Ministry of Finance [GoTL]) (2015) *State Budget 2015: Budget Overview*. Available at: laohamutuk.org/econ/OGE15/bksOct14/OGE15Bk 1Oct2014en.pdf.

Neves, G. (2011) 'Timor's oil: Blessing or curse?', Foreign Policy in Focus, 26 August. Available at: fpif.org/timors_oil_blessing_or_curse/.

Neves, G. (2013) 'Timor-Leste: The political economy of a rentier state', in Loney, H., Da Silva, A. B., Da Costa Ximenes, A., Canas Mendes, N. and Fernandes, C. (eds) *Understanding Timor-Leste*, vol. 2, 4th Timor Leste Studies Association Conference, 15–16 July, Dili, Hawthorn: Swinburne Press, pp. 22–26.

Neves, G. (2016) *The political economy of petroleum dependency*, SSGM In Brief 2016/6, Canberra: State, Society & Governance in Melanesia, ANU. Available at: ssgm.bellschool.anu.edu.au/experts-publications/publications/ 3630/political-economy-petroleum-dependency.

Nguyen, P., Cornwall, K., Inder, B., and Qu, N. (2017) *An economic perspective on people movement in Timor-Leste*, Centre for Development Economics and Sustainability, Monash University. Available at: drive.google.com/file/ d/0ByznZLkW5XMKSFpwMEdEcjFrRmM/edit.

NSD (National Statistics Directorate [GoTL]) (2012) *Business activity survey of Timor-Leste 2010*. Available at: www.statistics.gov.tl/wp-content/uploads/ 2013/12/BAS_202010_20ENGLISH.pdf.

NSD (2013) *Labor force survey 2013*. Available at: www.ilo.org/wcmsp5/ groups/public/---asia/---ro-bangkok/---ilo-jakarta/documents/publication/ wcms_417168.pdf.

NSD (2015) *Timor-Leste national accounts 2000–2014*. Available at: www. statistics.gov.tl/wp-content/uploads/2016/06/TL-NA-2000-2014.pdf.

NSD (2016) *Business activity survey of Timor-Leste 2014*. Available at: www.statistics. gov.tl/wp-content/uploads/2016/06/Bussines-Activity-Survey-2014-.pdf.

NSD (2017) *Poverty in Timor-Leste 2014*. Available at: www.statistics.gov.tl/wp-content/uploads/2018/02/Poverty-Report-2014-final.pdf.

OECD (Organisation for Economic Co-operation and Development) (2017) *Budgeting for a sustainable future: Towards a roadmap of budgetary governance reform in Timor-Leste* (presentation). Available at: www.slideshare.net/OECD-GOV/budgetary-governance-reforms-in-timorleste-ronnie-downes-oecd.

Owen, R. (2004) *State, power and politics in the making of the modern Middle East*, 3rd edition, New York: Routledge.

Ross, M. L. (2012a) *The oil curse: How petroleum wealth shapes the development of nations*, Princeton: Princeton University Press.

Ross, M. L. (2012b) *The political economy of petroleum wealth in low-income countries: Some policy alternatives*, Economic Research Forum Working Paper No. 708, Giza, Egypt: Economic Research Forum. Available at: erf.org.eg/wp-content/uploads/2014/08/708.pdf.

Ruak, T. M. (2016) 'Speech by His Excellency the President of the Republic, Taur Matan Ruak, to the National Parliament', *Life at Aitarak Laran*, 26 February. Available at: aitaraklaranlive.wordpress.com/2016/02/26/speech-by-his-excellency-the-president-of-the-republic-taur-matan-ruak-to-national-parliament-on-the-dismissal-of-major-general-lere-anan-timur/.

Scambary, J. (2015) 'In search of white elephants: The political economy of resource income expenditure in East Timor', *Critical Asian Studies*, vol. 47, no. 2, pp. 283–308. doi.org/10.1080/14672715.2015.1041281.

Scheiner, C. (2014) *How long will the Petroleum Fund carry Timor-Leste?* La'o Hamutuk – The Timor-Leste Institute for Development Monitoring and Analysis. Available at: www.laohamutuk.org/econ/model/ScheinerPetrolFund17Feb2014en.pdf.

Scheiner, C. (2015a) *Can the Petroleum Fund exorcise the resource curse from Timor-Leste?* La'o Hamutuk – The Timor-Leste Institute for Development Monitoring and Analysis. Available at: www.laohamutuk.org/econ/exor/ScheinerFundExorciseCurseJun2015en.pdf.

Scheiner, C. (2015b) 'Fiscal strategies and their implications for wealth distribution', Paper presented at ANU Timor-Leste Update Conference, 19–20 November 2015, Canberra. Available at: www.laohamutuk.org/econ/briefing/ScheinerANUNov2015.pdf.

Schwarz, R. (2008) 'The political economy of state-formation in the Arab Middle East: Rentier states, economic reform, and democratization', *Review of International Political Economy*, vol. 15, no. 4, pp. 599–621. doi.org/10.1080/09692290802260662.

Soares, A. de J. (2013) 'Combating corruption: Avoiding "institutional ritualism"', in Leach, M. and Kingsbury, D. (eds) *The politics of Timor-Leste: Democratic consolidation after intervention*, New York: Cornell University Press, pp. 85–97.

Soares, A. de J. (2015) 'A social movement as an antidote to corruption', in Ingram, S., Kent, L. and Andrew McWilliam, A. (eds) *A new era? Timor-Leste after the UN*, Canberra: ANU Press, pp. 203–212. doi.org/10.22459/NE.09.2015.13.

The Asia Foundation (2017) *Timor-Leste 2016 Tatoli! Public opinion poll.* Available at: asiafoundation.org/wp-content/uploads/2017/06/2016-Tatoli-Survey-Report-ENGLISH.pdf.

World Bank (2013) *Timor-Leste social assistance public expenditure and program performance report*, Report No. 73488-TP, Social Protection and Labor Human Development Sector Unit, East Asia and Pacific Region. Available at: documents.worldbank.org/curated/en/193531468117251571/pdf/734840 WP0P126300PER000240June00eng.pdf.

World Bank and Ministry of Finance (GoTL) (2015) *Democratic Republic of Timor-Leste public expenditure review: Infrastructure*, Report No. AUS6142, GMFDR, East Pacific and Pacific. Available at: openknowledge. worldbank.org/bitstream/handle/10986/22367/PERI0FINAL00WB0site0. pdf;sequence=1.

4

Piloting the experimental ZEESM megaproject: Performing the future in the Oecusse-Ambeno enclave[1]

Laura S. Meitzner Yoder

'So, what did you think of the inauguration?' I asked my young Oecusse friend as we joined hundreds of people walking home from Lifau. We were leaving the site of the district-wide Catholic mass and the dedication of a sizable ship monument depicting the disembarkation of Portuguese Dominicans and their first contact with several Oecusse men. It was 27 November 2015, the culmination of the week-long festivities of what the national government of Timor-Leste was calling a 'celebration of the affirmation of Timorese identity' (GoTL 2015). The purported reason for the event was the (approximately) 500th anniversary of the arrival of Portuguese clerics to Oecusse's shores, co-celebrated with the 40th anniversary of a Timor-Leste 1975 declaration of independence. This landing was celebrated because it symbolised the start of Portuguese presence on the island of Timor, which developed into a colonial presence that lasted until Portugal abandoned the region due to civil chaos

---

1   This paper draws on ZEESM publicity and public meetings from 2013 onward and focuses on events surrounding the celebration in Oecusse in late November 2015, as well as near-annual visits from 2011 to 2017. I conducted initial ethnographic fieldwork in Timor in 2001, and was based in Oecusse from 2002 to 2004.

at home. The Oecusse-Ambeno region had served as the first colonial capital from 1701 to 1769. It retained its ties to Portuguese rule even when the surrounding territories came under Dutch control from the eighteenth century, leaving Oecusse an enclave of the Portuguese territory that eventually became what is today the majority Catholic nation of Timor-Leste. The fledgling nation was under military occupation by its Indonesian neighbour from 1975 until 1999. Following a brief period under United Nations transitional administration, Timor-Leste became fully self-governing in 2002.

The previous week had featured multiple nights of international musical entertainment on a large stage, a local products fair, mass Catholic weddings and confirmations, and popular events like motocross competitions. This evening's festivities featured official actions (signing plaques, unveiling statues, short speeches and blessing the monument with holy water) by a range of visiting dignitaries from Dili, church leaders and envoys from Portuguese-speaking countries who had spent the previous hours – or days – ferried from one high-level event to another in VIP cars. An impressive fireworks display – launched from the beach and two boats some distance from the shore, and featuring a small drone dramatically hovering unscathed among the aerial explosions – had capped off the celebration. The volume of visitors and of public entertainment over the past four days exceeded the sum total of everything the largely agrarian Oecusse district had seen in the previous decade combined.

My friend was silent for a while, and then she responded:

> To be honest, it made me angry. The celebration was in Oecusse, but it was not about Oecusse. We, and our Oecusse cultural traditions, barely got mentioned. It was about Portugal, and run by Dili. All those guests did not even learn about our home; we didn't even get to see them. And there should have been *takanab* [one highly appreciated interactive form of Oecusse ritual speech that usually serves to open events] at the monument's inauguration.

This response illustrates some of the complexities facing the nascent government of the Special Administrative Region of the Oecusse-Ambeno enclave (RAEOA [*Região Administrativa Especial de Oé-Cusse-Ambeno*]). In addition to marking 500 years of Portuguese contact and 40 years since declaration of Timor-Leste's independence, the November 2015 celebration was simultaneously the major public 'opening event' of the Special Economic Zone of Social Market Economy of Timor-Leste

(ZEESM [*Zonas Especiais de Economia Social de Mercado de Timor-Leste*]), which came into being in 2014 and since 2015 has been in effect a radically decentralised government project. ZEESM exhibits a distinctly and deliberately futuristic vision, and the specific ways in which this vision is being expressed in Oecusse will have significant impacts on the current and near-future lives and livelihoods of Oecusse residents (Meitzner Yoder 2015). This chapter briefly explains the genesis of the ZEESM initiative and its overarching vision for transforming Oecusse realities. It then examines multiple actors' perspectives on the relationships between the past and the future, how the approach of 'investment enclaving' is being deployed in ZEESM as a pilot project, and the performative aspects of this initiative.

'Creating the future': From the National Development Plan to a regional government

The genesis of ZEESM lies in the 2011–2030 national strategic development plan; thus, the overarching vision for how this project transforms Oecusse bears implications for the rest of Timor-Leste. This document names the creation of special economic zones (SEZs) as central in the economic plan (Republica Democratica de Timor-Leste 2011). The plan lists six 'National Strategic Zones' that span the territory, and the Oecusse-Ambeno SEZ is the first to be implemented. In government speeches and documents, the creation of the Oecusse SEZ is frequently cited to be in line with the national development plan, billing Oecusse as a 'pilot project' that will set an example and a new path for the rest of the nation. A budget report and request to Parliament states that the new ZEESM concept will 'challenge the development paradigm and model in Timor-Leste and will start first from Oecusse-Ambeno' (RAEOA and ZEESM 2015: 2 [my translation]). The Oecusse-Ambeno zone is envisioned to introduce a multiplicity of novel changes:

> There are a variety of potential sectors that will be developed such as international trade, CIQS [Customs, Immigration, Quarantine, and Security], development at selected junction points, new plantation areas and new livestock extension services, new fish processing industries and a new creative industry, as well as new tourist sites. (Republica Democratica de Timor-Leste 2011: 116)

Tourism gets the most attention for economic development in the enclave (ibid.: 96). In the case of Oecusse, the plan to develop 'a special administrative policy and economic regime' for the district fulfils a 2002 constitutional mandate for attention to the unique situation of the enclave. In 2013, the Council of Ministers and Prime Minister Xanana Gusmão appointed former prime minister Mari Alkatiri to an undefined term of service in order to oversee the development of the Oecusse-Ambeno SEZ. Alkatiri began by enlisting the aid of international technicians and consultants, and seeking inroads with potential investors. From these practices emerged an ultramodern vision of Oecusse's future, in which foreign investment in as-yet-unidentified sectors would transform the largely agrarian district into an urban industrial hub. The initial stage centres on a massive revamping of the tiny downtown of the enclave's capital, Pante Makassar, replacing simple, functional existing buildings with architectural novelties and adding major infrastructure projects deemed foundational and necessary to attract foreign visitors and investors to the district. In May 2013, Alkatiri went on a publicity visit to Oecusse in which he unveiled this plan fully formed in a series of speeches and a public slide presentation, informing rather than consulting the local population of this futuristic vision for their district. From 2014 to early 2017, under the heading 'Creating the Future', the ZEESM website showed the same sketches of the projects currently underway that were shown to the population in public meetings since 2013 and still prominently displayed on Oecusse billboards in early 2018.[2] The widely publicised price tag for the entire ZEESM endeavour was estimated to be US$4.11 billion, with one-third coming (mostly at the outset) from public funding. From 2014 to 2017, ZEESM received US$544 million from the national government (La'o Hamutuk 2018). As discussed elsewhere in this volume, at present over 90 per cent of the national state budget comes from oil and gas revenues that became accessible within the past decade, so, in a real sense, the ZEESM endeavour is made possible by this petroleum income.

2   The ZEESM projects listed include only planned buildings and capital investments: the international airport; the Hotel ZEESM Timor-Leste; a tourism and cultural information centre; a multi-storey RAEOA administrative building; the expansive ZEESM villa and residential complex; a seafront park with free wi-fi; a ferry boat; a power station; a garden and sports park; a 200-metre dam and associated irrigation network; 50 kilometres of coastal and lowland urban roads, especially from Oecusse's eastern Indonesian border to the Lifau Monument; a 380-metre bridge along the coastal road; and an amphitheatre-style Lifau Monument 'for the celebration of the 500th anniversary of the arrival of Portuguese navigators and missionaries in Lifau-Oecusse, a fact that marks the beginning of construction of the new identity of Timor Leste' (ZEESM 2016).

The declaration of Oecusse as an SEZ brought about a major change in its governance structure. To enable the project, the enclave district was legally named a Special Economic Zone of Social Market Economy (ZEESM) in mid-2014. The RAEOA was created and formally implemented by law in January 2015. The RAEOA is presently tasked with implementing the ZEESM project; government letterhead lists both names and logos, indicating that the Regional Authority (the district's government) and the SEZ (an economic development project) are coterminous (RAEOA and ZEESM 2015). All power over governance and budget for the district (except the usual national matters of external defence, currency policy, etc.) were vested in the Regional Authority, and Alkatiri has a skeleton crew of seven Oecusse-based regional secretaries of various sectors. As the centrally appointed head of the ZEESM 'pilot project' as well as president of the Regional Authority,[3] Alkatiri oversees the district development plan to align all public spending – including schoolteachers' salaries, water supply, and health promotion and care facilities – with construction for the substantial public infrastructure projects underway. Importantly, civil servants in social services and public offices in Oecusse now report to the Regional Authority in Oecusse instead of to the national capital's Dili offices of their various sectors. The RAEOA-ZEESM entity was tasked with executing the November 2015 celebration as one of its first duties, simultaneously showcasing its plans and construction progress to date.

The beginning is the future; the future begins in the past

Nationwide, Oecusse is known primarily for being the place where the Portuguese first landed and where the Catholic Church first entered the island, and is often named as one of Timor-Leste's 'most traditional' districts (ZEESM 2013: 51). The enclave's historical importance is a source of great pride to Oecusse people, and modern political figures can reliably prompt an Oecusse crowd to cheer enthusiastically by repeating the refrain, 'Without Oecusse, there would be no Timor-Leste!' At the November 2015 celebration, as in ZEESM foundational documents,

---

3   As a result of mid-2017 elections, Alkatiri once again took the national position of prime minister; he left that post after the May 2018 elections. However, in 2017, he did not relinquish his role as Oecusse's president of the RAEOA, but instead appointed an interim president from among the regional secretaries.

then president Taur Matan Ruak extended the importance of these events to declare that Oecusse-Ambeno was where the groundwork for the modern nation-state of Timor-Leste was laid, and that the arrival of the Catholic Church and the Portuguese were foundational to the East Timorese as a people. The president's media report stated:

> In his speech, the Head of State designated Lifau as the place of birth and development of the Timorese identity, 'It was here that our relationship with the Portuguese people began and where it blossomed, thus shaping our identity – an identity built on two important pillars: the Portuguese language and Catholicism'.

> H.E. the President congratulated the people of Oecusse, as well as all Timorese, the Portuguese people and the peoples of all other CPLP [Portuguese-speaking] countries, and reminded them that Timor-Leste was born in Lifau and developed in Oecusse. The unveiling ceremony ended with a photo session with CPLP dignitaries and the bishops. (Presidência da República de Timor-Leste 2015b)

Capitalising on popular conceptions of Oecusse as 'the place where it all began', the ubiquitous tagline of the ZEESM project, featured on the letterhead logo as well as on hundreds of signs and banners throughout Oecusse, is *O inicio é o futuro* ('The beginning is the future'). Timorese political figures have drawn rhetorical parallels between the importance of Oecusse in national political history and its anticipated importance in Timor's economic future; the place credited with getting Timor-Leste started will now be the model for a new program of economic development and a new era of prosperity. The ZEESM website proclaims:

> Besides the history of the Timorese nation having started in Oé-Cusse, the fact is that it is one of the poorest regions, with more than 60% of the population living below the poverty line, was also one of the reasons why it was chosen to start a new future for the country. A future committed to Prosperity, Peace and Performance. (ZEESM 2016)

The future-oriented ZEESM project explicitly aims to be different from the past and to supersede the conditions of the present. Among Oecusse people, as is common throughout Timor and the broader region, the past is not disconnected from the future, but rather interwoven to create a comprehensible whole. The past informs the present (and future), providing a framework within which decisions are made and life makes sense. Writing about Oecusse's Atoni ethnolinguistic group in Indonesian West Timor, Schulte Nordholdt (1971: 61) explains, 'In his [Atoni] culture the past is normative and is considered the ideal situation – it cannot but have been better than the present'. The present is a by-product of an idealised past, which focuses less on the colonial connection than on indigenous authorities and polities. Topics under frequent discussion by Ambeno people involve folklore and legends about indigenous inhabitants, early rulers and leading figures.

In the middle of the November 2015 celebration, the local academics' Oecusse-Ambeno Intellectuals' Association presented the preliminary results of their inaugural research, entitled *Oral history of the Oe-Kusi–Ambeno people* (later published as Taçain et al. 2016). Alkatiri briefly attended to offer an opening speech with reflections on the conflictual nature of studying history, and joked how different it is from science, which now explains many things that people did not understand in the past. Mentioning that identity is dynamic, he said that he didn't want people to come to Oecusse to see the past, emphatically stating, 'We are missing the future, not the past'. Then, true to the Oecusse and Atoni predilection for history-telling, the research team proceeded to present their distinctly past-centric report. For more than two hours, the research report narrated the development of regionally diverse social structures present in Oecusse-Ambeno, weaving in the legendary indigenous rulers, the political rise and fall of local dynasties and the subsequent creation of sacred and politically important places throughout Oecusse. They explained why this research was their inaugural project: to provide information about the traditional social structure of their own Ambeno people, since within Oecusse there are many differences in perception about history; and to preserve 'for the generations today and in the future' the inherent variability in the data, as people in each region of Oecusse tell history in ways that put themselves in premier positions. Their project was based largely on interviews with 40 older men from various villages who are acknowledged as authoritative on matters of Oecusse-Ambeno history and custom, but the project's stated goal was not to present one standardised narrative, as none is possible. For the local researchers and for their participants, their descriptions acknowledge the past as critically important in giving meaning to and making sense of the present and the future – not as something to be superseded or supplanted by new, modern or scientific understandings of how the world operates.

Investment enclaving: Pilot projects and the source of future prosperity

Investment is the quintessential future-oriented activity. It involves present sacrifice for potential future gain, often forgoing some current use in hopes of yielding even more in the time to come. The entire Oecusse-Ambeno project is predicated on the premise that building infrastructure in Oecusse will enable the realisation of some types of economic development initiatives that will bring outside wealth into the district, which will in turn generate profit and economic growth. The early stages of the project are aimed at providing the basic infrastructure (e.g. roads, electricity, transportation) that the ZEESM leadership believes will enable the district to be sufficiently attractive to foreign investors.

The investment-oriented ZEESM-RAEOA entity – simultaneously infrastructure-building project and local government – complicates the state/corporate divide common in discussions of how global market rise affects the relevance of state governance. Speaking of extractive oil industries in Africa, Ferguson (2005: 378) writes, 'What is noteworthy is the extent to which this economic investment has been concentrated in secured enclaves, often with little or no economic benefit to the wider society'. He continues:

> The clearest case of *extractive enclaving* (and no doubt the most attractive for the foreign investor) is provided by offshore oil extraction, as in Angola, where neither the oil nor most of the money it brings in ever touches Angolan soil. (ibid.: 378 [my emphasis])

He describes a situation in which profits skip among global capitals rather than flowing through national economies, 'noteworthy for their ability to bypass the national-state frame altogether' (ibid.: 379). Oecusse's future wealth – unlike that of the Tasi Mane project described by Bovensiepen in this volume – does not depend on natural resource extraction, but rather on what I will call an intense *investment enclaving* by the state, and hoped-for foreign business interests in limited, circumscribed areas. In Oecusse, the enclaving of public spending – within Oecusse, disproportionately on coastal megaprojects; and on a national level, disproportionately in the SEZ – does not automatically lead to economic improvement in the whole of Oecusse, nor in the rest of Timor-Leste. And while Ferguson's (2005: 79) corporate extractive enclaves expect to provide all their own security, infrastructure and services, the Timorese state's investment enclave is oriented towards providing the basic infrastructure and services deemed essential precursors to attracting foreign investment.

National leaders have raised the matter of inter-district equity, justifying the disproportionate investment in this stage of the ZEESM development and calling upon Oecusse people to invest themselves. While visiting the new power plant in Oecusse, then president Taur Matan Ruak stated:

> I ask the people of Oecussi, authorities, scholars, the youth, community leaders, traditional leaders, the population in general, to support the establishment of the ZEEMS [sic]. All other municipalities had to tighten their belts so as to save up for Oecussi. This is a great opportunity for the people of Oecussi. The President asks you to contribute to the success of this project. (Presidência da República de Timor-Leste 2015a)

The former president Ramos Horta reminded the population that infrastructure is the necessary precondition to attract investors, and that the pilot project of ZEESM will be of eventual benefit to the other 12 districts (Matadalan Online 2015). While the present directionality of funding is being channelled from Dili to Oecusse (as expected in this stage of using public funds for major infrastructure projects), there is a clear expectation that this public spending on infrastructure will eventually yield financial gain to the nation as a whole.

The initial public spending on the Oecusse enclave's infrastructure is rarely framed as motivated by altruistic or humanitarian impulses; nor does it express a desire to bring this heretofore neglected district up to the level of other districts. The 2011 National Strategic Plan is explicit about the role of SEZs as central to national economic development strategy. These zones are expected to 'drive domestic development' and 'generat[e] national income' by contributing to the national coffers (Republica Democratica de Timor-Leste 2011: 155). ZEESM documents certainly demonstrate an understanding that the initiative is a novel approach to economic development that aspires to be a 'national model', a 'new paradigm', a 'pilot project' and an 'incubator' for what can be later replicated elsewhere in Timor-Leste (RAEOA and ZEESM 2015). Alkatiri has hailed the project as a 'development laboratory' and as a 'model' (*referência*) for Timor-Leste (Agência Lusa 2015).

THE PROMISE OF PROSPERITY

ZEESM is not only to serve as a pilot for a new national approach to economic growth, but also as a testing ground for new policies, laws and models of governance that may later be extended nationwide. Describing the project plans, Alkatiri noted that Oecusse would have a nationally distinct legal framework: 'The immigration law, labour, fiscal, trades, everything you need, it has to be different than the normal one here in Timor-Leste, to be a bit more attractive for investors' (Gabinete da Ex Primeiru Ministro Dr Mari Alkatiri 2013). In April 2014, the national Council of Ministers approved an accelerated legislative process to permit infrastructure preparations for the November 2015 celebration (Business Timor 2014). One of the pieces of legislation that passed concerned land, which is especially notable as Timor-Leste had yet to develop a comprehensive land policy or associated legislation on a national level until mid-2017, when Timor-Leste promulgated a national land law (Almeida 2016; Batterbury et al. 2015). Section IV, Article 26 of Law No. 3/2014 (published on 18 June 2014) has two clauses regarding land utilisation that focus on the state's right to take land for purposes of development and for investors in economic activity, but no mention is made of local residents' land rights or uses.

Just as not all expenditures are investments, not all pilot projects are built to fly. Pilots that are miniature, contained experiments may not contain the design elements that will enable them to be replicated elsewhere (Billé 2010). Is ZEESM meant to be replicable? This is clearly the stated intent as written in the national strategic development plan. A pilot project involves both connection and uniqueness, linkage and separation. A useful pilot will be conducted in conditions typical enough of the whole so that the results and lessons learned will not be explained away as effects of some anomalous quality of the pilot's context. The pilot project is also an opportunity to test various elements – economic models, policies, novel governance arrangements – in a relatively low-risk setting to deliberately contain failure so that major errors would not have catastrophic effects on the larger enterprise or setting. One very important function of a pilot project is to give rise to lessons that enable the implementer to learn from them and make corrections when expanding out or scaling up. Capturing such lessons learned, however, requires deliberate, dedicated effort by project overseers to document and to evaluate what is done – including naming unsuccessful aspects and identifying how they could be addressed in the future.

Oecusse's physical separation from other districts is what caused the region to be promised special administrative and economic treatment in Timor-Leste's 2002 constitution;[4] since 2014, this has taken the form of an explicitly investor-friendly incipient SEZ governed by an unelected regional authority. Since 1999, Oecusse's persistent logistical difficulties in communication with the eastern districts have necessitated some degree of self-governance in the enclave, as land and air access to the eastern districts are scant and transport by sea is erratic due to seasonal conditions and periodic unavailability of the boat service. From this perspective, Oecusse's *atypical* geographic isolation may have been its comparative advantage as a place to develop and implement untried governance practices for Timor-Leste, including significant upfront spending of public money in an effort to attract foreign investment.

Conclusion: Performing national visions

How might ZEESM illustrate the future vision of Timor-Leste? In the authors' workshop that gave rise to this book, several participants commented that Oecusse seemed to be serving as a testing ground for a new national vision of economic development embodied in ZEESM. Some initiatives of the international humanitarian and state-building community from the United Nations era treated all of Timor-Leste in this way – as a manageably small and compact entity in which it ought to (and just might) be possible to get everything right, as if histories did not matter and as if states, economies or societies could be built from scratch (Kammen 2009). The ZEESM miniature model for a state vision of prosperity has been enabled by the nation's present oil and gas wealth, even as it purportedly aims to attract a different income stream for the nation. Speaking of ZEESM in Oecusse as a pilot links the outcomes in Oecusse rhetorically to the rest of the nation, even though special legal and administrative regimes entrench the enclave's distinction and isolation. In contrast to the administrative era of the United Nations and international advisers, Oecusse could provide an opportunity for Timorese to develop laws and policies that suit the realities of a largely agrarian but recently urbanising context. On a national level, the president has emphasised the importance of investing in human capital, as it is more certain to provide returns than building infrastructure (*Decreto do*

---

4   Section 5, Clause 3, and Section 71, Clause 2, respectively.

Parlamento Nacional n.o 20/III 2016). Ferguson (2005) reminds us that it is not only possible, but common for hyper-networked fiscal enclaves to look like economic successes while leaving vast tracts of minimally governed hinterlands ignored or out of the picture – a situation that may be of low moral concern to an international offshore expatriate oil investor, but is an integral responsibility of a state apparatus.

There are multiple layers of performance in ZEESM. As a pilot project, many are watching and waiting to see how the district fares as the subject in this experimental economic laboratory. The 'show' must be good enough to impress and subsequently woo potential investors to buy into the company. For ZEESM project managers, part of the performance pressure for the early activities is to demonstrate competence and efficiency in modern governance, employing an ability to accomplish extraordinary transformation in a difficult setting. The November 2015 celebration was a performance of Timorese political visions of national identity for multiple audiences. With Oecusse as the stage, ZEESM is simultaneously playing the roles of building project contractor and regional government, performing a new iteration of the state vision of development, political consensus and a prosperous future.

References

Agência Lusa (2015) *Projecto de OeCusse deve ser referência para todo o país – Mari Alkatiri* [OeCusse project should be a model for the whole country – Mari Alkatiri]. Available at: portocanal.sapo.pt/noticia/50095/.

Almeida, B. (2016) *Land tenure legislation in Timor-Leste,* Leiden: Universiteit Leiden Faculty of Law and The Asia Foundation. Available at: asiafoundation.org/wp-content/uploads/2016/04/Land-Tenure_TL_EN.pdf.

Batterbury, S. P. J., Palmer, L. R., Reuter, T. R., de Calvalho, D. do A., Kehi, B. and Cullen, A. (2015) 'Land access and livelihoods in post-conflict Timor-Leste: no magic bullets', *International Journal of the Commons*, vol. 9, no. 2, pp. 1–29. doi.org/10.18352/ijc.514.

Billé, R. (2010) 'Action without change? On the use and usefulness of pilot experiments in environmental management', *S.A.P.I.E.N.S. [Online]* vol. 3, no. 1. Available at: journals.openedition.org/sapiens/979.

Business Timor (2014) 'Preparasaun Tinan 500 Portugal tama Timor, KM Hasai Pontu 12 ba ZEEMS' [In preparation for 500 years of Portugal's entry to Timor, Council of Ministers gives 12 points about ZEESM], *Jornal Bisnis Timor*, 28 April. Available at: www.jornalbisnistimor.com/notisia/politika/1990-preparasaun-tinan-500-portugal-tama-timor-km-hasai-pontu-12-ba-zeems.

Decreto do Parlamento Nacional n.o 20/III, Orçamento Geral do Estado para (2016) *Mensagem ao Parlamento Nacional do Presidente da República Democrática de Timor-Leste: Taur Matan Ruak na Promulgação do Orçamento Geral do Estado para 2016* [Message to national Parliament from the President of the Democratic Republic of Timor-Leste: Taur Matan Ruak on the Promulgation of the General State Budget for 2016].

Ferguson, J. (2005) 'Seeing like an oil company: space, security, and global capital in neoliberal Africa', *American Anthropologist*, vol. 107, no. 3, pp. 377–382. doi.org/10.1525/aa.2005.107.3.377.

Gabinete da Ex Primeiru Ministro Dr Mari Alkatiri (2013) *Special zones of social market economy: Pilot location Oecusse*. Available at: www.zeesm.com/zeesm-official-video/ (site discontinued) [accessed 11 January 2015].

GoTL (Government of Timor-Leste) (2015) *500th anniversary of the Affirmation of the Timorese Identity*. Available at: timor-leste.gov.tl/?p=13165&lang=en.

Kammen, D. (2009) 'Fragments of utopia: Popular yearnings in East Timor', *Journal of Southeast Asian Studies*, vol. 40, no. 2, pp. 385–408. doi.org/10.1017/S0022463409000216.

La'o Hamutuk (2018) *Rights and sustainability in Timor-Leste's development*, La'o Hamutuk – The Timor-Leste Institute for Development Monitoring and Analysis, Dili. Available at: www.laohamutuk.org/econ/briefing/RightSustain CurrentEn.pps [accessed 24 February 2018].

Matadalan Online (2015) 'Projetu ZEEMS La Deskrimina Munisípiu 12' [ZEESM Project does not discriminate against 12 municipalities], *Matadalan Online*, 22 August. Available at: matadalan.com/projetu-zeems-la-desk rimina-munisipiu-12/ (site discontinued).

Meitzner Yoder, L. S. (2015) 'The development eraser: Fantastical schemes, aspirational distractions and high modern mega-events in the Oecusse enclave, Timor-Leste', *Journal of Political Ecology*, vol. 22, pp. 299–321. Available at: jpe.library.arizona.edu/volume_22/Yoder2015.pdf. doi.org/10.2458/v22i1.21110.

Presidência da República de Timor-Leste (2015a) *H.E. the President of the Republic TMR Asks the Atoni People to Support ZEESM*. Pante Makassar: Ambeno. Available at: presidenciarepublica.tl/2015/12/01/h-e-the-president-of-the-republic-tmr-asks-the-atoni-people-to-support-zeesm/?lang=en.

Presidência da República de Timor-Leste (2015b) *H.E. the President of the Republic, Taur Matan Ruak, Unveils Monument in Lifau*. Dili. Available at: presidenciarepublica.tl/2015/12/03/h-e-the-president-of-the-republic-taur-matan-ruak-unveils-monument-in-lifau/?lang=en.

RAEOA and ZEESM (2015) *Audiência conjunta da Comissão C Parlamento Nacional* [Joint Hearing of Commission C of National Parliament], OGE RAEOA e ZEESM TL 2016.

Republica Democratica de Timor-Leste (2011) *Timor-Leste strategic development plan 2011–2030*, Dili: RDTL. Available at: www.laohamutuk.org/econ/SDP/2011/Timor-Leste-Strategic-Plan-2011-20301.pdf.

Schulte Nordholt, H. G. ([1966] 1971) *The political system of the Atoni of Timor*, Verhandelingen van Het Koninklijk Instituut voor Taal-, Land-, en Volkenkunde, 60, The Hague: Martinus Nijhoff. doi.org/10.1017/S00 41977X00110419.

Taçain, J., Bacun, P., and de Almeida, N. C. (2016) *Kultura no Natureza Ema Atoni-Oékussi-Ambeno* [Culture and Nature of Atoni-Oékussi-Ambeno People], Dili, Timor-Leste: UNTL.

ZEESM (2013) *Projecto piloto distrito Oecusse* [*First steps towards a new Oecusse*].

ZEESM (2016) Home page. Available at: zeesm.com/oe-cusse-ambeno/ (site discontinued) [accessed 30 January 2016].

5

Expropriation or plunder? Property rights and infrastructure development in Oecusse

Bernardo Almeida

The prerogative of state institutions to expropriate property for public purposes is established by virtually all national legal frameworks, but the specificities of this power vary substantially. In line with other countries, the Constitution of the Democratic Republic of Timor-Leste (RDTL, *República Democrática de Timor-Leste*, in Portuguese) gives the state the possibility of expropriating property, which is often presented by politicians and state officials as an unchallengeable power. 'Whether people like it or not' (*hakarak ka lakohi* in Tetun) is an expression that is invoked to argue that when the state needs people's property, they must surrender it with no contestation (see Bovensiepen, Chapter 6). But is this true? Does the RDTL Constitution give the state an almost absolute power to expropriate property? And can ordinary citizens contest expropriation?

This chapter debates the legal meaning and limits of the right to property (land and existing buildings and plantations) and the power of the state to expropriate it, as established by the RDTL Constitution and infra-constitutional legislation. Although required by the constitution, the development of legal and administrative mechanisms to secure people's property rights is very limited in Timor-Leste, and a legal process for expropriations is non-existent. This is particularly relevant under the government's current development strategy – that centres on the so-called mega infrastructure projects – for which obtaining access to land is paramount and is happening in several areas of the country. The debate proposed by this chapter is framed around ongoing state-led processes to obtain land for infrastructure projects for the Special Economic and Social Market Zone of Oecusse (ZEESM [*Zonas Especiais de Economia Social de Mercado de Timor-Leste*]). This case study will show, first, the state's failure to develop mechanisms that protect and, when necessary, expropriate individual and collective rights to property and, second, how this failure is used by the state to conduct illegal dispossession.

An important postscript note must be made. In 2017, a few months after writing this chapter, a new Land Law officially called Special Regime for the Determination of Ownership of Immovable Property, and an Expropriation for Public Purposes Law were approved by Parliament. Despite some limitations, these laws are an important step towards stronger protection of people's property rights and regulation of the state's prerogative to expropriate land, but their success is dependent on a difficult process of implementation. The next few years will show whether there is a real political will to strengthening people's property rights, or if these laws are only legal artefacts with little or no meaning in practice.

Right to property, expropriation and ZEESM

In 2013, the government announced the idea of developing a ZEESM in the Timorese enclave of Oecusse (see Meitzner Yoder, Chapter 4). The government presented ZEESM as an innovative pilot project that would transform the poor and neglected Oecusse enclave into a new regional hub for trade, industry and tourism. Central to the project is the state-led construction of multiple infrastructure projects, including roads, a hotel and an international airport, with an estimated budget of over US$4 billion for the next 20 years, one-third of which is supported by public funds. To implement this project, a vast area of land is needed – estimates range between 107 and 1,000 hectares (see *Independente* 2014; ZEESM 2013–2014: 11). In 2014, Parliament approved a new autonomous administrative status for the enclave, called the Special Administrative Region of Oecusse-Ambeno (RAEOA by its Portuguese acronym) to implement ZEESM (Law 3/2014, further regulated by Decree-Law 5/2015).

Infrastructure projects need land but legally obtaining access and rights to land is a difficult issue. Over three centuries of Portuguese colonialism, 24 years of Indonesian occupation, and displacement and dispossession caused by several waves of conflict have resulted in a complex scenario of overlapping land claims and unclear land rights (Fitzpatrick 2002). Since independence, little has been achieved in developing a property system that can clarify the validity of land titles issued by the Portuguese and Indonesian administrations, address the grievances caused by forced displacement and occupation, and clarify who has which property rights (Almeida 2016). A central point for the development of a fair property system is the legal recognition and protection of the rights of those who have never had any formal land title. Both the Portuguese and Indonesian administrations issued formal land titles, but the beneficiaries were mostly the elites close to these administrations. The great majority of Timorese have always accessed land through customary systems, characterised by complex networks of rights and obligations connected to customary groups, and have never seen their property rights recognised by state law. Under the current legal framework – especially the selectivity with which laws are interpreted and applied – they live under the real threat of seeing the land they live on, and to which they are culturally and spiritually connected, simply being classified as 'state land'.

Problems with land acquisition have contaminated the initial optimism that the population of Oecusse felt when ZEESM was announced (Rose 2016: 1; *Timor Post* 2015b). A preliminary ZEESM study concluded that 'almost all the land parcels [in the ZEESM area] are private land' and 'state land is negligible' (ZEESM 2013–2014: 17). This conclusion was based on the results of *Ita Nia Rai* ('Our Land'), a systematic land registration project from 2007 to 2012 supported by the United States Agency for International Development that registered urban parcels in the district capitals of Timor-Leste, but whose results were left in a legal limbo (Almeida 2016: 35). During the initial presentations of ZEESM to the Oecusse population in 2013, the project's main promoter stated that compensation for property rights would not be paid with money but by making land rights holders 'shareholders' of the project (Meitzner Yoder 2015: 308). This controversial idea for compensations has now been forgotten in favour of an even more controversial approach. Through an informal process and without sufficient previous consultation, written notice, adequate documentation or a clear time frame, the RAEOA administrative bodies compelled people to surrender the requested land, most of it used for housing and agriculture (Januario 2016a, 2016b, 2016c, 2016d; Meitzner Yoder 2015: 314, 2016: 1–2; Rose 2016: 2). People were offered construction materials and meagre sums of money to reconstruct structures built on the seized land, but at least to those without pre-independence land titles, no compensation has yet been paid. The rationale presented by the RAEOA representatives for the lack of compensation is that people without land titles are 'illegally' using the land; furthermore, the necessary legal framework to pay compensation is still missing, therefore none can be paid (*Jornal Nacional Diário* 2016; *Timor Post* 2015a). The registration conducted by the *Ita Nia Rai* project seems to have been ignored. The evictions proceeded without any prior social and cultural assessment or resettlement plan; in several cases, the construction materials provided were scarce and of poor quality and the money for reconstruction was insufficient to pay contracted labourers (a report from the Ombudsman's Office details some of these problems – see *Provedoria dos Direitos Humanos e Justiça* 2016). Many families have ended up living in tents or improvised shelters (Meitzner Yoder 2016: 2). There are also reports of people being threatened with the use of police force (*Jornal Nacional Diário* 2015). Rose (2016: 2) reports one case in which the land users managed to resist eviction and get some compensation from the construction company, but this seems to be an exception. Land has been taken for various projects, including widening of roads, an airport and a hotel constructed by the RAEOA. Future projects will require more land.

Interestingly, as in the case of Suai (detailed in this volume by Bovensiepen), the power of the state to take land for all kinds of purposes goes almost unquestioned both by state officials and the people affected. The debate is mostly centred on compensation and the lack of due process. In Oecusse, the lack of compensation for land was compared with the case of Suai, where US$3 per square metre were paid to land claimants, independent of whether or not they had land titles. The president of the RAEOA stated that if the affected people – most of them subsistence farmers – wanted to get compensation, they should appeal to the courts (*Jornal Nacional Diário* 2016). But with little knowledge about their rights and obligations in this process, no financial capacity to hire a qualified lawyer and no state legal aid offered to them, it is very unlikely that this problem will ever be analysed by a court. Furthermore, as the case of Suai well exemplifies, the payment of compensation to the affected people is often not enough to avoid the social problems caused by expropriation.

This case study raises the question: was the Authority of the RAEOA legally entitled to dispossess these people the way it did or was it, in fact, an act of plunder?

The legal framework for property rights and expropriation in Timor-Leste

The right to property in international law

The Universal Declaration of Human Rights (UDHR) from 1948 is the starting point for the protection of the right to property in modern international law. Despite not being a treaty, UDHR assumes a central role in the protection of human rights, and it is often referred to by scholars and practitioners as part of customary international law (constant and uniform practice of states). It is, therefore, a primary source of international law (Hannum 1996; Jacobs 2013: 91). Article 17 of UDHR, establishing the right to property, is central to this legal analysis. This right is divided into two points: (1) 'Everyone has the right to own property alone as well as in association with others'; and (2) 'No one shall be arbitrarily deprived of his property'. The drafting of this article was difficult and controversial, due to opposing political views of property (Jacobs 2013: 91; Dehaibi 2015: 17). The final text of article 17 is vague as result of this controversy, and the meaning and limits of the right to private property are still debated by academics and legal jurisprudence (Dehaibi 2015: 13; Golay and Cismas 2010: 11).

It is easiest to start by determining what the right to property is not. First, the right to property established in article 17 is not limited to individual rights to property but also includes collective rights (Golay and Cismas 2010: 3). This idea is relevant in contexts such as Timor-Leste, where collective forms of rights to property are widespread. Second, article 17 does not recognise unrestricted rights to property; however, limits can be imposed without an agreement between authors on where those limits should be placed (Dehaibi 2015: 17). While authors seem to agree on these two points, they do not significantly clarify the meaning of article 17. A strict interpretation sees the right to property as a right of individuals to keep the property already obtained by law but without any positive obligation of the state to provide property (Jacobs 2013: 97). Contrary to this view, some authors have called attention to the fact that protection of the right to property is not an end in itself but an instrument to protect human rights and achieve the self-realisation preconised by UDHR (Dehaibi 2015: 19; Joireman and Brown 2013: 168). Authors have pointed out at least three different perspectives on this instrumental role of property rights. Some have focused on the economic value of property as a way of protecting the human rights of the poorest (Commission on Legal Empowerment of the Poor and UNDP 2008: Chapter 2). Others have framed the right to private property as an intrinsic part of the right to an adequate standard of living, closely connected with the right to housing and food (Golay and Cismas 2010: 23). Finally, other authors maintain that some property has an intrinsic personal value for some people, and obtaining rights over that property is fundamental for their personhood and identity (Dehaibi 2015: 19; Joireman and Brown 2013: 166; Radin 1994: 71). Although coming from different perspectives, these three positions imply an active role of the state in legislating and acting to substantiate the two principles of the right to property; in other words, creating an enabling environment for fulfilling the right to property.

Ironically, the right to property is not part of the International Covenant on Economic, Social and Cultural Rights (ICESCR) from 1966 (Golay and Cismas 2010: 3). However, the right to property is implicit in the right to adequate housing established in article 11 of ICESCR. According to the General Comment No. 4 of the UN Committee on Economic, Social and Cultural Rights, legal tenure security is one of the criteria that defines adequate housing, and forced evictions can only proceed in very exceptional circumstances.

Furthermore, the right to property is part of key human rights treaties that Timor-Leste is signatory to, such as the international Convention on the Elimination of All Forms of Discrimination against Women from 1979 (ibid.: 4). The right to property and the right of states to expropriate it is further detailed by several soft-law instruments, such as the Basic Principles and Guidelines on Development-based Evictions and Displacement, the Association of Southeast Asian Nations (ASEAN) Human Rights Declaration, and the Voluntary Guidelines on the Responsible Governance of Tenure of Land, Fisheries and Forests in the Context of National Food Security.

Understanding the right to property in international law is fundamental to understanding the Timorese legal framework. The RDTL Constitution incorporates into the national legal framework all international treaties and agreements that Timor-Leste is party to, as well as customary principles of international law that prevail over national law (articles 9.1, 9.2 and 9.3 of the Constitution). As a result, international law sets the boundaries of the Timorese legislation and can be directly used in court, against or in absence of national law (Vasconcelos 2011: 52). Furthermore, the constitution incorporates UDHR as an interpretative element of the fundamental rights it prescribes. According to article 23 of the RDTL Constitution, the '[f]undamental rights enshrined in the Constitution … shall be interpreted in accordance with the Universal Declaration of Human Rights' (ibid.: 91).

In conclusion, article 17 of UDHR is central to understanding the right to property in the Timorese legislation. While the interpretation of this article is contentious, it is the author's view that this article obliges states to actively create the necessary conditions to guarantee the right to property, especially when this right is necessary to enforce other human rights. This obligation is especially strong when housing is at stake.

The right to property in the RDTL Constitution

This section analyses the right to property in the RDTL Constitution. This analysis divides the right to property into two parts: (1) the right to obtain and enjoy property; and (2) the right of the state to expropriate property.

The right to obtain, enjoy and transfer property

Article 54.1 of the RDTL Constitution establishes the basis for the right to property by determining that '[e]very individual has the right to private property and can transfer it during his or her lifetime or upon death, in accordance with the law'. While the second part of this article is straightforward, the first part follows an equivalent formulation of article 17 of UDHR, recalling the above-mentioned debate: Does the article simply create a state obligation to recognise existing rights to property, or does it represent a larger obligation to actively provide these rights?

Different methods of legal interpretation can help to answer this question. The first interpretative method is established by the RDTL Constitution: fundamental rights should be interpreted in light of UDHR. As debated above, article 17 of UDHR obliges states to provide rights to property; therefore, the same should be considered for article 54.1 of the Constitution.

This argument can be further strengthened by other methods of interpretation. A historical interpretation based on the minutes and documents of the Constituent Assembly in 2001 (available in the

Parliament archives) do not give much information about the origins and intentions of this article. Nevertheless, it is possible to see in these minutes a clear concern among members of the assembly to create a legal framework that can equitably address the injustices regarding legal rights to land left by colonialism and occupation (see also Devereux 2015: 246–254).

A systematic interpretation based on other articles of the RDTL Constitution can also help to clarify article 54.1. First, article 54.2 establishes that '[p]rivate property should not be used to the detriment of its social purpose'. This provision can have several interpretations. During the Indonesian occupation, the concept of 'social function' of the land was used to justify unfair dispossession by the state (Plessi and Leckie 2000: 7), one of the main concerns raised in 2001 by members of the Constituent Assembly (Devereux 2015: 250, 252). Furthermore, the prerogative of the state to take land from individuals is regulated in article 54.3. As such, the purpose of article 54.2 is not to justify any dispossession by the state. There are at least two other interpretations of this article: the first is to see it as a limit to the right to property, establishing that this right is not absolute and that the state can impose limitations on the use of property in order to safeguard collective interest – for example, restrictions on construction in protected areas (see Almeida 2016: 12; Vasconcelos 2011: 224). The second interpretation of this article is to see it as a guideline for the property system, determining that it should promote the reduction of inequalities in the distribution of wealth and income (compare with Miranda 2000: 526). These two interpretations do not exclude each other and both can be applied.

Article 141 should also be considered for the systematic interpretation of article 54.1. This article establishes that '[o]wnership, use and useful possession of land as one of the factors for economic production shall be regulated by law'. With economic production in view, this article again stresses the need for the state to develop and implement an adequate property system. Finally, article 2.4 of the RDTL Constitution determines that '[t]he state shall recognise and value the norms and customs of Timor-Leste that are not contrary to the Constitution and to any legislation dealing specifically with customary law'. As debated above, de facto customary systems regulate access to land for the great majority of Timorese. In light of this provision and in line with the previously analysed articles, there is an obligation – under the limits of the Constitution – to accommodate those customary systems into the property system. Finally, considering the debate around article 17 of the UDHR, and the role of the UDHR as a source of constitutional interpretation, it is clear that article 54.1 of the Constitution encompasses individual but also collective forms of ownership.

In conclusion, the first part of article 54.1 of the RDTL Constitution can be interpreted to mean various things. First, it can be interpreted as obliging the state to respect and protect the rights to property of those whose rights are already recognised by law. Second, it can be interpreted as the right of everyone to obtain rights to property and, once those rights are obtained, the right to use and enjoy that property. Third, this article can be interpreted as an obligation of the state to develop and implement the legal and administrative mechanisms to protect property rights not yet recognised by law. The range of rights to be protected is bound by the need to respect other fundamental rights, such as the right to adequate housing, the reduction of social inequalities, the respect for customary norms that do not contradict the constitution and the use of property as an economic factor. These three interpretations are not mutually exclusive; indeed, in the author's view, the first part of article 54.1 includes all of them. As a result, the lack of an adequate and functioning property system as described in the above case study represents a clear situation of unconstitutionality by omission. Thus, the constitution recognises the property rights of the people affected in the ZEESM case study, despite the state's failure to substantiate these rights. If by law people have these property rights, the state can only take them through an expropriation. The next section considers in which cases expropriation can legally happen.

The right of the state to expropriate property

Expropriation limits the right to property. Expropriation allows the state to acquire rights over property, against the will of the holder of that right, for reasons of public interest (Fonseca 2011: 10). The premise that justifies expropriation is that in some cases it is reasonable to disturb the right of one individual in order to provide a larger benefit to the community (Ronen 2013: 249). The right to expropriate encompasses two main questions: (1) In which situations can property be expropriated; and (2) Who has the authority to expropriate? When the right to expropriate *can* be exercised, a third question surfaces: (3) What is fair compensation? Expropriation should not be confused with situations of 'confiscation' in which private property is seized as a fine or forfeit, or 'nationalisation', in which a private business is taken by a government (Reeves 1969: 867).

Expropriation is regulated by article 54.3 of the RDTL Constitution. The initial text proposed by the political party, Fretilin, to the Constituent Assembly determined that '[r]equisitioning and expropriation of property can only take place in accordance with the law'. In this text, the limits of expropriatory power would be solely dependent on subsequent legislation. After the initial debates in 2001, a more detailed article including 'public interest' and 'compensation' was drafted (Devereux 2015: 247, 251). In the final plenary meetings after public consultation, the criterium of 'fair' compensation was added (Devereux 2015: 254). The final text of article 54.3 became the following: 'Requisitioning and expropriation of property for public interest shall only take place following fair compensation in accordance with the law'. As such, article 54.3 establishes three requisites for an expropriation: Expropriation can only happen (1) in the public interest, (2) upon the payment of fair compensation, and (3) according to the law. The following paragraphs analyse each requisite.

While the concept of 'public interest' is central to expropriation, the RDTL Constitution does not define it. This problem is not unique to Timor-Leste, and academics and practitioners have recorded various cases worldwide of unfair dispossession by the state based on unclear definitions of the public interest (Cotula 2013; Lund 2008). Those expropriations where 'economic development' is used to justify the public interest are especially controversial, and even more so if the beneficiary of the expropriation is a private party (Eisenberg 1995: 220; Wolford et al. 2013). For instance, Levien (2013) describes in detail how expropriation for private investment in special economic zones in India became a mechanism of making the poorest citizens subsidise investments that mostly benefited the investor elites. In 2005, the case *Kelo vs City of New London*, in which the Supreme Court of the United Sates allowed an expropriation of a private owner to another private owner for economic development, resulted in a strong movement against this kind of expropriation and, since then, many states have approved legislation that specifically prohibits it.

Although the RDTL Constitution does not define public interest, systematic and comparative interpretation can help to clarify this concept. First, the Indonesian law for voluntary land acquisition (not expropriation), in force before Timor-Leste's independence, provides a detailed list of infrastructure considered to have a public interest (article 5 of Presidential Decision No. 55/1993). Second, legal doctrine identifies some minimum principles that limit the concept. The first principle is that the general public should be the main beneficiary of the expropriation (Eisenberg

1995; Ronen 2013: 249). The expropriation can bring side benefits to individuals (for example, land values in a certain area go up because of new infrastructure), but the core beneficiary should be the general public. Proportionality is the second guiding principle that should define what is considered public interest; the benefit to the public should be bigger than the damage caused to individuals whose property is expropriated (Vasconcelos 2011: 94, 96, 203). Finally, the expropriation can only happen when there is no other viable alternative (ibid.: 94, 97; to compare, see Fonseca 2011: 15). Also, and in line with the above-mentioned debate about land as an element of personal identity, some authors sustain that the threshold of 'public interest' should be even stricter in cases of indigenous peoples' land rights (Golay and Cismas 2010: 16). As debated below, compliance with these principles must be justified in each case. Going back to the case study in Oecusse, we can ask whether the purposes for which property was taken fit the concept of public interest. Some, such as the hotel, raise serious doubts. What are their advantages for the general public? Are those advantages superior to the damage caused to individuals? Was there no viable alternative for those projects? The people affected by expropriation have the legal right to know what purpose the expropriation serves and to contest it. The expression '*hakarak ka lakohi*' ('whether you like it or not') makes less sense when seen in the light of the law; people have the right to refuse and contest expropriation.

The second requisite for expropriation imposed by the RDTL Constitution is fair compensation. Determining fair compensation is not easy and starts with the kind of compensation to be paid: money or replacement property – would this include shares in a company, as originally proposed by ZEESM? Other problems come with 'market value' solutions: what is the monetary value of property in an area where it is not transacted with money (for example, as in Timor-Leste, where often land is transacted inside customary groups, as part of long-term relationships)? Finally, how should things without monetary value be compensated for (for example, the sentimental value of the land; the social or ancestral connections lost with resettlement)? The minutes of the Constituent Assembly of 2001 show how, in light of all the unfair dispossessions experienced during the Indonesian occupation, the assembly was committed to adding 'fair' in the requisite of compensation, but no concrete principle was written in the Constitution. A reduced budget is sometimes used by Timorese state officials to justify low compensations. This justification is based on a misconception of expropriation. The idea behind expropriation is not that those unfortunate enough to be in the path of a public interest project have to contribute their property to the common good. The only imposition on those affected by an expropriation is that they agree on transacting the property. The costs of that transaction – the value of their right to property, the resettlement costs, the disturbance caused – are a burden on the public, not the affected individuals, and should be factored into the costs of undertaking the project that the expropriation serves (Fonseca 2011: 21). Therefore, compensation should fully compensate the affected people and leave them in at least an equal economic and social position as the one they had before expropriation.

Finally, article 54.3 establishes that expropriation should happen in accordance with the process regulated by law (Almeida 2016: 13; Oliveira et al. 2015: 521; Vasconcelos 2011: 203). Legally speaking, expropriation is a complex process, composed of several administrative acts, such as the decision to expropriate, the declaration of public interest and the determination of compensation (Guerreiro 2012: 18, 20). As with any administrative act, these are bound by several principles (for example, legality, transparency) and obligations, such as to justify the legal and factual grounds on which the administrative acts are taken (ibid.). The sequence of and specificities on these acts need to be detailed by law. Furthermore, it is paramount that the law defines which institutions have the power to perform each of these administrative acts. The principle of legality determines that public institutions can only carry out the administrative acts that the law explicitly authorises them to practise (ibid.: 6). In conclusion, the obligation of having a clear administrative process is not just a whim or a bureaucratic formality; it is these formalities that will give people the opportunity to participate in the decision to expropriate, to contest the foundations of the expropriation and to fight for better compensation (see Fonseca 2011: 12). These formalities are also necessary to assess whether an expropriation process respects the above-mentioned principles.

As will be described in the next section, the general legal framework set by the RDTL Constitution has experienced very limited development in infra-constitutional legislation.

The infra-constitutional legal framework

This section analyses the right to private property in the Timorese infra-constitutional legal framework. The right to obtain and enjoy property is only briefly analysed, while the right of the state to expropriate is debated in more detail.

The right to obtain, enjoy and transfer property

Timor-Leste does not yet have a consolidated property system that can address past grievances and protect its citizens' right to property (see Almeida 2016). If those with formal land titles from Portuguese and Indonesian administrations are uncertain of the legal validity of their rights, those *without* a formal land title – the great majority – are in a worse situation. Under the incipient infra-constitutional legal framework, even those with clear and deep customary connections to property run the risk of having their property classified as state land.

The Decree-Law 5/2015 that regulates RAEOA says that it has the power to administer the property cadastre of Oecusse (article 8.1[c]), but does not clarify which RAEOA administrative body has this power. In practice, there is no property cadastre functioning in Oecusse. In conclusion, the state is failing to create the legal framework to substantiate the property rights protected by the RDTL Constitution.

Expropriation

The RDTL Constitution requires that expropriation follow an administrative process predetermined by law. However, since Timor-Leste's independence in 2002, no expropriation law has been approved. The Indonesian law in force before 25 October 1999 was integrated into the Timorese legal system as subsidiary legislation and, therefore, the Indonesian Expropriation Law in force at that time is, in theory, still applicable (Almeida 2017: 176). However, the disconformity of this law with the current Timorese institutions and administrative practices makes its implementation in Timor-Leste very difficult, if not impossible. The Indonesian legal framework also has legislation for voluntary land acquisition by the state that could guide a pre-expropriation process of negotiation and acquisition of land (Presidential Decision No. 55/1993). However, this process has also been ignored.

Despite the lack of a general expropriation law, Law 3/2014, which created ZEESM and RAEOA, briefly mentions expropriation in article 27. However, this article does not have any procedural rules for expropriation and only adds to the confusion. Article 27.1 establishes that:

> the Authority [of the RAEOA] protects, according to the law, the right of the individual and collective/legal persons to acquire, use, transfer, and transfer by inheritance property, and the right to receive compensation in case of expropriation.

Such provision does not add any depth to what is established in articles 54.1 and 54.3 of the RDTL Constitution. Article 27.2 establishes that:

> [t]he value of compensation mentioned in the previous article should correspond to its real value at the moment of the expropriation, and should be freely convertible and paid without unjustifiable delay.

The expression 'real value' seems to refer to the market value of the property, but is not consistent with terminology commonly used by land evaluators. However, as debated above, market value raises problems in places where an open property market does not exist, such as Oecusse. The second part of this article is even less clear: what is freely convertible compensation, to be converted into what? What is an 'unjustifiable delay'? Article 27.3 establishes that '[t]he property rights of companies and investments from outside of the Region are protected by law'. While this article was probably drafted to assure foreign investors that their assets would not be arbitrarily expropriated, it does not add any more detail to what was already established in article 54 of the constitution.

Expropriation is also mentioned by Decree-Law 5/2015, which further regulates RAEOA. Article 6.1(f) establishes that the RAEOA administrative bodies are allowed, according to the competencies given to them by law, to conduct 'expropriation[s] verified as being in the public interest, under the terms established by law'. However, the attribution of this competency to the RAEOA administrative bodies has a number of problems. First, the constitutionality of article 6.1(f) is dubious: article 96.1(l) of the RDTL Constitution establishes that the government needs authorisation from Parliament to make decree-laws about 'means and ways of … expropriation … on grounds of public interest, as well as criteria for the establishment of compensations in such cases'. Article 6.1(f) of the decree-law gives RAEOA administrative bodies the power to expropriate, which is part of the 'means and ways of expropriation'; however, this decree-law was not preceded by legislative authorisation, which makes this article unconstitutional. Second, neither this decree-law nor any other legislation specifies which administrative bodies are competent to order an expropriation. As debated above regarding the principle of legality, the competency to practise acts cannot be presumed – it must be specifically determined by law. Furthermore, note that article 6.1(f) specifically mentions the power of the RAEOA administrative bodies to expropriate 'within the strict limits of the competencies given [to them]'. Therefore, there is currently no RAEOA administrative body with the power to order an expropriation. Furthermore, article 52.6(a) refers to the possibility of certain 'development companies' becoming beneficiaries of expropriation. Third, similar to article 54.3 of the constitution, article 6.1(f) of the decree-law establishes that expropriation should happen according to the law. However, as shown above, there is no law detailing the expropriation process. In conclusion, the authority given to the RAEOA administrative bodies to expropriate property has a very dubious constitutionality and, under the current legal framework, cannot be applied.

Another detail of Decree-Law 5/2015 deserves mention. Article 2.2 establishes that the decisions of RAEOA executive bodies have to be recorded in writing and adequately justified. Also, article 39.1 establishes that the decisions of the RAEOA Authority and its president detailed in article 35 and 36 have to be published in the first series of the Official Journal (*Jornal da República*), and the lack of publication makes these decisions legally inapplicable (see also article 40[a]). Until now, no publication about expropriations has ever been made in the Official Journal. Hence, it is safe to say that no legal expropriation was ever conducted in RAEOA.

We can, therefore, conclude that the infra-constitutional legislation necessary to conduct an expropriation is not in place and that the references to expropriation in the laws that govern ZEESM and RAEOA do not address this gap. Furthermore, the article that gives the RAEOA administrative bodies the power to expropriate property is unconstitutional. It is safe to say that the RAEOA administrative bodies did not access land in Oecusse through expropriation according to the constitutional criteria.

Conclusion

The RDTL Constitution and the international law that compose the Timorese legal framework demand legal and administrative mechanisms that can effectively protect the right to property. The exact scope of this obligation is not clear, but the protection of the right to housing, food and self-identity, as well as the objective of reducing inequality, should guide those mechanisms. Within the limits imposed by the constitution, the de facto customary property systems that rule most of the country must be acknowledged and be part of these mechanisms. However, in practice, little has been achieved in establishing these legal and administrative mechanisms.

By law, expropriation can only be used for clear public interest, upon payment of fair compensation and in accordance with a pre-established legal process. The necessary infra-constitutional legal framework is not yet in place, and the reference to expropriation in the RAEOA legislation does not provide any procedural guidance. Furthermore, the attribution of competency for expropriation to the RAEOA administrative bodies is unconstitutional in its current format.

The Oecusse case study shows that, despite the failure in protecting property rights, and despite not creating the necessary mechanisms for expropriation, state institutions are moving forward with infrastructure projects. Worse, these failures are deliberately used by these state institutions, together with a selective use of the law, to justify illegal dispossession. The affected people have no real means to challenge the legality of dispossession. As in other cases, politicians justify this disrespect of the law by invoking the country's young independence, the need to create jobs and the demands of economic development. State institutions cannot cherry-pick the 'rights' that the RDTL Constitution gives them and forget the obligations that come with the exercise of those 'rights'. The legitimacy of state institutions is based on the powers given to them by the constitution, and these powers are limited by clear obligations (for example, expropriation should be based on a process established by law), and clear regulations for exceptional situations (for example, article 24 about restrictive laws). By not respecting these obligations, state institutions undermine their own legitimacy and the rule of law principles established in the Constitution. In other words, they break what Canotilho (2003: 253) called the 'the chain of legal legitimacy' (see also Oliveira et al. 2015: 345). When economic development or job creation is used to justify the disrespect of the Constitution's basic rules, as has happened in the Oecusse case study, a very dangerous precedent is set.

In the face of the total disarray in which property rights and state administration were left after the violence and destruction that followed the 1999 popular consultation, one could not expect that, at this point in time, the country would have perfect mechanisms for determining land rights and conducting expropriations. But it is the obligation of the state to not proceed with infrastructure projects without the minimum legal basis to implement them. For instance, if the mechanism for identifying property owners is not in place, everyone residing in the affected area should be compensated as owners. Moreover, the situation of Timor-Leste is not unique, and there are many lessons to be taken from other developing countries. More than on infrastructure, the development of Timor-Leste depends on respecting the rights of its people.

As mentioned in the introduction, a new Land Law and Expropriation for Public Purposes Law were approved a few months after the writing of this chapter. Despite some limitations, these laws provide a stronger legal framework than previously existed for protecting people's property rights and regulating the prerogative of the state to expropriate land, but the success of these laws will be dependent on a complex process of implementation. Nevertheless, the laws are now in force, and 'waiting for the law' is no longer a reason for not recognising people's rights to the people. The next years will show whether there is a real political will to strengthen people's property rights in Timor-Leste.

References

Almeida, B. (2016) *Land tenure legislation in Timor-Leste*, Leiden: Van Vollenhoven Institute, The Asia Foundation.

Almeida, B. (2017) 'The main characteristics of the Timorese legal system – a practical guide', *Verfassung und Recht in Übersee VRÜ*, vol. 50, pp. 175–187. doi.org/10.5771/0506-7286-2017-2-175.

Canotilho, J. J. G. (2003) *Direito constitucional e teoria da constituição* [*Constitutional law and constitutional theory*], 7th edition, Coimbra: Almedina.

Commission on Legal Empowerment of the Poor and UNDP (2008) *Making the law work for everyone*, vol. 2, Working Group Reports. Available at: www.undp. org/content/dam/aplaws/publication/en/publications/democratic-governance/ legal-empowerment/reports-of-the-commission-on-legal-empowerment-of-the -poor/making-the-law-work-for-everyone---vol-ii---english-only/making_the_ law_work_II.pdf.

Cotula, L. (2013) *The great African grab? Agricultural investments and the global food system*, London: Zed Books.

Dehaibi, L. (2015) 'The case for an inclusive human right to property: Social importance and individual self-realization', *Journal of Legal Studies*, vol. 6, no. 1, article 5. Available at: ir.lib.uwo.ca/cgi/viewcontent.cgi?article=1159& context=uwojls.

Devereux, A. (2015) *Timor Leste's Bill of Rights: A preliminary history*, Canberra: ANU Press. doi.org/10.22459/TLBR.05.2015.

Eisenberg, A. (1995) '"Public purpose" and expropriation: Some comparative insights and the South African Bill of Rights', *South African Journal on Human Rights*, vol. 11, no. 2, pp. 207–221. doi.org/10.1080/02587203.1995. 11827560.

Fitzpatrick, D. (2002) *Land claims in East Timor*, Canberra: Asia Pacific Press.

Fonseca, G. da (2011) 'A expropriação por utilidade pública, o poder político e a Constituição' ['Expropriation for public interest, the political power, and the Constitution'], *Revista do Ministério Público*, vol. 126, April/June, pp. 9–25.

Golay, C. and Cismas, I. (2010) *Legal opinion: The right to property from a human rights perspective*. Available at: papers.ssrn.com/sol3/papers.cfm?abstract_id= 1635359.

Guerreiro, S. (2012) *Colectânea de direito administrativo Timorense com comentários de conteúdo Parte II – Actividade administrativa em Timor-Leste* [*Compilation of Timorese administrative legislation with comments on its content – Part II: the administrative activity in Timor-Leste*]. Provedoria de Direitos Humanos e Justica, UNDP.

Hannum, H. (1996) 'The status of the Universal Declaration of Human Rights in national and international law', *Georgia Journal of International and Comparative Law*, vol. 25, no. 1, pp. 287–397. Available at: digitalcommons. law.uga.edu/gjicl/vol25/iss1/13/.

Independente (2014) 'Projetu ZEESM Oekusi okupa rai ektare rihun ida' ['The Oecusse ZEESM project occupies 1,000 hectares of land'], 28 April.

Jacobs, H. M. (2013) 'Private property and human rights: A mismatch in the 21st century?', *International Journal of Social Welfare*, vol. 22, S85–S101. doi.org/10.1111/ijsw.12044.

Januario, R. (2016a) 'Catarina: Hau laiha kbiit hodi koalia, hau pasensia ho situasaun ida ne'e' ['I'm not able to express my patience with this situation'], *Rede Ba Rai*, 2 June. Available at: redebarai.org/?p=304 (site discontinued).

Januario, R. (2016b) 'Francisco Salu: Hau nia esperansa mohut' ['My hope is dead'], *Rede Ba Rai*, 2 June. Available at: redebarai.org/?p=310 (site discontinued).

Januario, R. (2016c) 'La fo valor ba maluk alezadu [sic.] hodi moris justu' ['Not giving value for disabled friends to live fairly'], *Rede Ba Rai*, 2 June. Available at: redebarai.org/?p=300 (site discontinued).

Januario, R. (2016d) 'Marius Fuca: Sistema fahe material la transparansia' ['The system to disburse materials isn't transparent'], *Rede Ba Rai*, 2 June. Available at: redebarai.org/?cat=6 (site discontinued).

Joireman, S. F. and Brown, J. (2013) 'Property: Human right or commodity?' *Journal of Human Rights*, vol. 12, no. 2, pp. 165–179. doi.org/10.1080/147 54835.2013.784662.

Jornal Nacional Diário (2015) 'Presiza espasu ba projetu autoridade justifika desizaun – ZEESM muda povu ho forsa' ['Authority justifies the decision that they need land for the project – ZEESM uses force to move people'], 9 October.

Jornal Nacional Diário (2016) 'Alkatiri: Kompensasaun laos atu sai riku' ['Alkatiri: compensation is not to get rich'], 13 June.

Levien, M. (2013) 'Regimes of dispossession: From steel towns to special economic zones', in Wolford, W., Borras Jr., S. M., Hall, R., Scoones, I. and White, B. (eds) *Governing global land deals: The role of the state in the rush for land*, Milton, QLD: Wiley-Blackwell (Kindle version). doi.org/ 10.1002/9781118688229.ch9.

Lund, C. (2008) *Local politics and the dynamics of property in Africa*, New York: Cambridge University Press. doi.org/10.1017/cbo9780511510564.

Meitzner Yoder, L. S. (2015) 'The development eraser: Fantastical schemes, aspirational distractions and high modern mega-events in the Oecusse enclave, Timor-Leste', *Journal of Political Ecology*, vol. 22, pp. 299–321. doi.org/ 10.2458/v22i1.21110.

Meitzner Yoder, L. S. (2016) *Oecusse's special economic zone and local governance*, SSGM In Brief 2016/5, Canberra: State, Society & Governance in Melanesia, ANU. Available at: dpa.bellschool.anu.edu.au/sites/default/files/publications/ attachments/2016-04/ib-2016-5-meitzneryoder.pdf.

Miranda, J. (2000) *Manual de direito constitucional, tomo IV: Direitos fundamentais* [*Constitutional law manual, part IV: Fundamental rights*], 3ª Edição, Coimbra: Coimbra Editora.

Oliveira, B. N., Gomes, C. and Santos, R. dos (2015) *Os direitos fundamentais em Timor-Leste: Teoria e prática* [*Fundamental rights in Timor-Leste: Theory and practice*], Coimbra: Coimbra Editora.

Plessis, J. du and Leckie, S. (2000) *Housing, property and land rights in East Timor: Proposals for an effective dispute resolution and claim verification mechanism*, UN Habitat.

Provedoria dos Direitos Humanos e Justiça (2016) 'Resultado monitorização da PDHJ sobre a implementação do projeto do alargamento das estradas e irrigação da barragem da Ribeira de Tono em RAEOA' ['PDHJ monitoring results on the implementation of the road widening project and Tono River dam irrigation project in RAEOA'], 13 June.

Radin, M. J. (1994) *Reinterpreting property*, Chicago: University of Chicago. doi.org/10.7208/chicago/9780226702292.001.0001.

Reeves, W. H. (1969) '"Expropriation," "confiscation," and "nationalization": – What one can do about them', *The Business Lawyer*, vol. 24, no. 3, pp. 867–886.

Ronen, Y. (2013) *Transition from illegal regimes under international law*, Cambridge: Cambridge Books Online. doi.org/10.1017/cbo9780511978142.

Rose, M. (2016) *ZEESM: Destructive 'development' in Timor's special economic zone*, SSGM In Brief 2016/4, Canberra: State, Society & Governance in Melanesia, ANU. Available at: bellschool.anu.edu.au/sites/default/files/publications/attachments/2016-04/ib-2016-4-rose_12.pdf.

Timor Post (2015a) 'Uma kain 270 afeitadu ba projetu ZEESM' ['270 households affected by ZEESM project'], 12 October.

Timor Post (2015b) 'ZEEMS konsege sulan komunidade iha lona okos' ['ZEESM managed to house the community under canvas shelters'], 18 October.

Vasconcelos, P. C. B. de (ed.) (2011) *Constituição anotada da República Democrática de Timor-Leste* [*Annotated Constitution of the Democratic Republic of Timor-Leste*], Direitos Humanos – Centro de Investigação Interdisciplinar.

Wolford, W., Borras Jr., S. M., Hall, R., Scoones, I. and White, B. (eds) (2013) *Governing global land deals: The role of the state in the rush for land,* Milton, QLD: Wiley-Blackwell (Kindle version). doi.org/10.1002/9781118688229.

ZEESM (2013–2014) *Oecusse Special Economic Zones of Social Market – First steps towards a new Oecusse*, La'o Hamutuk – The Timor-Leste Institute for Development Monitoring and Analysis. Available at: www.laohamutuk.org/econ/Oecussi/ZEESMSituationAnalysisMar14en.pdf.

6

Just a dream? The struggle for national resource sovereignty and oil infrastructure development along Timor-Leste's south coast[1]

Judith M. Bovensiepen

In May 2015, I was driving with a friend through Timor-Leste's capital, Dili. It was around lunchtime and the streets were buzzing with traffic, with cars entering the road from all sides and in all directions, incessantly honking and often squeezing into a fourth or fifth lane on the three-lane road. We got stuck right in front of Timor Plaza – a relatively new multi-storey shopping mall that, despite high prices, attracts many visitors every day. A *mikrolet* (minibus) stopped in front of us that carried almost double the passengers it was built for, with quite a few young men hanging on outside. Loud Indonesian pop music was blasting from the speakers. It looked like most other *mikrolets* in Dili. However, three words stood

1   This article is based on research carried out in collaboration with, and with the support of, Monis Filipe, Flaviano Freitas and Evya do Carmo; they do not necessarily share the views expressed in this article. This research is based on seven months of fieldwork in Timor-Leste carried out in 2015 and 2016, which involved interviews with government officials, members of the oil industry, civil society and the 'affected community' of the Tasi Mane project in Suai and Betano. All interviews are anonymised. I would also like to thank all the participants of the University of Kent workshop 'Visions of the Future in Timor-Leste' for their helpful feedback, as well as Bernardo Almeida for his comments on this chapter. The research was funded by the Economic and Social Research Council (grant no. ES/L010232/1).

out that were written in gigantic pink letters in English across the back: 'just a dream'. My companion turned to me, let out a loud laugh and said, 'the perfect metaphor for the Tasi Mane project – really just a dream'.

The Tasi Mane project is a state-led development scheme, aimed at developing the south coast through heavy investment in infrastructure, industry and tourism. The project envisages the development of three industrial clusters on the thinly populated south coast of the country (La'o Hamutuk 2011; SDP 2011; TimorGap 2015; see Figure 6.1). Its centrepiece is the construction of petroleum infrastructure with an oil refinery and a liquefied natural gas (LNG) plant to be completed by 2020. Its goal, as a respondent who is one of the main drivers behind its implementation explained, is to 'unleash the potential of the south coast' and to turn the south into the 'power house' of the country. The Tasi Mane project is one articulation of growing resource nationalism in Timor-Leste, the government's endeavour to assert control over the natural resources in its own territory inspired by a sense that East Timorese should benefit from profits derived from their own resources. The project is controversial and has been strongly criticised by civil society groups. However, scepticism among foreign observers has also been met by an increasing sense of frustration in the country about what is seen as a patronising attitude by outsiders towards attempts to realise plans for a prosperous future.

Plans to build a large petroleum infrastructure are not the only manifestations of resource nationalism; another instance was the government's bold strategy to try and force Australia to re-enter negotiations with regards to the maritime boundary between both countries. Timor-Leste's largest oil and gas reserves are located offshore, including the Sunrise and Troubadour gas and condensate fields, collectively known as Greater Sunrise, which lie about 450 km north of Australia and 150 km southeast of Timor-Leste. According to the Law of the Sea's median line principle, the majority of the reserves would belong to Timor-Leste, but, until recently, Australia refused to negotiate maritime boundaries and had proposed a resource-sharing agreement that would provide Timor-Leste with only 50 per cent.

Immediately before Timor-Leste regained independence in 2002, Australia withdrew from a key aspect of the United Nations Convention on the Law of the Sea in order to avoid the juridical determination of the border between both countries. In January 2015, the East Timorese

Government launched a series of campaigns to garner support for a median line agreement and triggered a non-binding but compulsory conciliation process (Leach 2018). In March 2018, Timor-Leste secured a landmark agreement, settling the Australia–Timor-Leste maritime border along the median line and agreeing on a fairer Greater Sunrise revenue split. The decision was widely celebrated as an unprecedented breakthrough.[2]

This chapter examines some of the dynamics and effects of resource nationalism in Timor-Leste. More specifically, it looks at the relationship between state-led onshore oil infrastructure development plans (the Tasi Mane project) and the desire for full national resource sovereignty through boundary negotiations with Australia. While it has been argued that these two are in principle separate issues, this chapter illustrates that resource nationalism tends to conflate the issue of boundaries and the issue of infrastructure. This conflation must be understood in the context of two forms of domination: first of all, resource nationalism gains traction through 'occidentalism' – a term developed by Coronil (1997: 14) to describe the 'stereotypical representations of cultural difference', which form part of 'the West's self-fashioning as an imperial power'. Negative stereotypes about Timor-Leste's supposed inability to govern itself, and presumed inevitable 'squandering' of resources, form part of the reproduction of geopolitical power asymmetries. These are arguments that have been used to delegitimise Timor-Leste's legitimate claims to full sovereignty.

Second, resource nationalism is a fertile ground for what Reyna and Behrends (2008: 11) have called 'crude domination' – namely, the 'struggles to dominate the flow of value produced by oil' (ibid.: 15), which can be examined by paying attention to how different groups (local, national and transnational) seek to assert their dominance in the struggle over resources. As will be examined later in this chapter with regards to the Tasi Mane project, nationalist arguments about resource sovereignty are used by politicians and members of the oil industry in order to stifle internal critique of ongoing development plans. While occidentalist representations intensify nationalist sentiments, these very nationalist

---

2   This article was written in 2015 and revised in 2016 and hence does not include a detailed discussion of the most recent developments. The focus is on the campaign to re-enter boundary negotiations with Australia as an expression of resource nationalism, rather than on the outcome of these negotiations.

arguments (that derive from legitimate grievances) in turn enable 'crude domination' by presenting those who criticise current infrastructure development projects as 'anti-nationalist'.

Resource nationalism

In the *Timor-Leste Strategic Development Plan 2011–2030* (henceforth SDP), launched in 2011, the Sixth Constitutional Government of Timor-Leste formulated a clear vision for the future. As one member of this government told me, this vision is one where Timor-Leste will be an internationally recognised upper-middle–income country, with transparent institutions and a diversified economy. The SDP is a key policy document that is seen to have been developed and designed with the strong personal involvement by the former prime minister Xanana Gusmão. The document includes plans to improve education and health, and develop cultural heritage as well as Timor-Leste's oil and non-oil economies. It also contains plans for the development of human resources for the petroleum industry, for the establishment of a national petroleum company and for the so-called Tasi Mane project (SDP 2011: 136–138). These ambitious development plans by the government are (at least at this point) largely to be financed by oil revenue from the Timor-Leste Petroleum Fund. The plans were made despite warnings that at current spending levels, the Petroleum Fund will be exhausted by about 2025 (La'o Hamutuk 2015).[3]

In Suai, the planned scheme stipulates building a supply base including a port, an international airport and a crocodile farm (La'o Hamutuk 2011). Furthermore, the Ministry for Petroleum and Mineral Resources has been reviewing business plans that include carpentry and forestry projects; a cattle slaughterhouse; and discussions with an Australian cruise ship company, which is thinking of bringing up to 2,000 tourists at a time to Suai, who could then be taken by helicopter to interesting tourist sites throughout the country, such as the Marobo hot springs in the west of Timor-Leste.

---

3   Revenues from Greater Sunrise are likely to extend this prediction, though La'o Hamutuk (2018) has recently pointed out that 'Even according to the most optimistic credible projections, Sunrise will only finance Timor-Leste's state and economy for less than one generation'.

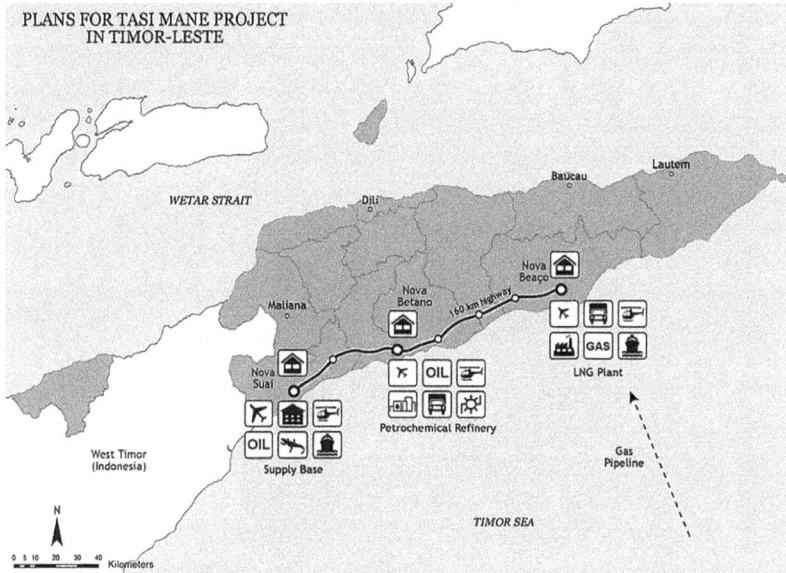

Figure 6.1. Plans for the Tasi Mane project.
Source: Map by Helder Bento, used with permission.

In Betano, there is supposed to be an oil refinery and a petrochemical plant. In Beaço, plans include an industrial complex and an LNG plant, and marine facilities for offloading goods. The refinery will provide fuels, such as diesel, gasoline and jet fuel. There are plans for three new cities – Nova Suai, Nova Betano and Nova Beaço – to administer these projects, and a large, 160 km four-lane highway connecting these three industrial clusters (La'o Hamutuk 2011; SDP 2011; TimorGap 2015).

The Tasi Mane project involves resettlement of people who are living in the affected areas, as well as the 'liberation' (as it is called) of vast stretches of land for the construction of the oil and gas infrastructure. Residents living in areas, affected by the construction work are to receive financial compensation for their land (see Bovensiepen and Meitzner Yoder 2018; Crespi and Guillaud 2018). At the time of writing, the identification of land and compensation payments were almost complete in Suai, and land to be 'liberated' was identified in Betano; least progress had been made in Beaço, where the pipeline from Greater Sunrise is to lead to. A series of community meetings had been held in all three locations, so-called 'socialisations', in order to inform the affected population about the process.

In 2015, I took part in a series of these 'socialisations' in Suai and Betano. During the speeches given by members of government and representatives from the oil industry, the language of nationalism, resistance and sacrifice were prominently used to motivate the participants to give their support (and land) to the Tasi Mane project. The same was true during mediations to resolve land conflict, and consultations organised to provide training and information to community members about how to deal with the large sums of money they had received as 'compensation' for their land.

The speech during one of these 'socialisations' by the subdistrict administrator I mentioned in the Introduction was a clear example of this. Through the Tasi Mane project, he said, Timor-Leste will move 'out of darkness, into light' (*husi nakukun, ba naroman*). He repeated this phrase again and again throughout the speech and connected it to the struggle for Timor-Leste's self-determination. The past was the darkness and the future will bring light. 'This is what we fought for during the independence struggle', he continued. 'The darkness is now behind us, and the light ahead of us.' At the time of Portuguese colonialism, Timor went 'from darkness to darkness' (*husi nakukun ba nakukun*). But since independence has been achieved, since there has been self-determination, 'everything has been moving forward' (*buat hotu lao ba oin*). The administrator told the audience that they needed to give something up, so that the country could go ahead and develop, so that the country could move out of darkness and into the light. His speech was greeted by enthusiastic cheers from the audience.

After the subdistrict administrator's speech, it was the turn of a senior member of the national oil company TimorGap. First, he led a short prayer, saying, 'We pray that this pipeline project will be successful'. Then he expressed special respect to former resistance fighters (*veteranos*). References to veterans and to the resistance struggle against Indonesia were a prominent feature of many of the speeches during the 'socialisation' events I attended, and often individual veterans were invited to sit on the front podium to show their support for the project. During these events, arguments about sovereignty and oil infrastructure construction were treated as the same issue.

More specifically, oil and gas infrastructure development was represented as an inherent part of the country's long history of resistance against foreign occupation, and this also emerged in interviews I carried out with a number of politicians. One high-level politician involved in the implementation of the Tasi Mane project argued that the development along the south coast was part of achieving independence (*ukun rasik aan*) – it was 'through development that people are liberated'. Another interviewee and member of the previous government argued along similar lines when he said:

> Claims to the oil of [the] Timor Sea is [a] normal ambition for countries where the oil companies call the shot[s] … if Australia chooses to continue with the illegal 'occupation' of the Timor Sea, [it is] stealing the oil from the rightful owners.

The struggle for independence was seen as incomplete until the country's borders are clearly defined. A respondent from Timor-Leste's Ministry for Petroleum and Mineral Resources maintained that the 'struggle for a pipeline' was a continuation of the resistance struggle, operating 'on three fronts'. Whereas resistance against Indonesia was fought on 'clandestine, diplomatic and military fronts', the 'struggle for Greater Sunrise' was fought on 'technical, legal and commercial fronts'.

I frequently asked research participants how and when the idea of the Tasi Mane project emerged. The most common response was that this idea emerged long before Timor-Leste regained independence, during the resistance struggle against Indonesia. The idea of building a pipeline from Greater Sunrise oil and gas fields to the south coast of Timor-Leste was one of the most important aspects of the Tasi Mane project mentioned. One respondent suggested that this idea of a pipeline came to former resistance leader Xanana Gusmão in a dream while hiding from the Indonesian military. Others said the idea to develop the south coast was conceived by members of the 'diplomatic resistance' who were living in Australia during the Indonesian occupation. Those who suggested that the vision of south coast development and the pipeline arose during the resistance also indicated that it was and essentially is still a part of resistance against foreign domination, and economic and political dependency on foreigners, including donors.

Concrete historical experiences drive the vision of resource sovereignty, especially with regards to the boundary with Australia. In scheming for the oil and gas reserves in the Timor Sea, Australia employed 'win-at-all-costs tactics' (McGrath 2014: 2) – for example, ordering raids (in the interests of 'national security') against a Canberra lawyer who was investigating allegations that Australia had been spying on Timor-Leste to gain a commercial advantage in the negotiations about Greater

Sunrise. Calls for the permanent delimitation of maritime boundaries with Australia initially came from the activist community in Timor-Leste, which had been criticising Australia's stance long before the issue received such widespread national attention. Activists pointed to the interconnections between Australia's acknowledgement of Indonesia's illegal occupation and its entering into negotiation with Indonesia over Timor's oil and gas (see McGrath 2017). Australia was the only western country to recognise Indonesia's annexation of East Timor, but even prior to Indonesia's invasion, the Whitlam Government used oil and gas reserves in the Timor Sea as the main reason to plead in favour of East Timor's 'integration' into Indonesia, arguing that it was easier to negotiate with Indonesia than with Portugal about a seabed border (Aditjondro 1999: 18). In 2015, a series of campaigns and protests were launched against Australia's refusal to negotiate a permanent maritime boundary. Arguments made by the activist community were appropriated and used to argue not just for boundary negotiations, but also in favour of Tasi Mane onshore infrastructure plans. Advocates of the project drew on the sentiments and frustrations that had built up around the boundary.

In the Introduction to this volume, I made the case that the negative consequences of oil dependency are more severe in some countries than in others. Gledhill (2008: 57) has argued that (at the time of his writing), several Latin American countries could mitigate the negative effects precisely through policies of resource nationalism, expressed in the notion that 'our oil belongs to the people'. This notion connected calls for national resource sovereignty to campaigns for social justice. In these cases, nationalist imaginaries successfully managed to ward off arguments that development can only go ahead if all remaining barriers to foreign investment are abandoned. The situation in Timor-Leste is clearly different – nationalist arguments are not used to protect the economy from market liberalisation; in the implementation of the Tasi Mane project, nationalist arguments seem to displace social justice concerns, rather that connect with them.

Occidentalism

In 2013, an incident occurred that caused a lot of consternation in government circles. A member of staff at the National Petroleum Authority (ANP [*Autoridade Nacional do Petróleo*]) of Timor-Leste is said to have thrown the Field Development Plan for the Greater Sunrise oil and gas fields back into a car driven by representatives of Woodside Petroleum, the Australian oil and gas company. The representatives had gone to the ANP offices to present what were supposed to be Woodside's options for the safest, technically possible and economically most viable way of developing Greater Sunrise. However, to the disappointment of the East Timorese interlocutors, Woodside only came up with two options: first, a floating LNG platform; and second, a pipeline to Darwin. What they had left out of the Field Development Plan was the option for a pipeline from Greater Sunrise to Timor-Leste's south coast.

Members of Timor-Leste's government and of the oil and gas industry frequently recounted the 'document-throwing' incident to me; the incident had clearly provoked intense emotions of anger and frustration. I was told that when the ANP representatives noticed that Woodside's Field Development Plan did not contain the Timor pipeline option, they tried to stall the meeting. When the Woodside staff realised what was going on, they simply left the document at the ANP offices and walked out of the meeting room. They are said to have moved quickly out of the building, trying to reach their car. After their sudden exit from the offices, the Woodside representatives could not find their car, and walked distraught up and down the car park. Staff at ANP saw this as an opportunity: a security guard was sent to follow the Woodside representatives and hand the documents back. As one of my respondents recounted, 'there was "shuffling", the car was right in front of the building, but they [Woodside staff] could not find it'. The local media was present to film the entire incident. He continued:

> So for us it was 'the ancestors are helping us … the past people are blinding these guys'. And then we threw the books back into their car. And it was all over the media. And it was a big drama. So they [Woodside] left. Officially they could not say [anything] because we got offended … But we understood that they were just going to push us aside.

I heard several different variations of this incident. However, most accounts stressed how insulting Woodside Petroleum's behaviour was, and how offensive their position was, to not include the option for a pipeline from Greater Sunrise to Timor-Leste's shores in their Field Development Plan. And yet there was another political aspect to the dispute: the incident took place just before an important deadline. There had been an agreement that Timor-Leste or Australia had the right to suspend the controversial CMATS Treaty (Certain Maritime Arrangements in the Timor Sea –

a treaty that instated a 50/50 resource-sharing agreement for upstream revenues from Greater Sunrise) if no Greater Sunrise development plan had been approved by 23 February 2013 (La'o Hamutuk 2016; Leach 2013). One commentator I spoke to argued that by throwing the document back into the car, Timor-Leste made a first step towards forcing renegotiations with Australia over Greater Sunrise, as it meant refusing to accept the proposals for the Greater Sunrise development. If there was no development plan, negotiations could be opened again. In April 2013, there was a request by the Timor-Leste Government to invalidate the CMATS agreement, because Australia had bugged the East Timorese prime minister's meeting room during the negotiations – a case that was later taken for arbitration to The Hague (for details outlining the history of CMATS and other agreements, see La'o Hamutuk 2016).[4]

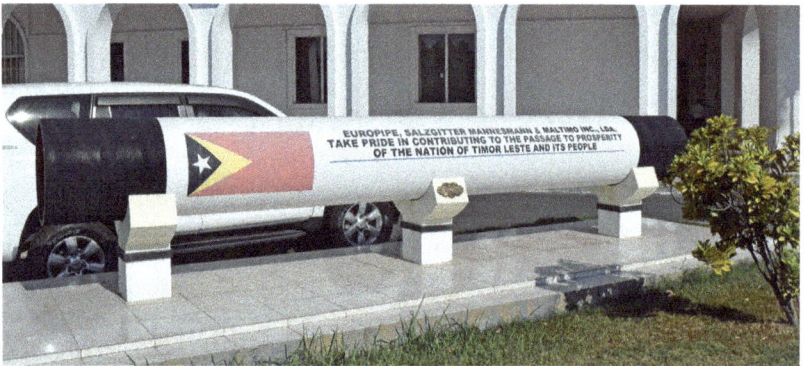

Figure 6.2. Sample pipeline in front of the Palácio do Governo in Dili.
Source: Photo taken by author in August 2016.

The East Timorese Government commissioned their own study into the feasibility of a pipeline from Greater Sunrise to Timor-Leste's south coast. This included commissioning a sample pipeline constructed by Europipe, which now stands in front of Timor-Leste's government office (see Figure 6.2). Printed on the outside of the pipe, it says in English that the producers of the pipe 'take pride in contributing to the passage to prosperity of the nation of Timor-Leste and its people'. The 'document-throwing' incident was not just about who would benefit economically from the Greater Sunrise oil and gas fields, valued at several billion dollars,

4   Despite having reached the landmark agreement to settle the maritime boundary in March 2018, by the time this chapter was finalised for publication, no agreement had been reached about the location for the processing of LNG from Greater Sunrise.

it was also closely enmeshed with the boundary dispute between Australia and Timor-Leste. The document-throwing incident and, later, spying allegations are seen as matters of both national resource sovereignty and the sovereignty of Timor-Leste's national borders. The Tasi Mane project is connected to the question of the pipeline because it is partly based on the idea of producing LNG from Greater Sunrise onshore, in Beaço. The project, like the pipeline, centres on the idea that Timor-Leste itself should be involved in benefiting from the extraction and processing of its natural resources.

In March 2015, a debate ensued on Facebook. An American-educated academic based in Dili had allegedly said to a reporter that Timor-Leste would not be the next Singapore as the country was not strategically located. The vision of Singapore had been prominent in relation to infrastructure construction plans, including the Tasi Mane project. The comment appeared in print and outraged many, including a prominent Timorese politician, who posted an angry comment asking, 'Did anyone in Timor-Leste ever dreamed [sic] loud to be another Singapore?' Comments by other Facebook users strongly condemned the academic (who may well have been quoted out of context), expressing a very sincere sense of frustration that I think is symptomatic of a wider sentiment in the country. Saying Timor-Leste will not be the next Singapore was understood by some to mean that Timor-Leste is not allowed to envisage a prosperous future for itself. Some commentators asked why they, as East Timorese, were not allowed to dream and have ambitious plans. After all it was precisely the unrelenting ability to imagine a different future (one independent from Indonesia) that was such a motivating vision during the resistance struggle. The fact the Timor-Leste had regained independence was interpreted as evidence that dreams *can* come true. The comments revealed an intense dissatisfaction with the continuous dependence on foreign advisers and experts in both politics and the development industry. They also exposed a strong irritation at the negative assessments of Timor-Leste's future by the outside world. Social media platforms allowed people to counter occidentalist representations and thus served to invigorate resource nationalism.

A very different kind of debate ensued on Facebook in August 2016 about a newspaper article citing the prime minister at the time, Rui Maria de Araújo, who addressed an audience of academics at the national university by asking 'in 15 years from now, can we be like Singapore?' Interestingly, the social media response was again critical. Rather than reaffirming their right to 'dream', commentators mocked the prime minister. One of the biggest points of critique was the suggestion that Timor-Leste would want to become like another nation, rather than developing its own specific trajectory. 'Why don't we have our own dream?', was one of the comments. What is really interesting about the two debates is that the response differed based on the identity of the person making the initial remark. A foreigner saying Timor-Leste would be no Singapore caused outrage, yet when the prime minister encouraged his audience to have precisely this dream, people mocked him and urged him to be realistic. It might also be worth noting that the article also stated that the prime minister had insisted that the country must diversify, and should not only rely on income from oil and gas – an aspect mainly neglected in the commentaries on social media.

In the classic anthropological study of the Venezuelan state from the perspective of oil booms and busts, Fernando Coronil (1997) effectively examined the interactions of national and international political struggles and how they have shaped the way Venezuelan governments managed the country's oil resources. In Venezuela's nationalist imaginary, the state became the unifying agent of the nation, which would act as the guardian of the country's oil wealth. The idea was that, through its oil wealth, the state would be able to magically bring about a prosperous and diversified society, hence Coronil's notion of the 'magical state'. In addition to his fine analysis of the internal political struggles connected to this imaginary, Coronil critically examined how the state might be dominant within the Venezuelan context, though in the global system it remains economically and politically marginal and dominated through notions of occidentalism.

'Occidentalism', according to Coronil (1997: xi), refers to the representational practices that portray non-western peoples as the 'Other' of the western self. His book develops 'a perspective from which to view societies that are central to the formation of what has been called the modern world and yet are cast as marginal to it' (ibid.). My argument is that East Timorese resource nationalism is not just a response to geopolitical inequalities that made it difficult for the government to negotiate a fair agreement over borders and resources for so many years. It is also a response to discursive practices of occidentalism that deny Timor-Leste the ability to govern its own resources. This became clear in a comment by a Timorese politician, who said he was told by an

Australian counterpart in 2015 – off the record – that Australia would not give in regarding the maritime boundary, because Timor-Leste would just 'squander the money anyway'. As Coronil (1997: 14) put it:

> While any society may produce stereotypical representations of cultural difference as part of its own self-production, what is unique about Occidentalism is that it entails the mobilisation of stereotypical representations of non-Western societies as part of the West's self-fashioning as an imperial power. Occidentalism is inseparable from Western hegemony not only because it establishes a specific bond between knowledge and power in the West.

Crude domination

The second mode of domination that characterises resource nationalism in Timor-Leste is what Reyna and Behrends (2008: 11) call 'crude domination' – namely, the internal dynamic between different local and national actors seeking to assert control over profits from natural resources. Local struggles largely manifest themselves in concerns about the loss of land, and conflicts emerging from money received through government compensation. Landowners expressed deep concern about the fact that they would only receive US$3 per square metre of land that they gave up for the Tasi Mane project. Arguments were made that the land prices had gone up to between US$4 and US$15 per square metre, depending on where the land was located, so they would struggle to buy land for the same price (see also Crespi and Guillaud 2018). It is also questionable whether financial compensation is really the best form of compensation for loss of land, because such cash injections can produce conflicts between or among families and do not necessarily provide people with livelihood security in the long term.

While interviewing residents affected by the Tasi Mane project in Suai, I was repeatedly told by local residents that they felt they simply did not have a choice. *Hakarak ka lakohi* ('whether we want to or not'; which might be more loosely translated as 'like it or not') was a sentence that I heard over and over again from people we interviewed: 'Whether we want to or not, we need to give our land' or 'Whether we want to or not, the project will go ahead anyway' (see also Almeida, Chapter 5 for Oecusse). Quite a few residents worried that the project might have potentially negative consequences. However, they had a sense that there was nothing they could do; the development would go ahead anyway. Hence, symptomatic of the domination of oil, their strategy was to get as much out of the government as they could (mainly in terms of monetary compensation for land). Some residents of Covalima I spoke to had received US$10,000, US$15,000 or, more rarely, even US$60,000 in compensation for their land (US$3 per square metre). Some had made good investments and bought land elsewhere, others did not and the problem of livelihood insecurity was an issue raised by many as a potential future problem.

During a 'socialisation' in 2015, participants also expressed concerns about the possible environmental impact the highway and accompanying pipeline may have (a pipeline is to lead from Suai to Betano alongside the highway). After TimorGap representatives explained some of the health and safety risks of the construction work, including fire risk, members of the affected community asked: 'How will you be dealing with the environmental problems if they occur on our land?' Local residents were also concerned about trees that would be cut down for the building project. People worried about losing their livelihood and not receiving adequate compensation. There were also concerns about access to water, especially if the highway cut people off from water resources. Locals were also concerned about how many of those working for the project would be local, and what percentage of workers would be foreigners. There were questions about how to deal with sacred (*lulik*) sites in the area designated for development, and how places where crocodiles (considered to be *lulik*) reside would be affected.

Although government officials and TimorGap employees clearly took into account the important cultural value of certain sites and were open to discuss how people's losses could be compensated, both financially and through the appropriate rituals, some research participants from the oil industry that I interviewed also suggested people were suddenly over-valuing sites of customary significance in order to increase benefits to themselves. There was a sense, by some of those charged with implementing the project, that people were invoking culture for economic gain.

The concerns of people attending the 'socialisations' are reflected in some of the critical literature on the project and in critiques formulated by a number of non-governmental organisations working in Timor-Leste (e.g. La'o Hamutuk 2011; Fundasaun Mahein 2013). Meabh Cryan (2015: 8–12), for example, stressed the potential negative impacts of the Suai Supply Base, including landlessness, homelessness, increased vulnerability of specific groups that are already vulnerable, impacts on gender equality, food insecurity, loss of livelihoods, joblessness, marginalisation and increased political and economic inequality. This echoes the possible problems Laura Meitzner Yoder (2015) identified with the plans to develop a special economic zone in the enclave of Oecusse, which, she argued, focus largely on the coastal regions and are designed to cater to foreigners, leaving rural populations in the highland marginalised and excluded from development. This echoes my own observation in Suai, where risks of joblessness, greater inequality, changed gender relations and potential for social envy and conflict seemed to be pertinent problems in the making.

Spokespeople for the Tasi Mane project promised economic development and employment opportunities to local people. And yet critics have argued that there is little employment in the oil industry, that Timor-Leste's oil and gas is running out and it is not worth spending so much on an infrastructure program such as this, until it is clear whether the pipeline from Greater Sunrise is actually going to Timor-Leste's shores. The government's argument against the latter point is that the pipeline would only come to Timor-Leste if the infrastructure is in place: hence the Tasi Mane project was, to an extent, represented as a pre-emptive plan designed to force Australia's hand.

Figure 6.3. Motorbikes in Suai market.
Source: Photo taken by Mathijs Pelkmans in 2015, used with permission.

In Suai, residents I spoke to joked, saying, 'in three years from now, people will be eating motorbikes'. This was a comment on the large numbers of motorbikes people had purchased with the money received in compensation for land. There were also reports of prices for land and food (vegetables, meat and other staple foods) having gone up rapidly in Suai since the compensation payments had been made and of people taking out loans on the basis of future compensation payments. There were worries people would spend the money they received rather than invest it in a more sustainable means of income for the future. There were also reports that some people had stopped pursuing some of the regular work they had been engaged in after having received money from compensation – perhaps a symptom reminiscent of the resource curse, which is known to stifle productivity in non-oil–related sectors. There have also been criticisms that suggest the entire project is technically and financially unviable, that the project would destroy local cultural heritage and leave people landless with few prospects for the future. Supporters of the Tasi Mane project maintain that it is important to take some risks in order to produce benefits for everyone, and they expressed sincere worries that the criticisms voiced towards the project will end up scaring off investors.

In June 2015, a team from the government and from TimorGap travelled to Betano to present local residents with their plans to build an oil refinery there. A large tent had been erected in front of a house close to the sea, where small waves were gently splashing against the shores. The presentation of the refinery plans was quite similar to previous 'socialisation' events, and time was allowed for local residents to ask questions. As in previous meetings, most of the questions focused on issues relating to land ownership and the compensation schemes for loss of land. However, there was one question from a member of civil society, who asked the organisers about recent reports that Timor-Leste's oil and gas were running out as the Bayu-Undan field is close to depletion. (This was before the Boundary Treaty of 2018.)

The responses to what was a legitimate question at the time (see La'o Hamutuk 2015) were revealing. One of the leaders of TimorGap and a high-ranking member of the national government at the time argued that suggesting Timor-Leste's oil was running out was basically a false rumour spread by 'foreigners' – the goal of such rumours was to undermine Timor-Leste's struggle for resource sovereignty. References were made to the Australian spying scandal and those who criticised the Tasi Mane project were represented as anti-nationalist. The nationalist rhetoric representing the Tasi Mane development project as an extension of the resistance struggle was, in this case, used to deflect and perhaps even silence critics.

Despite some attempts to understand and connect with those affected by the Tasi Mane project, the project's representatives, responding to local people's questions, demanded their unwavering support. The audience was told that if people did not support the project, the government would take this fantastic scheme elsewhere and they would not get any benefits at all. With a sense of passion, the speaker from TimorGap at the Betano 'socialisation' responded to people's questions by saying: 'by 2020 we will no longer be importing gas or gasoline – you will be using your own gas and oil'. He added, 'You will not be hungry … Your motorbike will always have petrol … And we as a nation will no longer have to buy oil from foreign nations'. He then added:

> At the moment, the government spends millions of dollars a year on buying petroleum from outside. When the pipeline is here, this money will go to you, because the government will no longer have to buy the petroleum from the outside … This is why the state wants this project. It is about minimising the involvement of foreigners [*estrangeiros*].

Multiple references to the struggle for self-determination were made and the audience was asked to give up something for the good of the nation. Again, the nationalist rhetoric and the appeal to patriotic capitalism were very clear: the Tasi Mane project is represented as making Timor-Leste independent from outsiders, thereby strengthening the country's sovereignty overall. Giving up their land was one of the sacrifices that people were asked to make.

During my research in Suai, I repeatedly heard from members of civil society that their attempts to establish a critical dialogue with affected community members about the development project and accompanying land dispossession were being thwarted. Some of them even felt intimidated and were critical of the prominent role veterans played in some of the developments and consultations. Critics also reported having been publicly admonished for warning against the negative consequences of oil dependency. One of the intended or unintended consequences of growing resource nationalism has been the attempt to sideline voices critical of megaproject development.

Conclusion

For many East Timorese citizens, it would seem that dreams can indeed come true. In March 2018, Timor-Leste secured an agreement to create a permanent maritime boundary with Australia along the median line and confirmed a resource-sharing agreement that benefits Timor-Leste 70–80 per cent. This extraordinary achievement seemed impossible just a couple of years earlier. While this chapter was written prior to these recent events, in many ways they confirm the immense appeal and efficacy of Timor-Leste's resource nationalism discussed (for an analysis of the factors that led to the breakthrough in the negotiations with Australia, see Leach 2018).

This chapter has analysed the pertinence of resource nationalism in the contemporary political landscape of Timor-Leste. It has examined how the political discourse of resource nationalism conflates two issues: the issue of boundaries and the legitimacy and feasibility of onshore oil and gas infrastructure development. It has argued that 'struggles to dominate the flow of value produced by oil' (Reyna and Behrends 2008: 15) emerge out of the interlacing of national and international processes of domination. On the one hand, nationalist arguments are used internally to suppress critical voices of the Tasi Mane project; on the other hand, arguments about the dangers of oil dependency and profligate spending are used internationally to delegitimise Timor-Leste's legitimate claims to resource sovereignty. Occidentalist representations of East Timorese future visions intensify resource nationalism, which has thus far had limited success in connecting with campaigns for greater equality and social justice or in warding off aggressive market liberalisation. Yet, unlike in parts of Latin America, where in the past (during the time of high oil prices) resource nationalism has mitigated some of the more drastic impacts of the resource curse, in Timor-Leste, there is a risk that heightened nationalist sentiments around the issue of resource sovereignty could stifle more effective articulations of critique towards the ways in which oil profits are allocated internally. A disentangling of the issue of borders from the issue of onshore infrastructure development might allow more thorough scrutiny of contemporary development plans and thus ensure that the dream of resource sovereignty does not turn into a nightmare.

References

Aditjondro. G. J. (1999) *Is oil thicker than blood?* New York: Nova Science Publishers.

Bovensiepen, J. and Meitzner Yoder, L. (2018) 'Introduction: Political dynamics and social effects of megaproject development' in Bovensiepen, J. and Meitzner Yoder, L. (guest eds), *Megaprojects and national development models in Timor-Leste*, Special issue of *The Asia Pacific Journal of Anthropology*, vol. 19, no. 3, pp. 381–394. doi.org/10.1080/14442213.2018.1513553.

Coronil, F. (1997) *The magical state: Nature, money, and modernity in Venezuela*, Chicago and London: The University of Chicago Press.

Crespi, B. and Guillaud, D. (2018) 'Oil and custom: Impacts of the Tasi Mane oil project on the local communities in Suai, 2011–2017', in Bovensiepen, J. and Meitzner Yoder, L. (guest eds) *Megaprojects and national development models in Timor-Leste*, Special issue of *The Asia Pacific Journal of Anthropology*, vol. 19, no. 3, pp. 412–431. doi.org/10.1080/14442213.2018.1513060.

Cryan, M. (2015) *Dispossession and impoverishment in Timor-Leste: Potential impacts of the Suai supply base*, SSGM Discussion Paper 2015/15, Canberra: State, Society & Governance in Melanesia, ANU. Available at: ssgm.bell school.anu.edu.au/sites/default/files/publications/attachments/2016-07/dp_2015_15-cryan.pdf.

Fundasaun Mahein (2013) 'Projetu Suai supply base: Dezenvolvimentu ka ameasa?' [The Suai supply base project: Development or danger?], *Mahein Nia Lian Nú*. 57, 29 August.

Gledhill, J. (2008) '"The people's oil": Nationalism, globalization, and the possibility of another country in Brazil, Mexico, and Venezuela', *Focaal: Journal of Global and Historical Anthropology*, vol. 52, pp. 57–74. doi.org/10.3167/fcl.2008.520104.

La'o Hamutuk (2011) 'South Coast petroleum infrastructure project', *La'o Hamutuk – The Timor-Leste Institute for Development Monitoring and Analysis*, 16 September (updated 19 June 2016). Available at: www.laohamutuk.org/Oil/TasiMane/11TasiMane.htm.

La'o Hamutuk (2015) 'Timor-Leste's oil and gas are going fast', *La'o Hamutuk – The Timor-Leste Institute for Development Monitoring and Analysis*, 15 April. Available at: laohamutuk.blogspot.co.uk/2015/04/timor-lestes-oil-and-gas-are-going-fast.html.

La'o Hamutuk (2016) 'Information about the treaty between Australia and Timor-Leste on Certain Maritime Arrangements in the Timor Sea (CMATS)', *La'o Hamutuk – The Timor-Leste Institute for Development Monitoring and Analysis*, 1 August. Available at: www.laohamutuk.org/Oil/Boundary/CMATSindex.htm.

La'o Hamutuk (2018) 'The Timor-Leste-Australia Maritime Boundary Treaty', *La'o Hamutuk – The Timor-Leste Institute for Development Monitoring and Analysis*, 21 March. Available at: www.laohamutuk.org/Oil/Boundary/Treaty/18TreatyArticleEn.htm.

Leach, M. (2013) 'Turbulence in the Timor Sea: Australia could benefit too from a renegotiation of the maritime boundary', *Inside Story*, 6 December. Available at: inside.org.au/turbulence-in-the-timor-sea/.

Leach, M. (2018) 'Timor-Leste: Architect of its own sunrise', *Inside Story*, 8 March. Available at: insidestory.org.au/timor-leste-architect-of-its-own-sunrise/.

McGrath, K. (2014) 'Oil, gas and spy games in the Timor Sea. Australian scheming for the Greater Sunrise oilfield has a long history', *The Monthly*, April. Available at: www.themonthly.com.au/issue/2014/april/1396270800/kim-mcgrath/oil-gas-and-spy-games-timor-sea.

McGrath, K. (2017) *Crossing the line: Australia's secret history in the Timor Sea*. Carlton: Redback.

Meitzner Yoder, L. S. (2015) 'The development eraser: Fantastical schemes, aspirational distractions and high modern mega-events in the Oecusse enclave, Timor-Leste', *Journal of Political Ecology*, vol. 22, pp. 299–321. doi.org/10.2458/v22i1.21110.

Reyna, S. and Behrends, A. (2008) 'The crazy curse and crude domination: Toward an anthropology of oil', *Focaal: European Journal of Anthropology*, vol. 52, pp. 3–17. doi.org/10.3167/fcl.2008.520101.

SDP (Democratic Republic of Timor-Leste) (2011) *Timor-Leste strategic development plan 2011–2030*. Available at: sustainabledevelopment.un.org/content/documents/1506Timor-Leste-Strategic-Plan-2011-20301.pdf.

TimorGap (2015) *Southern coast project*. Available at: www.timorgap.com/databases/website.nsf/vwAll/SOUTHERN%20COAST%20PROJECT.

7

Reconsidering reintegration: Veterans' benefits as state-building

Kate Roll

In Timor-Leste, newspaper columns, blog posts and roadside debates crackle with questions about the relationship of the past to the present: Why should former resistance members give up their weapons and cede control to young police officers? What is the benefit of replacing efficient 'jungle justice' with lengthy court processes? On what grounds can state administrators tell former resistance members that they do not qualify for a pension? These are questions about legitimate domination and justifying a new regime. These are questions about the relationship of the past to the future.

Many Timorese look to the resistance movements that fought against the Indonesian occupation (1974–1999) for political legitimacy, indigenous governance models and structures, and narratives for what independence should mean. In the vision of those who participated in the resistance, the past provides a template for the new state. As one former leader argued:

> We need an organ to clear up and organise [the state] … the body should be structured like it was in the jungle. If you spoke you had to pause first; you had to speak truthfully, to the point. And everyone understood this.[1]

However, efforts to preserve the resistance-era political order clash with the development and consolidation of a neoliberal statist order. This can be observed in a lack of resolution about where authority should reside, as well as in repeated clashes between state authorities and former combatants.

While the independent Democratic Republic of Timor-Leste has been internationally recognised for over a decade, the process of state-building is ongoing. Not sewn from whole cloth, the new state depends upon artefacts of the pre-existing order; simultaneously, it is also defined in opposition to the resistance movement. In particular, the state-building challenge has revolved around renegotiating the relationship between the new state and the resistance movement, which until the end of the 24-year Indonesian occupation served as the legitimate site of authority, popular sovereignty and coercive force. The central puzzle of state-builders in Timor-Leste thus has been *how* to consolidate power with the state. This entails the delicate dance of moving from multiple sites of legitimate force and authority towards a Weberian monopoly, while also continuing to draw upon the symbolic power of the resistance movement and its leadership. In the context of pervasive state weakness, this process has involved incorporation and 'grafting' as well as exclusion and delegitimisation.

Reintegration programs, which connect the nascent state and former resistance members, are a key technology for state-building. More specifically, I examine registration and the performative elements of data verification practices and demobilisation ceremonies through this lens. I connect reintegration programs and state-building by arguing that reintegration programs exemplify Aretxaga's 'local encounters' (2003), which communicate the presence of the state in people's lives and shape their actions accordingly. In a country with poor infrastructure and non-existent or destroyed personal records, reintegration programs are

---

1   All quotations are derived from the author's fieldwork, unless indicated otherwise. This fieldwork took place in two waves in 2010 and 2012, during which the author conducted 224 survey interviews using randomised cluster sampling and a further 90 elite interviews using purposive sampling. The interviews were conducted in Tetum when possible.

a significant state undertaking, engaging a powerful cohort. Since the early 2000s, reintegration programs in Timor-Leste have registered 250,000 former resistance members, bringing them into contact with the state.

This chapter seeks to contribute to the literature on both Timor-Leste and its future, as well as to broaden the way scholars think about state-building and its mechanisms. Reintegration programs relocate centres of legitimate authority from conflict-era institutions to the inchoate state; viewed this way, they are not about controlling spoilers or rewarding heroes. I identify reintegration programs as an example of how states are built from – but also destroy – the power structures of the past. Reintegration programs enlist a vision of the modern bureaucratic state, one with all the tools of technocratic power: registration forms, ID numbers, stamps and pension databases. This perspective moves beyond a narrow, security-driven view of disarmament, demobilisation and reintegration (DDR) as the monopolisation of coercive force. Instead, it looks at the role of reintegration in drawing new boundaries between state and non-state, defining and regulating veterans, and extending the state's reach. This argument is supported by critical and anthropological theories of the state.

Reintegration in Timor-Leste

On 20 May 2002, Timor-Leste achieved independence following a brutal Indonesian invasion and occupation (1974–1999) and a period of United Nations trusteeship (1999–2002). Independence marked the putative end of the resistance movement that had fought against the occupation. Diverse and dynamic, the movement went through major strategic shifts and periods of fracture and rebuilding. In the post-conflict period, key leaders of resistance organisations, including clandestine groups, the diplomatic front and the armed resistance, sought office and became the backbone of the country's new political elite. These former resistance members brought with them longstanding alliances and tensions (often in the same relationship), as well as obligations to their networks of men and women who served under their command.

Undergirded by both a normative obligation to support those who served and the political mobilisation of potential beneficiaries, state benefits programs for former resistance members – namely, pensions and one-off payments – have been a core yet costly feature of the state's post-conflict development. In 2013, the Timorese pension program accounted for over

14 per cent of the social protection budget and 5 per cent of the total state budget. Since 2002, over 250,000 self-identified former resistance members – approximately 60 per cent of the population over the age of 30 – have registered. This number far outstrips historical estimates of participation (CAVR 2005: 39). This level of investment cannot be explained through conventional understandings of DDR programs as a strategic response to spoilers, concerns with security, or even political pressures.

As an alternative, I suggest that reintegration programs are a means of the state to exert control over 'unruly' subjects. The 'veterans problem' hinges on the rival status of ex-combatant networks in relation to state power, and the state has sought to gain control over these subjects through techniques that register, categorise and track them. As former prime minister Gusmão acknowledged, registration is important – as 'once there is oversight, we'll know who's who' (*Timor Post* 2010). This process of capturing 'who's who' has driven state-building: first, by necessitating the expansion of the state's institutional apparatus – more cars, databases, enumerators and ministry offices – and second, by increasing state power through the 'knowing' and ordering its subjects (see Widder 2004). The growth of state power can be understood to occur when 'more power relations are referred through state channels – most immediately, that more people must stand in line and await rubber stamps to get what they want' (Ferguson 1994: 274). Similarly, Loveman (2005: 1679) describes the extension of disciplinary state power through 'infrastructural penetration and administrative "ordering" of everyday life'.

Veterans' reintegration has also entailed the exertion of new practices that model the state's 'verticality' as above civil society, a concept borrowed from Ferguson and Gupta (2002). The authors argue that through 'spatialization', state actors 'help to secure their legitimacy, to naturalize their authority, and to represent themselves as superior to, and encompassing of, other institutions and centers of power' (ibid.: 982). From the construction of matching memorials and ossuaries in each of the country's subdistricts to demobilisation ceremonies in the capital, these performances draw upon a language of authority and communicate the modernity and centrality of the state. In the following two sections, I will first explore the extension of disciplinary power through the registration process and will subsequently address state performance in data verification processes and demobilisation ceremonies.

Registration and disciplinary power

In Timor-Leste, the identification and classification of individuals through registration provides a key example of how the new state has extended its disciplinary power. Once classified, groups such as 'veterans' are naturalised, becoming 'problems' for the state and thus the objects of intervention and regulation. State actors first actively define the population subject to the intervention by producing knowledge on the cohort. This expert 'knowledge' becomes the source of power ('knowledge/power'), as it justifies and facilitates differential treatment and intervention (see MacKinnon's excellent summary, 2000: 296). Technologies for creating these identities include enumeration, classification and mapping. These practices engender standardisation, radical simplification and institutionalisation, and make state surveillance and control possible (see Anderson 1991; Bernal 1997). The legal development of identity categories in Timor-Leste used for administering pension benefits also provides an example of this knowledge/power nexus.

The creation of these identity categories allows for a range of disciplinary action, particularly through the exercise of 'biopower' – the control of bodies and populations – and the creation of docile bodies (see O'Neill's analysis, 1986: 43). As Ferguson argues, government services extend disciplinary state power into the realm of how people live and how they control their bodies. He writes:

> 'Government services' are never simply 'services'; instead of conceiving this phrase as a reference simply to a 'government' whose purpose is to serve, it may be at least as appropriate to think of 'services' which serve to govern. (Ferguson 1994: 253)

The view of the state as instrumentalised through the extension of disciplinary power is of particular relevance to this thesis; here, government services, including benefits programs, are a means of regulating identities and bodies, reframing reintegration programs as a form of disciplinary biopolitics. In this light, the introduction of state controls or programs (e.g. permits, forms, taxes, identification, services) marks the extension of state power and thus a form of state-building.

In Timor-Leste, the development of comprehensive registries began with non-state veterans' associations.[2] Of the new groups, the Association of Resistance Veterans (AVR [*Associação Veteranos dos Resistência*]) boasted over 18,000 members by 2002 (McCarthy 2002: 91), many of whom would have had extremely limited fighting experience. The Association of Former Combatants (AAC [*Associação dos Antigos Combatentes*]) also registered putative former fighters, 'demanding cash payments from those who registered in return for an ID card' (World Bank 2008: 9). The engagement of these associations in state-like functions (e.g. issuing identity papers or promising benefits) increased the state's need to establish its own registration program and reassert control over who would take part in these programs. As one Member of Parliament summarised: '[Resistance members] served the state, now it is the state's obligation. They could organise themselves … this would be a problem!'

Accordingly, Timorese programs have focused on creating authoritative data, 'official' records that control who is offered benefits and who is not. More broadly, these data drives have helped the Timorese state account for its populace. Prior to the registration drive, most Timorese registrants had no formal 'identity' in relation to the state apparatus. But registration has done more than just put individuals on the state's radar: the resulting identity categories set the lens through which the state approaches subjects. Here the summation of disciplinarity as *fixing* individuals within institutions is again apt (Hardt and Negri, quoted in Widder 2004: 414). These discursive processes – the categorisation of individuals – fundamentally augment the state's 'control over the production, unification, codification and dissemination of knowledge' (Loveman 2005: 1660).

In Timor-Leste, the registration programs identify subjects who merit special attention and interventions, including recognition and payments, using categories and criteria relevant to state purposes. Legal instruments draw the lines defining and excluding civilians and collaborators, separating high-status 'veterans' from 'former national liberation combatants'. These determinations centre on questions around types of service, with particular emphasis on use of weaponry; the criteria favour the politically powerful (older men) over the less so (women, young people). The title of 'veteran',

2   These included the FALINTIL Veterans' Foundation (FVF), the Ex-Combatants Foundation (AAC), and the Association of Resistance Veterans (AVR), in addition to resistance-era groups, including RENETIL and CPD-RDTL.

which has a distinct legal meaning, establishes subjects' relationships to the state. The categorisation is double-edged, however. As discussed in regards to demobilisation, such an assignation both honours the subject and marginalises him or her, simultaneously underscoring the subject's heroism and marking it as from a bygone era.

The emergence of the state in making these determinations marks a very specific extension of state power. Nationwide registration establishes the state as the maker and keeper of official – and thus consequential – histories, identities and knowledge. Here, state actors draw black-and-white distinctions in a conflict marked by shades of grey, resolving thorny questions around identity and service. This power to resolve ambiguities is, somewhat ironically, highlighted by the state's complicity in 'laundering' fraudulent or inflated service claims. As Scott notes, 'fictitious facts-on-paper' matter: they 'can often be made eventually to prevail on the ground, because it is on behalf of such pieces of paper that police and army are deployed' (1998: 83). The state renders these classifications 'true' by deploying the state apparatus and conferring special treatment on fraudulent registrants. As discussed above, the state's ability to remove people from the list marks a similar expression of this power.

In addition to simply determining who gets benefits (who 'counts'), registration renders subjects visible – countable, measurable – to the state. This allows for the treatment of registered individuals as a coherent group and facilitates monitoring, as well as control through targeted benefits distribution. For example, the provision of financial benefits to identified individuals can be used to disperse – the 'pay and scatter' DDR approach (Alden 2002: 345) – or concentrate problematic populations. In Timor-Leste, benefits payments are disbursed in the subject's subdistrict of birth, requiring regular pilgrimages back to areas in which the subject is 'known'. Veterans' benefits programs have also, for both surveillance and cultural reasons, often focused on housing, placing residences near the road for ease of state visits or envisaging 'veterans' villages' in which former fighters are concentrated. In this manner, data gathering and analysis is disciplinary and key to the extension and effectiveness of the state apparatus.

Finally, the classification of 'veterans' also makes possible the articulation of a 'veterans problem'. This problematisation both sets the stage for and justifies intervention. In interviews, state officials depict former resistance members as infirm and doddering, or hot-blooded and not modern – of a different era. This contrasts with state actors, who – despite often having been in the resistance themselves – now identify with the state and with hybrid organisations like Gusmão's National Congress for Timorese Reconstruction party. This idea of former resistance members as being anachronistic has emerged as the heart of this 'problem', the clash between the old ways of doing things and the 'new' state. The focus of policymakers has thus been on excluding these actors from driving the political process and instead finding more 'appropriate', state-run venues in which they could express themselves – most notably the National Veterans' Council, which was under development at the time of fieldwork in 2012. Settling or solving the 'veterans problem' in this perspective thus revolves around redefining their relationship to the state, and undercutting or coopting these forms of authority.

Incorporation of the resistance into the state

Tied to the process of extending state power through the constitution of subjects, a key area in which the performance of modern, bureaucratic statehood can be seen is the process of registering and verifying the data of former resistance members. Here, the theatre of this process must be considered independently of its efficacy as a tool of enumeration and authentication. As Appadurai (1993: 316–317, my emphasis) discusses in the context of colonial India, the use of numerical tools such as censuses 'rather than being a passive instrument of data-gathering … became an important part of the *illusion* of bureaucratic control'. Even if the forms and folios have been lost, what matters in this instance is the impression or 'illusion' of modern statehood that the registration and data verification process itself makes on the participants. In Timor-Leste, the audience is considerable, with approximately 250,000 individuals having registered and thousands having participated in data verification.

In the case of data verification, the Commission for Homage, Supervision of Registration and Appeals, observed during fieldwork in 2010, arrived from the capital in a large government vehicle with a driver. The members stayed with local leaders, were fed first and held their audiences from behind a table set up within a commandeered school building. The Data Verification Team's commissioners, many of whom were former resistance leaders, wielded all the tools of officialdom. They slid forms in and out of plastic sleeves, displayed identification cards on patriotic lanyards and had mobile phones clipped onto their belts; they thumped down rubber stamps with percussive authority. They also trafficked in the currency of the formal state, rewarding the production of official documentation, including birth records and voter identification cards, and looking askance at those who had none. In the wake of these visits, state-authored registries issued from the capital were publicly displayed, advertising the new, singular and official record of the resistance.

The authority and modern rationality of the Homage Commission, and thus the state from which they emanated, were communicated in everything from the organisation of the room to the use of formal documents. It painted the picture of a strong, modern and opaque central state, and marked off boundaries between state actors (commissioners) and subjects (registrants). The hierarchies established by the Data Verification Team recall Ferguson and Gupta's (2002) description of how states are performed as vertical – above civil society and other social groups – and encompassing. Nevertheless, one Timorese academic noted in a 2010 interview with the author that this process had been partial: 'They have not received [benefits] because the government does not yet have control over the data. Some people have given false documents … data is needed for recognition'.

It is important to note, however, that this performance of a modern, apolitical state also masks continuities in conflict-era power relations and the political content of the reintegration program. This dynamic is evident in the widespread appropriation of reintegration resources for patronage, whether the awarding of construction contracts to former comrades or the inflation of years of service in pension registration. This is made possible through the transformation of former resistance leaders into commissioners, the bureaucratic actors working on behalf of the state. Yet this transformation, achieved in part through the theatre of state authority described above, is illusory or partial (reflecting, in part, the very fiction of the autonomous technocrat). While their transformation into 'commissioners' may appear to be a victory for state consolidation, it obscures how non-state actors and institutions that precede the new state gain access to resources in the post-conflict period.

While these actors 'act' on behalf of the state, many have used their positions to advance their interests, as well as the resistance-era networks that they support and that in turn maintain their status. Wearing 'two hats', non-state actors – whether as traditional authorities, through patronage networks or via ex-combatant groups – embody state institutions and retain authority in both state and non-state spheres. Crucially, this result is not entirely unforeseeable. Indeed, the commissioners tasked with gathering and verifying former resistance members' registration data were chosen from the resistance leadership precisely because of their authority within those networks, as well as their knowledge of the area and of those who had participated in the resistance. This dual source of authority adds to their perceived omniscience, again evoking the vertical, encompassing state. The expansion of the state system through the registration program has, ironically, depended upon engaging resistance-era authority and legitimising it by dressing up former leaders.

Here, state actors have increased the impression of the encompassing, omniscient state by incorporating former resistance leaders and their networks – bodies still associated with coercive force and active surveillance. As Dorman (2006: 1086) argues, the institutions and styles of leadership that define the conflict era carry forward in post-conflict styles of politics and governance. I argue that the structures and networks carry over as well. In the case of Timor-Leste, we are reminded that even as the state enacts these boundaries, marking itself as distinct and autonomous from civil society and non-state resistance-era networks, these lines are both strategic and illusory. Rather, the exercise and currency of power remain rooted in relationships and narratives that extend through the state apparatus, and the perception of the state as unitary and autonomous is produced through specific practices.

State consolidation through exclusion

While the extension of the state's reach is made possible through the transformation of former resistance leaders into 'commissioners', the imagination of the state is also achieved through the *exclusion* of certain non-state actors. Indeed, a key element of the performance of statehood is the articulation of lines separating the state from society: it is via these boundaries that the state takes form and is attributed with autonomy. As Mitchell (1991: 95, my emphasis) argues, '[t]he state should be addressed as *an effect* of detailed processes … which create the appearance of a world fundamentally divided into state and society'. Of particular relevance to this discussion, as I will examine in more detail below, is the use of demobilisation ceremonies to rearticulate lines of authority and reclassify former resistance actors as 'non-state' and thus as illegitimate authors of coercive force.

To study this boundary, Mitchell (1991: 78, 90; see also Torpey 1998) suggests looking at the 'detailed political processes through which the uncertain yet powerful distinction between state and society is produced' and 'through which a certain social and political order is maintained'. In this reconceptualisation, a key element of state-building is how and where the line defining state and society is drawn. Who can act on behalf of the state? Who is a subject of the state? More broadly, I contend that the key to the modern state's performance and the idea of state autonomy depends on the creation of standard, mutually exclusive roles. These include citizen/bureaucrat, politician/technocrat, veteran/soldier and rebel/soldier, among others. The assignment of such roles as a form of disciplinary state power will be discussed in the next section.

One of the best examples of the redrawing of lines of authority is the demobilisation of armed resistance members, the FALINTIL (the *Forças Armadas da Libertação Nacional de Timor-Leste* [Armed Forces for the National Liberation of East Timor]). In 2006, 2011 and 2013, the Timorese Government demobilised 205, 236 and 219 high-level former resistance members, respectively. In 2012, a further 30,000 diplomas were distributed to former resistance members with shorter terms of recognised service. These ceremonies included the awarding of medals, presentation of new uniforms and martial displays by the new generation of the Timorese military, the F-FDTL. The theatrical ceremonies communicated a passing of the torch – a shift in authority from former fighters (the FALINTIL resistance) to the new state actors (the F-FDTL). The new uniforms, for example, made clear the separation of and distinction between the active troops and those now 'demobilised'. The protracted, expansive and iterative nature of this 'demobilisation' highlights the difficulty of reshaping the relationship between a resistance movement and a 'new' state army.

Comments by the Japanese ambassador to Timor-Leste, Iwao Kitahara, highlight the underlying narrative of these ceremonies and underscore the fundamental challenge of such a proposition:

> We are entering to a new era. Until now, there were F-FDTL soldiers who were also members of the FALINTIL. But from now on, the F-FDTL will be organised only by F-FDTL soldiers. (Kitahara 2011)

Yet, can such a line distinguishing the two identities be so clearly drawn? The point seems to have been lost that the name FALINTIL remains – as the first 'F' in F-FDTL. Indeed, this ambiguity or overlapping of the FALINTIL and F-FDTL authority was deliberately incorporated in the name. The military was first formed in 2001 as the East Timor Defence Force through the recruitment of 650 cantoned FALINTIL members; under public pressure to acknowledge the FALINTIL resistance, it was renamed the F-FDTL in 2002 (see ICG 2011: 4). The FALINTIL's authority remains, as does its symbolic power; as an institution, it is difficult to raze.

For those being 'honoured', demobilisation has served as a form of exclusion. These ceremonies confer an official status on the demobilised, symbolised through their medals and uniforms, but, concomitantly, they delegitimise these individuals' roles in the active state security apparatus. Even the bowing of each veteran's head to receive his or her medal signals a submission to the supremacy of the new state. Accordingly, some have refused to participate, viewing the ceremonies as a way to mark the resolution of their claims to government assistance. This displacement and delegitimisation of non-state resistance-era actors extends beyond demobilisation. The centralisation of information – for example, the determination of the years and types of service recognised in the demobilisation ceremonies – reproduces these lines of official (state) and unofficial (non-state) knowledge, only one of which 'counts'. These processes result in the alienation of these fighters and *clandestinos* from their histories.

The drawing of state and non-state boundaries and lines of authority is particularly complicated in post-conflict states. As Mitchell (1991: 88) argues, 'the edges of the state are uncertain; societal elements seem to penetrate it on all sides, and the resulting boundary between state and society is difficult to determine'. Many resistance-era actors have parlayed their authority into positions within the state. This is evident for both political leaders, who have drawn upon their conflict-era status to legitimise their claims as well as mobilise former followers politically, and 'Brown Shirt' security guards, who reportedly are often former resistance members who have received their positions through patronage networks. Even in the registration process, as discussed above, the incorporation of former resistance members as commissioners has merged and blurred the authority of resistance-era leaders and state actors. In such a fluid environment, activities that draw the lines between state and non-state are particularly powerful.

Conclusion

In drawing upon anthropological and post-structural concepts of the state, this chapter has sought to shed new light on state-building and the role of reintegration and benefits programs therein. This lens shifts attention from what is being built (the state as an object or assemblage of institutions) to what effect these processes have (the idea of the state; the drawing of boundaries). And it is worth emphasising that the idea of the state in state-building carries with it a vision of the future, one of Weber's modern autonomous state, exercising bureaucratic power. In this manner, it is a rejection of the patrimonial relations of the resistance era. Analytically, this places focus on 'how the state is performed and experienced in the everyday encounters of state agencies and functionaries with the citizenry or population' (Metsola 2006: 1119).

The re-identification of the state thus reanimates the study of post-conflict reintegration and benefits programs in Timor-Leste, transforming our perspective on seemingly mundane practices such as queuing for registration. This framework, in complicating notions around state autonomy and agency, exposes the complexity around sites of authority, with state and non-state actors appearing to be in competition, but also often highly integrated, with some former resistance leaders 'wearing two hats'. Here we see, ironically, that building the modern state is a process in which resistance-era actors and structures are essential. The idea of the state, expectations of state action and the legitimacy imparted by acting on behalf of the state remain highly relevant – the state maintains this 'meta-capital' – even in a situation like that of Timor-Leste, where state institutions are weak and the reach of the state apparatus, such as through policing, is limited.

In their discussion of state development in Timor-Leste, Richmond and Franks argue:

> East Timor appears increasingly to be a hollow liberal state: the state structure certainly exists, but its liberal substance is virtual and has even been described as a 'Hollywood film set'. (Richmond and Franks 2008: 196)

This chapter, with its focus on the performance of the state and engendering the state-as-idea, recognises a similar theatricality – the 'film set' of state governance – but in that performance, it also finds substance. If we reject a purely institutional view of the state and recognise that governance extends through the actions of people and infrastructural power, these performances and mythologies are important, drawing new lines between the past, present and future.

References

Alden, C. (2002) 'Making old soldiers fade away: Lessons from the reintegration of demobilized soldiers in Mozambique', *Security Dialogue*, vol. 33, no. 3, pp. 341–356. doi.org/10.1177/0967010602033003008.

Anderson, B. (1991) *Imagined communities: Reflections on the origin and spread of nationalism*, London: Verso.

Appadurai, A. (1993) 'Number in the colonial imagination', in Breckenridge, C.A. and Van der Veer, P. (eds) *Orientalism and the postcolonial predicament: Perspectives on South Asia*, Philadelphia: University of Pennsylvania Press, pp. 314–340.

Aretxaga, B. (2003) 'Maddening states', *Annual Review of Anthropology*, vol. 32, no. 1, pp. 393–410. doi.org/10.1146/annurev.anthro.32.061002.093341.

Bernal, V. (1997) 'Colonial moral economy and the discipline of development: The Gezira scheme and "Modern" Sudan', *Cultural Anthropology*, vol. 12, no. 4, pp. 447–479. doi.org/10.1525/can.1997.12.4.447.

CAVR (Timor-Leste Commission for Reception, Truth and Reconciliation) (2005) *Chega! The final report of the Timor Leste Commission for Reception, Truth and Reconciliation (CAVR)*, Dili, Timor-Leste: KPG in cooperation with STP-CAVR.

Dorman, S. R. (2006) 'Post-liberation politics in Africa: Examining the political legacy of struggle', *Third World Quarterly*, vol. 27, no. 6, pp. 1085–1101. doi.org/10.1080/01436590600842365.

Ferguson, J. (1994) *The anti-politics machine: Development, depoliticization, and bureaucratic power in Lesotho*, Minneapolis: University of Minnesota Press.

Ferguson, J. and Gupta, A. (2002) 'Spatializing states: Towards an ethnography of neoliberal governmentality', *American Ethnologist*, vol. 29, no. 4, pp. 981–1002. doi.org/10.1525/ae.2002.29.4.981.

ICG (International Crisis Group) (2011) *Update briefing Timor-Leste's veterans: An unfinished struggle?* Crisis Group Asia Briefing No. 129, Dili/Jakarta/Brussels.

Kitahara, I. (2011) *Ambassador of Japan to Timor-Leste*, comments on 23 August 2011. Available at: www.timor-leste.emb-japan.go.jp/newera_e.htm.

Loveman, M. (2005) 'The modern state and the primitive accumulation of symbolic power', *American Journal of Sociology*, vol. 110, no. 6, pp. 1651–1683. doi.org/10.1086/428688.

MacKinnon, D. (2000) 'Managerialism, governmentality and the state: a Neo-Foucauldian approach to local economic governance', *Political Geography*, vol. 19, no. 3, pp. 293–314. doi.org/10.1016/S0962-6298(99)00086-4.

McCarthy, J. (2002) *FALINTIL Reinsertion Assistant Program: Final evaluation report*, Dili, East Timor: International Organization for Migration.

Metsola, L. (2006) '"Reintegration" of ex-combatants and former fighters: A lens into state formation and citizenship in Namibia', *Third World Quarterly*, vol. 27, no. 6, pp. 1119–1135. doi.org/10.1080/01436590600842407.

Mitchell, T. (1991) 'The limits of the state: Beyond statist approaches and their critics', *The American Political Science Review*, vol. 85, no. 1, pp. 77–96.

O'Neill, J. (1986) 'The disciplinary society: From Weber to Foucault', *The British Journal of Sociology*, vol. 37, no. 1, pp. 42–60. doi.org/10.2307/591050.

Richmond, O. P. and Franks, J. (2008) 'Liberal peacebuilding in Timor Leste: The emperor's new clothes?', *International Peacekeeping*, vol. 15, no. 2, pp. 185–200. doi.org/10.1080/13533310802041436.

Scott, J. (1998) *Seeing like a state: How certain schemes to improve the human condition have failed*, New Haven: Yale University Press.

Timor Post (2010) 'PM Xanana husu veteranus hakmatek' [PM Xanana asks for calm from veterans], 19 July.

Torpey, J. (1998) 'Coming and going : On the state monopolization of the legitimate "means of movement"', *Sociological Theory*, vol. 16, no. 3, pp. 239–259. doi.org/10.1111/0735-2751.00055.

Widder, N. (2004) 'Foucault and power revisited', *European Journal of Political Theory*, vol. 3, no. 4, pp. 411–432. doi.org/10.1177/1474885104045913.

World Bank (2008) *Defining heroes: Key lessons from the creation of veterans policy in Timor-Leste*, Report No. 45458-TP, Washington, DC: World Bank.

Part III: Alternative moral economies of prosperity

8

Expressions of the 'good life' and visions of the future: Reflections from Dili and Uatolari

Josh Trindade and Susana Barnes

In this chapter, we take up Arjun Appadurai's (2013) call for a better anthropological understanding of the construction of the future as a 'cultural fact' and the implications of this for what he calls people's 'capacity to aspire' (ibid.: 290) – their ability to mobilise resources in order to make strategic decisions about their future. Appadurai argues that debate and discussion around 'futures' is often dominated by 'plans, goals and targets' – language that is associated with development. Culture, on the other hand, is too readily associated with 'habit, custom, heritage and tradition', and therefore dismissed as grounded in the past. Yet the future cannot be other than 'cultural' because it is 'in culture that ideas of the future, as much as the past, are embedded and nurtured' (ibid.: 179–180). It is within 'culture', understood broadly as local systems of value, meaning and communication, that people are enabled or constrained in their 'capacity to aspire'.

In our exploration of the construction of the future as a cultural fact, we consider the significance of three Tetun idioms – *matak-malirin* ('the green and cool'), *tempu rai-diak* ('the tranquil time') and *halerik* ('lament') – in shaping people's hopes and desires of the future in the context of the widespread revitalisation and recalibration of customary beliefs and practices in independence-era Timor-Leste. Drawing on fieldwork conducted in Dili and Babulo, Uatolari subdistrict, we suggest that while the material articulation of these hopes and desires and the individual or collective capacity to mobilise resources to achieve them are enabled or constrained by people's structural position in society, ideas about the future continue to be shaped by a shared cultural framework and vision for what constitutes a 'good life'.

Customary renewal in post-occupation Timor-Leste: The case of Babulo

Since 1999, the rebuilding of ancestral or origin houses in Babulo has occurred at a remarkable rate. As of 2015, at least 26 houses have been rebuilt. The length and complexity of the house-building process is determined by a variety of factors: the choice of particular types of timber and roofing materials; their procurement from specific forested areas; the need to follow a certain order of construction and conduct the relevant rituals; and the necessity of involving all house members, representatives from other houses of the same origin group and houses related through marriage to ensure no outstanding conflicts exist between these groups. If we consider the time, effort and resources invested in every house reconstruction, we can begin to understand the centrality of this process to post-occupation social and ritual life.

Acts of customary renewal represent a cultural response to the uncertainties and opportunities created by independence (see Barnes 2017; Bovensiepen 2015). By 'cultural response', we mean that these acts are motivated by 'aspirations and desires' that 'grow out of [people's] own structures of life' (Ortner 2006: 147). These 'structures of life' constitute the cultural framework within which the people of Babulo operate. This framework is not immutable or fixed, but rooted in human experience and continually shaped by it. Moreover, it is inseparable from patterns of distribution of material resources, and therefore intimately bound to issues of power (Appadurai 2013; Bourdieu 1979; Ortner 2006). This 'cultural' response to independence is not motivated by a desire to re-create the past in the present; rather, it represents an attempt to draw on the past in order to negotiate the future (Appadurai 2013; Geertz 1973; Weiner 1992). We consider the significance of three cultural expressions – *matak-malirin* ('the green and cool'), *tempu rai-diak* ('the tranquil time') and *halerik* ('the lament') – in the context of the experiences of the people of Babulo, living both in Dili and their native village, to explore their engagement with local processes of customary renewal and the implications of this for their 'capacity to aspire'. We argue that renewed participation in customary practices reveals a continued commitment to a shared cultural framework and shared vision for what constitutes a 'good life'. However, acts of customary renewal are also sites for the production of consensus and demonstrate the open and dynamic nature of local culture (Appadurai 2013).

Matak-malirin ('the green and cool')

One local understanding of the 'good life' is expressed in the concept of *matak-malirin* – *matak* meaning 'newly green' or 'sprouting', and *malirin* meaning 'cool'. The concept of *matak-malirin* refers to 'a state of good health and productive life energy' (see Kehi and Palmer 2012: 447; Trindade 2014; Vroklage 1952). Also referred to in Naueti as *bua-malu* (betel leaves and areca nuts), this concept combines a sense of 'coolness', associated with calm and peace, with the 'newly green' or 'sprouting', which represents the idea of fertility and bounty (Trindade 2014). The categorical opposite of 'coolness' is 'heat', which symbolises danger and potential violence – a state of disorder in which categorical distinctions run the risk of mixing or being blurred (Bovensiepen 2015; Douglas 2005).

The concept of *matak-malirin* draws on a vision of society where life, understood as generative potential, is continually given, received, reciprocated and renewed through exchange or transmission (Traube 1986: 130). This in an 'inclusive' society that involves a cycle of exchanges across human-to-human and human-to-non-human relations (Palmer 2015; Barnes 2017; Trindade 2015). A state of *matak-malirin* can be achieved through participation in ritual and adherence to local norms and practices that serve to regulate these exchanges or, in other words, to sustain the 'flow of life'. In the context of communal rituals, such as rice or corn harvest (Tetun: *sau hare* or *sau batar*), *matak-malirin* is distributed to participants in the form of a portion of the sacrificial meal and ritually blessed betel leaves and areca nut.

Yet the practical and visible articulation of how *matak-malirin* might be achieved is contextually contingent, influenced by individual and familiar life trajectories and structural positions within society. What constitutes a state of *matak-malirin* for a person from Babulo living in Dili with regular employment is not necessarily the same as a person living in the village, whose livelihood depends on near-subsistence agriculture and foraging. Those who live a modern life in Dili no longer hope for a better harvest, but instead aim to have a nice job in an air-conditioned office, a nice car to drive and a comfortable house, etc. Influenced by global images of what constitutes a 'good life', a government employee from Babulo, living in Dili or moving between rural and urban areas, may aspire to a degree of commercial and wealth-based prosperity, social mobility, personal autonomy and recognition. A farmer in Babulo, on the other hand, may hope for a successful harvest and an opportunity to earn some cash income in order to send his or her children to school. However, the aspirations of both employee and farmer continue to be textured by deeply embedded local values, beliefs and ethics that require investment in social and symbolic resources, rather than material ones.

People from rural areas living in Dili regularly return to their village to participate in collective rituals, such as the corn and rice harvest (Naueti: *masi eka rae* and *masi hare*). Additionally, they contribute in cash or kind (usually collectively) to house rebuilding and maintenance, and they partake in the life cycle ceremonial exchanges (Tetun: *lia moris, lia mate*) that involve families and houses related by birth or marriage. They do so for the same reasons as those who remain in rural areas and also participate in these rituals: they believe that failure to engage in the social and symbolic promotion of life increases the risk of both social exclusion and ancestral or divine retribution in the form of infertility or death.

As Palmer points out, continued participation and investment in the 'customary economy' runs counter to 'neoliberal logics' and 'capitalist certainty' (Palmer 2015: 23). Surplus from agriculture, wage labour, remittances and business enterprises is revitalising the customary economy and redistributing wealth in ways which challenge capitalist principles (ibid.). Within this customary economy, people seek to reinvigorate relations (with the living and the dead), not necessarily for the short-term economic benefits these might provide, but for the long-term security they represent (Gudeman 2001; McWilliam 2011: 755).

This process is not without its imbalances and tensions. A conception of society based on the generation and regeneration of life provides a cultural framework for structuring action in the social world, but is also the basis of social distinctions and inequalities (Bourdieu 1979; Ortner 2006).

The resurgent 'customary economy' has also become a site of struggle over symbolic and material resources. Ceremonial occasions and ritual exchanges become opportunities for relative ostentation and competitive gift-giving aimed at affirming, contesting, negotiating or recalibrating status and/or political influence (see also McWilliam 2011). Many people complain of the burden of the multiple and often costly demands for contributions to the cycle of life and death rituals, which underpin the customary economy and constrain rather than enable their vision of the 'good life'. Nevertheless, it is the excesses of the system rather than the system itself that tend to be the object of resentment and criticism.

Tempu rai-diak ('the tranquil time')

One of the distinctive features of customary renewal in Babulo is the reprisal of domain-wide ceremonies, including the seasonal corn and rice harvest festivals and a ceremony of thanksgiving, usually conducted only every 10–15 years, to the founder-ancestors of the ritual domain of Babulo Mane Hitu, which encompasses much of the territory of the present village (*suku*) of Babulo. These constitute key ceremonies during which *matak-malirin* is requested from the founder-ancestors of the domain and symbolically distributed to participants in the form of blessings with water and betel-nut spittle as well as ritually prepared meat, corn and/or rice, betel nuts and betel leaves (Naueti: *bua nua malus*). When people are blessed with *matak-malirin*, they believe they are living in *tempu rai-diak*.

The driving force behind this reprisal has come from members of the senior houses of the Daralari origin group, who are considered to be the descendants of the founder-ancestors of the ritual domain. The Naueti term *rea netana*, meaning 'source of the earth', is used to describe members of the senior houses of the Daralari origin group, and the formal ritual title *rea mumu, rea uatu* ('iron rod of the earth, stone of land') is bestowed on one representative of this group who operates in collaboration and consultation with two or three elders, ritual specialists of his descent group. The notion of *rea netana*, understood as 'source of the land' or 'master of the land', exists in varying forms throughout East Timor and the Austronesian cultural sphere more broadly (Lewis 1988; Vischer 2009). It is said that in the not-so-distant past, the source of the land held overarching rights to the allocation and apportionment of land and natural resources. In some cases, they also collected tribute and were afforded the right to demand labour and other services from those living within their domain. Their principal role, however, was that of overseeing collective rituals to ensure the prosperity of their domain and its people as a whole (cf. McWilliam 1991). In parts of Timor-Leste, the ritual management of customary domains complemented and supported the maintenance of a distinct executive political authority (Traube 1986). In other areas, it is claimed that ritual and political authority were one and the same.

Daralari claims to emplaced authority are based on narratives of origin that establish the founder-ancestors of the domain as a source of life and fertility (see Barnes 2017). The power and authority of the Daralari source of the land depend on their capacity to ensure that the basis of their claims is recognised and accepted by others. It is by asserting their direct relationship to the founder-ancestors through the possession of sacred objects and knowledge that the Daralari source of the land maintain their control over the means to access the source of life and fertility and bestow *matak-malirin* on others (cf. Godelier 1999: 187).

Since independence, the Daralari source of the land have been extremely strategic in the way they have sought public acknowledgement and recognition of their status in relation to other groups living within their domain, as well as to outsiders. For example, they have sought to reassert their claims to emplaced authority in relation to displaced communities living within their domain regarding the management of local water sources; in relation to neighbouring groups regarding the demarcation of sacred ancestral sites; and in relation to the Church regarding the right to receive baptismal certificates – which remain the most accessible means of obtaining legal recognition as a person by the state (see Barnes 2017).

The Daralari source of the land are motivated by a desire, which also shaped their political choices during the process of decolonisation that followed the Carnation Revolution in Portugal, as well as during the Indonesian occupation. In conversation with the most senior Daralari elder about his choice to join Fretilin (*Frente Revolucionária de Timor-Leste Independente*) in 1974, he described how representatives from all the major parties came to Babulo during the brief yet tumultuous period of time between the Carnation Revolution in April 1974 and the Indonesian invasion in December 1975:

[T]hey [the parties] came distributing party membership cards. I listened to what they all had to say, but I chose Fretilin because they used the phrase *ukun rasik a'an* ['self-government']. They were the only ones who told us we should govern ourselves, according to our own customs. That is what we wanted then and what we want now. (Carlos Amaral, pers. comm., 2006)

The implication of Carlos's statement was a desire to return to a pre-colonial (or, at the very least, pre-1910) past, when the land and its people were ruled by the law of *ukun* (literally, 'rule, regulate') and *bandu* (literally, 'forbidden'), and the source of the land held both ritual and political power over the domain.

The concept of *tempu rai-diak* is often used to refer to an 'imagined' or idealised past. For example, *tempu rai-diak* is frequently used to describe *tempu beiala sira* ('the time of the ancestors') – an imagined time of peace where there was no shortage of food, no war and no violence, when people could 'freely go to their farms without fear'. As Babo-Soares (2003: 89) describes it:

[L]ife in the *beiala* period is portrayed as peaceful, calm and governed by the rules of *ukun* (lit., rule, regulate) and *bandu* (lit., forbidden) or customary law. Emphasis is placed on the point that in the time of the ancestors life was peaceful, calm and bountiful. There was no shortage of food and the people lived a good life. This is the kind of life later interrupted by the invasion of outsiders. In public conversations, people refer back to the period of *beiala* as the time of *rai diak* (lit., earth/soil good) or peaceful times without making a reference to the opposite period, *raia at* (lit., earth/soil bad) or bad times. The colonial period is generally referred to as the time of war, famine and so on.

It makes sense why the time of the ancestors might be portrayed in such a way. In the pre-colonial past, the population of Timor was much smaller; competition for food, land and other natural resources was not as intense as it is today. While there were undoubtedly conflicts during this time, peace and tranquillity tend to be more easily created and maintained, or at the very least contained, when natural resources are abundant.

Tempu rai-diak does not necessarily place emphasis on the lack of conflict, but rather on the existence of a stable social order regulated by the law or the rules of *ukun* and *bandu*. When used to differentiate between colonial periods, some people of an older generation refer to the Portuguese colonial period as *tempu rai-diak*, despite the fact that during this time there was intra-Timorese conflict, people were traded as slaves in exchange for gunpowder, and ammunition and rebellions were mounted against the colonial order and bloodily repressed. Yet, in comparison to the Indonesian occupation, when over 200,000 people died as a direct consequence of war and famine (CAVR 2013), the Portuguese period – particularly when the colonial authorities ruled the country indirectly through local kings and potentates (*liurai*) – was relatively peaceful. Nevertheless, for those born or raised during the Indonesian occupation and those who did not experience the real or imagined 'peace' of the Portuguese colonial era, such as former slaves, *tempu rai-diak* does not lie in the past, but in the present.

Contemporary processes of customary renewal draw on particular interpretations of the past not in order to re-create the past in the present, but rather to provide moral validation to contemporary institutions or political interests; they can even serve as a basis for the creation of new values (Reid and Marr 1979, cited in Babo-Soares 2003: 108).

Halerik ('lament')

When the Timorese sense that they are not blessed with *matak-malirin* or are not living in *tempu rai-diak*, they may *halerik* ('sing their lament'). *Halerik* (*ha*: 'to do', *lerik*: 'lament') refers to the singing or chanting of suffering. It is used to seek external assistance, and it represents the voice of the powerless (*ema kbi'it laek*) to the powerful (*ema bo'ot*). Often it is women, children or the elderly who perform or vocalise *halerik* when they face difficulties in their life. *Halerik* speaks out the truth and describes social, economic and political problems. When watching local television news in Timor-Leste, it is common to hear people say '*Rona netik ami nia halerik*' ('Please listen to our *halerik*').

This chanting of suffering, or *halerik*, can be expressed as song, poetry, crying (during funerals) or singing with dancing (*dahur*). It also sung in church during mass. In song, for example, we can see the famous Timorese *halerik* '*E Foho Ramelau*' ('Eh Mount Ramelau') in the lines '*Tansa Timoroan atan ba bebeik, tansa Timoroan terus ba bebeik*' ('Why are Timorese still enslaved, why do Timorese still suffer?'). When people sing this song and repeat such an expression over and over, it gives them strength to fight for a better future.

There are differences between the uses of *halerik* during the Indonesian occupation and after independence. During Indonesian occupation, *halerik* focused on the fight for freedom or self-determination (*ukun rasik an*), the end of violence (*terus*) caused by the Indonesians, and the economic burden (*susar*) caused by war and displacement. After independence, the tone of *halerik* has changed – today's *halerik* revolves around the basic needs of the *ema kbi'it laek sira* (powerless).

Domain-wide ceremonies such as the aforementioned seasonal corn and rice harvest ceremonies (Naueti: *masi eka rae* and *masi hare*) are performed by the source of the land on behalf of the origin groups that live within the ritual domain of Babulo. These communal ceremonies, which involve invocation, sacrifice, commensality and the redistribution of *matak-malirin* in the form of *bua-malus* (areca nut and betel leaves) and ritually transformed food, also serve to create and reaffirm the social organisation of the domain. At the same time, these occasions articulate and emphasise the differences in rank and status that exist between groups.

By taking part in these ceremonies (and other acts of customary renewal, such as house-building, which recognise hierarchy and precedence between houses) and investing considerable resources in them, participants from the various origin groups involved appear to accept the cultural framework upon which the power and authority of the Daralari source of the land is constructed and, consequently, their position of relative subordination in relation to the Daralari source of the land (see Rappaport 1999). Yet the pursuit of *matak-malirin* does not necessarily imply 'over-attachment' or misplaced loyalty towards dominant cultural norms (Appadurai 2013). Acceptance is often circumscribed, and the same acts of renewal that play a critical role in enabling the Daralari source of the land to reassert their claims to emplaced authority also provide a performative medium for negotiation and contestation (see Bourdieu 1979; Bovensiepen 2015).

During the rice harvest ceremony in 2008, the people of Roma hamlet, descendants of a group of former slaves (Naueti: *ata*) who formerly held no position in local orders of precedence, were called by name to receive their portion of the ritual meal and ancestral blessings. Although the Roma people usually receive ancestral blessings during ritual cooling ceremonies in the form of holy water and betel-nut spittle, this was the first time they had been called out by name to receive a portion of the ritually transformed meal. The conditions of their incorporation – on this occasion, at least – were related to the particular context in which the rice harvest was taking place.

The ceremony took place a few weeks after a number of settlements in Babulo and the neighbouring village of Uaitame had been attacked and burnt down, allegedly by radical members of the Fretilin party, during the course of the presidential election campaign. During the unrest, the Daralari source of the land had decided to remove sacred objects from the sacred Daralari houses for safekeeping in the forest. It was decided that during the rice harvest ceremony, the objects would be replaced and the land would be 'made cool' once again. At the time of the attacks, the people of Roma hamlet had rallied around the Daralari source of the land and joined other groups in the defence of the *suku*.

The people of Roma hamlet are sometimes referred to by other groups as the '*aldeia* [hamlet] without land'. Unlike the majority of the rest of the *suku* population, the people of Roma hamlet are largely of Makassae, rather than Naueti, descent. According to one history of the origins of this group, the Roma ancestors served a *liurai* from Babulo who lived in exile near Quelicai. When this *liurai* was invited to return and rule over the people of Babulo, it is said he agreed on the condition that he could bring his 'own people', who 'stuck to him like seeds of a long grass'. There are no Roma 'house' structures in Babulo. Historically, members of this group were incorporated into their masters' houses, albeit without the same privileges and duties. The Roma were not granted specific areas of land on which to farm or settle, but instead were servants to the chiefly houses of Babulo. Their main task was to watch over the herds of buffalo that belonged to their masters. In time, the descendants of the Roma started farming near the animal pastures and enclosures they guarded. Many among this group now claim these plots of land as their own based on long-term occupancy rights.

The hamlet of Roma was created after independence by the then– Fretilin-dominated government in recognition of the Roma people's role in the struggle for independence. There is no doubt that the aspiration of the people of Roma hamlet resonated with Fretilin's rhetoric concerning putting an end 'to all forms of domination of our people' (Jolliffe 1978: 331). However, despite their gains in achieving recognition in the eyes of the state and (to a degree) the Daralari source of the land, the people of Roma hamlet remain marginalised within the *suku*. Although there is a general consensus that they should no longer be referred to as such, members of core origin groups, including the Daralari source of the land, continue to identify the people of Roma hamlet as former slaves. Senior Daralari men and women suggest that slavery disappeared during the Indonesian occupation. They argue that during this time, people 'like the Roma' were given the same opportunities as everybody else. In particular, they were able to access education and improve their situation through economic activity and employment.

Nevertheless, social exclusion remains a reality for many members of Roma hamlet. In 2006, members of the principal house of Aha Bu'u (the ancestral house of the former *liurai* and *chefe suco* of Babulo) began collecting material to rebuild their ancestral house. In the past, the descendants of the people of Roma hamlet who served that house of Aha Bu'u as slaves would have done much of this work without payment. However, in recognition of their right to receive remuneration for their labour, the headman of Aha Bu'u had arranged with the new headman of Roma hamlet to recruit members of the hamlet to collect *unu* (Tetun: *tali metan*; botanical: *Arenga pinnata*), a type of fibre obtained from black sugar palm, for which they would receive cash in exchange. But not all those who collected *unu* were treated equally.

In 2007, a man from Roma, who had collected *unu* for the house at Aha Bu'u but was refused payment, killed the hamlet chief of Roma. In the village, rumours began to spread about the incident. The general agreement was that the suspect, who immediately turned himself in to the local police, had acted out of desperation. A witness to the incident said that the suspect had approached the hamlet chief to discuss the payment for some *unu* he had collected for the house of Aha Bu'u, but the hamlet chief informed the suspect that he was not permitted to collect *unu* and refused to pay him. At this, the suspect grew agitated, threatening the hamlet chief and declaring, 'What can I do? I have no land to farm and I cannot collect *unu*? How am I going to feed my family?' He then struck the hamlet chief with his machete and broke down. The man's desperation was echoed in the lament (*halerik*) of his distraught wife.

The incident prompted much discussion about the predicament of those who do not have access to land or depend on others to gain access to land and other resources within the village. It transpired that the suspect did in fact farm a small piece of land; furthermore, he had 11 children to clothe, feed and send to school, and no means of earning cash. There were some in the village who suggested that, as citizens of independent Timor-Leste, everyone had the same rights to access land and other natural resources, while a member of one of the senior Daralari houses argued that if the Roma wanted land and other resources, they should return to their village of origin.

The people of the hamlet of Roma have sought recognition from both the state and the Daralari source of the land. While these two paths to recognition might seem incommensurable, they are both critical to the people of Roma's vision of the future and their capacity to aspire to greater opportunity. The people of Roma hamlet continue to seek ancestral blessings from the Daralari source of the land because they continue to rely on the fertility and bounty of the land – and because they believe that there is more at stake than their livelihoods. In seeking recognition and protection of state-sanctioned rights, however, they have been able to open up an arena for debate and inquiry regarding their position within the ritual community. Change will not happen overnight, but it is possible to suggest that a platform for the 'production of consensus' is in the making (Appadurai 2013: 184).

Conclusion

Although the pursuit of *matak-malirin* may continue to be a common aspiration of all the people of Babulo, the material articulation of this desire and individual or collective 'capacity to aspire' to achieve their goals, expressed as *tempu rai-diak*, is enabled or constrained by their structural position within society. The 'capacity to aspire' for people of Babulo is deeply relational: the Daralari source of the land realise that their authority and legitimacy rely on the acknowledgement and recognition of others, yet they are well aware that their efforts to revitalise customary relations and practices are of little importance if people living within their domain do not *fiar* (Portuguese: 'trust, rely on'), in the sense of both belief and trust (see Traube 2017: 47). Similarly, the people of Roma hamlet also know that their access to land and resources within the domain of Babulo depends on seeking recognition from the state and the Daralari source of the land realise that their authority and legitimacy rely on the acknowledgement and recognition of others, yet they are well aware that their efforts to revitalise customary relations and practices are of little importance if people living within their domain do not *fiar*

(Portuguese/Tetum: 'trust, rely on'). The loan-word *fiar* has a complex meaning, which encompasses both belief and trust (see Traube 2017: 47). Under these circumstances, a solution to the challenge of improving the socioeconomic conditions of subaltern groups may lie in working with these structures rather than against them (Appadurai 2013).

References

Appadurai, A. (2013) *The future as cultural fact: Essays on the global condition*, New York and London: Verso Books.

Babo-Soares, D. (2003) 'Branching from the trunk: East Timorese perceptions of nationalism in transition', unpublished PhD thesis, The Australian National University.

Barnes, S. (2017) 'Customary renewal and the pursuit of power and prosperity in post-occupation East Timor: A case study from Babulo, Uato-Lari', unpublished PhD thesis, Monash University.

Bourdieu, P. (1979) *Outline of a theory of practice*, Cambridge, New York and Melbourne: Cambridge University Press.

Bovensiepen, J. (2015) *The land of gold: Cultural revival and post-conflict reconstruction in independent Timor-Leste*, Ithaca: Cornell University Press, Southeast Asia Program Publications.

CAVR (Timor-Leste Commission for Reception, Truth and Reconciliation) (2013) *Chega! The final report of the Timor-Leste Commission for Reception, Truth and Reconciliation (CAVR)*, Jakarta: KPG in cooperation with STP-CAVR.

Douglas, M. (2005) *Purity and danger: An analysis of concept of pollution and taboo*, London and New York: Routledge.

Geertz, C. (1973) *The interpretation of cultures: Selected essays*, New York: Basic Books.

Godelier, M. (1999) *The enigma of the gift*, Chicago: University of Chicago Press.

Gudeman, S. (2001) *The anthropology of economy: Community, market, and culture*, Malden: Blackwell.

Jolliffe, J. (1978) *East Timor: Nationalism and colonialism*, St Lucia: University of Queensland Press.

Kehi, B. and Palmer, L. (2012) 'Hamatak Halirin: The cosmological and socio-ecological roles of water in Koba Lima, Timor', *Bijdragen tot de taal-, land-en volkenkunde*, vol. 168, no. 4, pp. 445–471. doi.org/10.1163/22134379-90003552.

Lewis, E. D. (1988) *People of the source: The social and ceremonial order of Tana Wai Brama on Flores*, Dordrecht, Holland, and Providence, RI: Foris Publications.

McWilliam, A. (1991) 'Prayers of the sacred stone and tree: Aspects of invocation in West Timor', *Canberra Anthropology*, vol. 14, no. 2, pp. 49–59. doi.org/10.1080/03149099109508467.

McWilliam, A. (2011) 'Exchange and resilience in Timor-Leste', *Journal of the Royal Anthropological Institute*, vol. 17, no. 4, pp. 745–763. doi.org/10.1111/j.1467-9655.2011.01717.x.

Ortner, S. B. (2006) *Anthropology and social theory: Culture, power, and the acting subject*, Durham, NC, and London: Duke University Press. doi.org/10.1215/9780822388456.

Palmer, L. (2015) *Water politics and spiritual ecology: Custom, environmental governance and development*, London: Routledge. doi.org/10.4324/9781315883250.

Rappaport, R. A. (1999) *Ritual and religion in the making of humanity*, Cambridge: Cambridge University Press. doi.org/10.1017/CBO9780511814686.

Reid, A. and Marr, D. (eds) (1979) Perceptions of the past in Southeast Asia, Singapore: Heinemann Educational Books.

Traube, E. G. (1986) *Cosmology and social life: Ritual exchange among the Mambai of East Timor*, Chicago and London: University of Chicago Press.

Traube, E. G. (2017) 'Returning to origin places in an expanding world: Customary ritual in independent Timor Leste', in Viegas, S. M. and Feijó, R. G. (eds) *Transformations in Independent Timor-Leste: Dynamics of social and cultural cohabitations*, London and New York: Routledge.

Trindade, J. (2014) 'Matak-malirin, Tempu Rai-diak and Halerik: Expressions of what Timorese longed for in life', in Loney, H., Da Silva, A. B., Da Costa Ximenes, A., Canas Mendes, N. and Fernandes, C. (eds) *Understanding Timor-Leste*, 4th Timor-Leste Studies Association Conference, 15–16 July 2013, Dili, Hawthorn: Swinburne Press, pp. 55–59.

Trindade, J. (2015) 'Relational dimensions within Timor-Leste customary society', in Loney, H., Da Silva, A. B., Da Costa Ximenes, A., Canas Mendes, N. and Fernandes, C. (eds) *Understanding Timor-Leste*, 4th Timor-Leste Studies Association Conference, 15–16 July 2013, Dili, Hawthorn: Swinburne Press, pp. 239–243.

Vischer, M. P. (ed.) (2009) *Precedence: Social differentiation in the Austronesian world*, Canberra: ANU E Press. doi.org/10.26530/OAPEN_459471.

Vroklage, B. A. G. (1952) *Ethnographie der Belu in Zentral-Timor*, Leiden: E. J. Brill.

Weiner, A. B. (1992) *Inalienable possessions: The paradox of keeping-while-giving*, Berkeley: University of California Press. doi.org/10.1525/california/9780520076037.001.0001.

9

Looking back into the future: Temporalities of hope among the Fataluku (Lautém)

Susana de Matos Viegas

In July 2012, one of my interlocutors in Lautém (the easternmost district of Timor-Leste, where the Fataluku live) told me of his 15-year experience fighting the Indonesian occupation army in 'the bush', which he saw as closely associated with his current expectations:

> We went to the bush; we went back and forth in the bush. All the party leaders told the people they had to resist in the bush to guarantee the liberation of the land, and the people. With that phrase we were fighting for two objectives: first to liberate the land; second to liberate the people. We have liberated the land, now we need to liberate the people.

And he added:

> To liberate the people means to lead the people into a better life – and that is our goal: to liberate the people in intellectual, economic and social terms, to free civil society and adopt a sustainable economy, and guarantee a healthy environment and life.

During the Indonesian occupation there were several moments when he believed his struggle would come to a positive end; at other times, he became hopeless. These were times when he was humiliated by several of his relatives and friends who did not side with the resistance and looked at him as a defeated, weak man fighting without any justified hope.

The occupation is regarded by my friend in a way that epitomises visions common to other interlocutors in Lautém: as a time in which the hope that drove people was not confined to obtaining political independence but encompassed a model for future livelihood based on a stable economy and 'healthy environment'. As Rui Graça Feijó and I heard time and again, the choice of those days was between a sustainable future and none at all.[1] Those who fought for independence expressed such radical feelings in the well-known expression 'Independence or Death'.

Life experiences among the East Timorese Resistance are similar to other historical experiences of oppression and despair, such as apartheid, which led Vincent Crapanzano (2003: 5) to claim 'the extraordinary resilience humans have to the insupportable, to hopelessness and despair'. However, hope also acquires ambivalent forms under certain circumstances, eventually becoming a mechanism of resistance to oppression (Sarró 2015: 226–27). Another perspective, from Judith Bovensiepen (2016: 77) analysing the current megaprojects of the Timorese state, sustains the view that the utopian hope of the independence struggle is being retrieved: 'the utopian hopes for radical societal transformation once associated with Independence … are now associated with oil wealth'. Elizabeth Traube (2011: 131) shows that nowadays hope among the Mambae (the people originating from Timor-Leste's western highlands) is associated with the idea of repaying the efforts made during the resistance. Rui Graça Feijó and I have also considered the relevance of repayments to understand the investments of the relatives of 'martyrs' (people who were killed in open fighting or died as a direct cause of being involved in the liberation struggle) made in reconstructing graves (Viegas and Feijó 2016, 2018).[2]

In this chapter, I focus on expressions of hope understood in the context of a complex, non-linear connection with the resistance struggle in the past. Taking as my main axis Crapanzano's (2013: 4) proposal – 'to give possible shape to a notion of hope as a category of both experience and analysis'– I discuss how prosperity and hope are experienced at the level

1   Fieldwork in Lautém was undertaken together with Rui Graça Feijó (2012–2014) and supported by the Portuguese Foundation for Science and Technology (FTC) through the grant FCT-PTDC/ CS-ANT/118150/2010. We also benefited from support provided by *Fundação Oriente* in Dili and the Timorese State Secretariat for the Arts and Culture. I would like to thank Rui for his insights, which were precious, to deepen the argument. I also thank all the participants at the seminar in Kent for their generous comments and, of course, Judith's review suggestions, which were of great help.
2   The Timorese make a clear distinction between victims of war and martyrs. The Portuguese word *martir* is a very clear-cut category used in Timor-Leste to refer to those who died in the fight for independence (cf. Viegas and Feijó 2018).

of a family economy in present-day Lautém. The enactment of hope in Lautém, a region where a great majority of the population was engaged in the resistance fight against Indonesian occupiers, reveals a number of other economic, temporal and spiritual dimensions, such as the personal strategies of action and social relations developed during the resistance, as well as the political tensions that are rooted in the occupation period. Hope also expresses different scales of time and activates certain networks – not just those developed in the resistance, but also those involving the ancestors. This chapter seeks to tease out the temporal dimensions that are implicit in the hope for a more prosperous future. It does so by following Eric Hirsch and Charles Stewart's (2005: 263) idea of historicity, as the 'relevant ways in which (social) pasts and futures are implicated in present circumstances'.

The ethnographic analysis of hope is advanced here by analysing the acquisition of a minibus (*mikrolet*) by a family who inhabit the village of Assalaino to operate in the capital of Dili. Describing the different aspects involved in this event is a way of deepening our understanding of the experience of prosperity involving relatives in Lautém, Dili and migrant communities. Of particular interest are the dynamics of people's networks (networks that include both the living and the ancestors). I take hope as a central category to explore these different dynamics and agencies given that, as Crapanzano also noted, hope entails the involvement and/or dependency of other agencies and/or other individuals in achieving one's goals. When making a distinction between desire and hope, Crapanzano underlines that the category of hope implies an action which:

> … depends on some other agency – a god, fate, chance or other – for its fulfilment. Its evaluation rests on the characterization – the moral characterization – of that agency. You can do all you can to realize your hopes, but ultimately they depend on the fates – on someone else. (Crapanzano 2003: 6)

Hope and prosperity may be used here as interchangeable words. The literal meaning of prosperity also involves both an appeal to the forces of dependency on 'someone else' or on some other agency - destiny and fortune - and to a propositional amelioration of material conditions. Hope in the case described here involves a hope for a more prosperous life.

The first section of this chapter presents a very brief overview of subjective experiences of lived economic conditions under the Indonesian occupation, showing how impossible prosperity was then for the average family, according to current concepts. The second section is an ethnographic description of the *mikrolet* acquisition by a close interlocutor, arguing that this cannot simply be described as a financial investment. A deal that apparently pertains to the domestic realm and involves a couple, their daughter and son-in-law is shown to mobilise different social networks and temporalities. The third section examines the integration of this process into the set of relations with the ancestors, to whom the minibus is presented in a ritual ceremony. This ceremonial procedure implies an extended network of kinship and its historical spectre, akin to the one that Bloch and Parry (1989) called 'long term transactional orders'. The concluding section develops the idea of the temporality of hope, specifically with regards to the chain of past events that inform the enactment of hope in the present.

Family prosperity pre- and post-independence

In Lautém, persons frequently situate themselves in the world and evaluate their perspectives of the future by contrasting the social and economic restrictions experienced under the Indonesian occupation and the overture of new possibilities that independence has generated. Economic precariousness, resulting from marginalisation and oppression, had particularly negative outcomes in the 1980s when estimates indicate more than 300,000 Timorese in Indonesian-occupied 'Timor Timur' were secluded in 'internment camps' or 'resettlement villages' (Nixon 2012: 87). In Lautém, the concentration of the surviving population was profoundly felt in some villages more than in others, and in Assalaino for only one year. However, the destruction of food supplies was widespread. From the mid-1980s, direct violence tended to subside, but the conditions for the recovery of family-based economies were not reinstated, which is now regarded as a major form of oppression given that, with the destruction of domestic livelihoods, local economies were set to zero. Food gardens were destroyed and the restrictions on movement meant people were often unable to tend agrarian plots. In addition, the regular diet, which now includes pork, goat and water buffalo meat (namely in ritual occasions), was made impossible by the decimation of livestock.

In the 1990s, many people report that the local population's access to development investments in the region was, at most, precarious. Besides family-based initiatives, state jobs (for example, a teacher) were not easily accessible to locals. Healthcare provisions were available, but most people did not use them for many different reasons, including the fear that they would be under surveillance. People feared that doctors had connections with the regime, portraying a situation acknowledged by Rod Nixon (2012: 97) that 'villagers, at least at this time, were often afraid to go to the health clinics, while public health staff had similar concerns about visiting the villages'. Nixon shows that the Indonesian development policies in the 1990s did not reach the vast majority of the Timorese population, making this 'a period of mostly poor development outcomes, despite substantial capital flow and a mostly high economic growth rate' (ibid.: 89). The idea that national emphasis on rapid economic growth did not have positive effects 'for many who lived at the geographical and political margins of the nation' has also been reported for other marginal regions of Indonesia in the same period (cf. Keane 2002: 67).

In 1999, the wave of destruction – from the scorched-earth policy unleashed after the results of the popular consultation were publicised – struck Lautém quite severely. Reporting on his visit to Timor at that time, James Fox (2000: 25) claimed that the districts most affected were Lautém, Bobonaro and Covalima: '[t]he local populations of these districts will take longer to re-establish themselves and rebuild their way of life'.

As Andrew McWilliam (2011) shows, the economic hardship from the destruction in 1999 has been superseded in Lautém mostly thanks to the reinvigoration of exchange networks. It is a process parallel to that described by Keane for Sumba, where he observed money being channelled to the 'thriving system of ceremonial exchange' as a form of reinvigorating domestic life (Keane 2002: 67). In addition, such activities are remarkably adapted to combining 'modernist aspirations with revivalist ancestral spirit ontologies', namely ritual blessing for 'instrumental ends' (McWilliam 2009: 174, 2012: 82). This should also be connected to the way the power of the ancestors is seen across Timor-Leste as ambivalent darkness, as highlighted in many contributions to this volume (see Palmer, Chapter 10; Trindade and Barnes, Chapter 8; Bovensiepen's Introduction; and McWilliam's Afterword). In Lautém, activating ceremonial exchange networks, combined with grave reconstruction, have fulfilled a similar role of revitalising social networks. As Rui Feijó and I have argued (Viegas and Feijó 2016, 2018), and as I address later in this chapter, economic renewal was advanced by several monetary activities, among which are state pensions (including those for 'veterans' and 'martyrs'). Remittances from the flourishing transnational chains of young Timorese migrants in Portugal, Ireland and the United Kingdom are also a key to this process (McWilliam 2009, 2012: 74). A generation of youth seeking 'freedom and opportunities' in Dili and abroad send remittances, which articulate their aspirations for modernity that, as McWilliam (2012: 73) observes, may satisfy desires for modern consumption. This is also part of the phenomenon of the rural–urban flux, which has seen Dili grow by 33 per cent between 2004 and 2014 (McWilliam 2015: 227). In fact, several researchers have observed that Dili has become a catalysing point for modernity, quickly moving away from the rest of the rural territory of the 'districts', transforming this new nation into a country marked by what Douglas Kammen (2009: 390) named 'the primacy of the capital'.

The family event of buying a *mikrolet*, which I followed in 2014 and will discuss in detail here, made me aware of the centrality of Dili in contemporary family dynamics in Lautém, dynamics that are subject to the flux and continuity of the rural milieu of Lautém and the urban capital. As we shall see, the apparently simple acquisition of a minibus for a family enterprise was intertwined with a specific form of hope (the expectation that the vehicle would lead to domestic prosperity), and hence makes explicit the event's historicity – 'the manner in which persons operating under the constraints of social ideologies make sense of the past, while anticipating the future' (Hirsch and Stewart 2005: 262).

Buying a *mikrolet*

Using his teacher's salary from his position at Assalaino's primary school, his family's 'veteran' pension and remittances from a relative in Ireland, Pitinumalai[3] has ventured into several family businesses since independence. He built a cement house, adjoining which he later constructed a *kiosk*, and bought a small truck. His economic standing seems well above the average for the region, but his diversified domestic economy epitomises several family dynamics encountered in Lautém. The labour activities in Pitinumalai's domestic economy involve almost all the categories enumerated by the non-governmental organisation La'o Hamutuk, the Timor-Leste Institute for Development Monitoring and Analysis, for the sources of income in Timor-Leste as shown in Figure 9.1.

3　This is not his real name, but comes from a stock of Cailoru people's personal names.

What do Timorese people do for work?
Population aged 15-64: 672,000

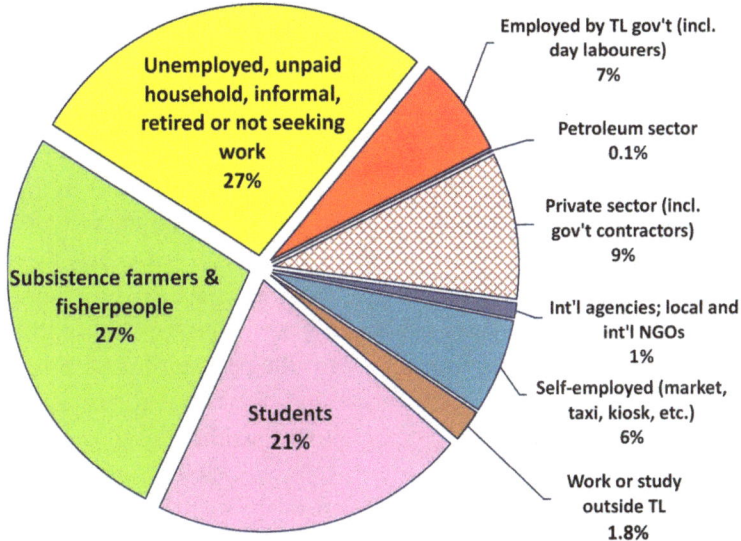

Employed by TL gov't (incl. day labourers) 7%

Petroleum sector 0.1%

Private sector (incl. gov't contractors) 9%

Int'l agencies; local and int'l NGOs 1%

Self-employed (market, taxi, kiosk, etc.) 6%

Work or study outside TL 1.8%

Students 21%

Subsistence farmers & fisherpeople 27%

Unemployed, unpaid household, informal, retired or not seeking work 27%

Figure 9.1. Graph by La'o Hamutuk based on information from the 2017 State Budget and 2015 Census.

Source: Scheiner (2017: 5). Based on information from the 2017 State Budget, 2015 Census, 2015 Business Activities Survey, 2013 Labor Force Survey and La'o Hamutuk research and estimate, March 2017.

As a teacher, Pitinumalai belongs to the 7 per cent of the population employed directly by the government; his daughter is among the 21 per cent who are students; himself (with the small truck) and his son-in-law (who was to drive the minibus he was about to buy) pertain to the 6 per cent of self-employed; and his cousin, who migrated to Ireland, is part of the around 2 per cent who work abroad. Living in rural Assalaino, he is also among the 27 per cent of subsistence farmers and fisherpeople in Timor-Leste.

In 2014, Pitinumalai decided to make a new investment, buying a *mikrolet* to provide transport in Dili. This vehicle was to be driven by his daughter's husband in Dili, where the couple lived. Pitinumalai placed the business management in the hands of his wife in Assalaino. By June 2014, the month we arrived in Lautém, Pitinumalai had already bought his vehicle. This enabled me to witness some of the difficulties that arose during the process of actually taking full possession of the minibus. Pitinumalai bought his vehicle in Kupang (Western Timor, Indonesia) at a cost of

US$7,500. He expected his business in Dili would make US$2,000 per month, which in our view was a realistic estimate. In fact, as Dili represents a growing urban centre, the *mikrolet* business flourishes every year. It should also be noted that since 2008 *mikrolet* business may gain support from the government.[4]

Although the acquisition of a motor vehicle is an act primarily determined by financial capacity, there were complications that meant the process of buying the *mikrolet* and taking it to Assalaino took several months. Unexpectedly, when the *mikrolet* (already paid for Pitinumalai) arrived at the Timorese–Indonesian border in July 2014, it was seized by the authorities. Legislation, of which he was unaware, prevented the import of vehicles more than 10 years old, and his was manufactured in 2003. For two months, Pitinumalai tried to solve the problem from his home in Lautém, but he finally realised he had to travel across the country to the border post in order to sort it out. In September, he took off and spent two weeks in the border town of Atambua. He later explained he was trying to implement a strategy similar to the one he was used to as an active member of the resistance against Indonesia. He took part in festivities with the border officers, attempting to find a Timorese or, better still, a Fataluku-speaker from his native Lautém. He needed 'accomplices' to turn a blind eye to the fact that the number plate of his *mikrolet* was hidden, thus allowing him to transport the vehicle across the border. He also directly confronted the Indonesian officers at the border by raising the issue of the tense Timor-Leste–Indonesia relations, challenging his opponents with moral questions, such as: 'What is the nature of the bilateral relations between Timor-Leste and Indonesia?! Is Timor-Leste a garbage depot?!' When he was finally on the Timorese side of the border, he took the route to Dili, where he was helped by former combatants from the resistance era – also from Lautém – to get legal paperwork for the *mikrolet*. In October, four months after its purchase in Kupang, his *mikrolet* finally arrived in Assalaino.

4   It was possible that he might receive a state grant for 'providing a social price to the public' as a *mikrolet* operator, as is in the legislation *Decreto-Lei* 28/2008 (in *Jornal da República* 2008: 2560–2561).

Lutur mara: The ceremony for the prosperity of the *mikrolet* business

A ceremony organised for Pitinumalai's minibus, was supposed to take place in July, but had been continuously postponed. In Fataluku, this sort of ceremony is called *lutur mara* ('to go to the grave'). Ressiloro, one of Pitinumalai's kinsmen, was in charge, since he is the person responsible for any ceremony that involves people in their kin group. In general terms, *lutur mara* corresponds to a 'flow-blessing ceremony' (Schefold 2001). This involves thanking the ancestors for the benefits they have provided and, critically, asking for the ancestors to protect the new business. However, the *lutur mara* for Pitinumalai's *mikrolet* integrated various other facets of action directed at future prospects, relevant for an ethnographic analysis of hope.

On 5 October 2014, the much-anticipated ceremony finally took place. We all drove to Assalaino's old village (*lata matu*) where the graves and tombs of the direct descendants of a particular ancestor are located. Among them was Pitinumalai's father's father – Zemalai. Zemalai was the main focus of the ceremony, which took place around his grave. On arriving at the 'entrance' to the *lata matu* (the old village), Ressiloro got out of the *mikrolet* and started circling it with two coins in his hand, speaking ritual words in a low voice. The role of the coins was to break any existing link with the *mikrolet*'s previous owner. As Pitinumalai argued: 'We bought it from other people who may have used it for stealing or other wrongdoing, so we have to cleanse it with coins'. Cleaning it from the former owner was also the final act in the transaction of the *mikrolet* – to effect a proper change of ownership. It reveals a lot about temporality, creating a drastic rupture to any history still contained within the vehicle – creating a separation from the vehicle's past – and its present and future, placing it within the new family network. After circling the vehicle with the coins, Ressiloro placed the coins, together with an egg and some rice by the entrance to the cemetery, and the *mikrolet* moved ahead to stand next to the grave around which the remainder of the ceremony was performed (see Figure 9.2).

Figure 9.2. The *mikrolet* next to the graves.
Source: Photo taken by the author in 2014.

As soon as the vehicle parked, five men climbed onto the grave of Pitinumalai's father's father, Zemalai. Subsequently, Ressiloro started addressing the ancestor. A circle of men stood on top of the grave and participated in a conversation, partially in ritual speech. The ancestor Zemalai was part of this conversation, not just because the relatives talked to him, but also through his material presence in the *na'otu* – a stone placed on the grave at the time of his burial and meant to serve as a communication device between the living and the dead. Through the *na'otu*, Zemalai was offered food, cigarettes and drinks, and this presented a way in which those standing on top of the grave who were drinking beer established a connection with their paternal forefather. While this rather informal conversation was going on, Ressiloro spoke in a constant rhythm of ritual speech evoking many names, including those of other ancestors, but also 'general' names of people from the kin groups from which the ancestors' spouses had come (the 'wife-givers', or *ara ho pata*). This is relevant inasmuch as it helps to understand how these ceremonies – even if restricted to what Schefold (2001: 369) names an 'ancestral flow' blessing – also integrate forces of an 'affinal flow' blessing. Ancestrality is first of all a matter of belonging to the same *ratu* (clan or origin group). *Ratus* are patrilinear descent groups, excluding women for most matters, such as direct communication with ancestors. They are, however, mentioned as affines and, as this case study will make clear, they may become important mediators between male agnatic kin.

As these informal conversations and ritual speech were taking place on the grave, a group of youths, Ressiloro's and Pitinumalai's sons, slaughtered a sacrificial pig. They did so with expertise, accompanied by the sound of loud, funny music. After being dismembered, the pig was cooked in a great pan over a fire under a tree. Then men climbed down from the grave and gathered around the fire, joining their sons and other men from different villages, but of the same *ratu*. Members of the same *ratu* share a 'common grandfather/ancestor', *calu ukane*, sharing sacrificial meat. Pitinumalai's son in-law (who belongs to a different *ratu*) and the women (who also come from a different *ratu*), and myself, moved away towards the *mikrolet*, where we drank coconut water. Half an hour after the sharing of sacrificial food had started, and men were chatting and laughing seated in a circle, I had been kindly asked to go away. Pitinumalai then explained to me I had to bring the fruit juices (which I had bought in the village, under his instructions, before the ceremony started), and give personally one can of juice to each man seated in the circle. This, I imagine, closed my involvement. The following day, Pitinumalai's daughter gently offered me a film she made of the full ceremony and so I have been able to watch the final moment when the head of the pig, already clean of meat, was put on Zemalai's *na'otu*.

An important ceremonial element took place before sharing the meat, namely the divinatory act (*ari*) performed by reading the sacrificial pig's pancreas. This means that it was critical that the pancreas be left intact when the pig was slaughtered. By then, young men brought the pancreas to Ressiloro who, in front of everyone (including myself, called to witness it), inspected it from all angles numerous times. Some people present became agitated: Pitinumalai said they had received 'a signal'. 'He has received it, but they [that is, Ressiloro and the others] are still in doubt about its full meaning'. It is important to understand how this sort of *ari* institutes tensions between kin. In fact, as Pitinumalai would later explain, the pancreas readings were all in his favour, but not all those involved – including Ressiloro – were happy about it. The reading meant Zemalai claimed a rehabilitation of his grave. This was a sensitive issue among Pitinumalai's relatives. In his own words, he had acted in a 'strategic' manner, first rehabilitating the graves of the spouses who did not require any ceremonial attention, hoping this would make the ancestors Zemalai and Nomalai jealous, subsequently claiming, as they did, for their own graves to be rehabilitated. Pitinumalai knew that if he had asked Ressiloro and the other elders to rehabilitate the ancestors' graves, they would not comply. In the following week, Pitinumalai bought cement to renovate the graves in question, thereby contributing to existing *lutur uhupai* (literally, rehabilitating a grave).

In sum, if the *mikrolet* ceremony's goal was to address 'the uncertainties and contingencies of social life' (McWilliam 2011: 71), and to protect the new business venture, assuring its prosperity, it also constituted new relationships between kin alive and dead. The ceremony for the *mikrolet* revealed specific ways in which prosperity and hope intertwine with negotiations of relationships in the present and future – a case I have put forward through the focus on the demand of the rehabilitation of graves.

Conclusion

Among the Fataluku in Lautém, a region in Timor-Leste where no major investment project is anticipated in the near future, and where resistance to Indonesian occupation was particularly generalised, domestic economies become the focus of practices to bring about prosperity. This means that, on the one hand, hope for prosperity emerges from a contrast with past times (that is, the Indonesian occupation), which is regarded as a period of obstruction, poverty and humiliation. On the other hand, I have emphasised how prosperity and hope is inserted in small-scale family economies, showing it actually depends on webs of relationships throughout the country and intense relations of kin between Lautém and Dili.

Lutur mara and *ari* allow us to understand the role of the ancestors in this temporal connection between the past and the future. Communication with the ancestors goes well beyond the purposes of controlling destiny or requesting blessing. Resuming Bloch and Parry's argument on different transactional orders, one may claim that, in this case, there is a clear complementarity between transactions inscribed in the more material and short-term forms of retribution, and those in the long term, in which 'the two cycles are represented as organically essential to each other' (Bloch and Parry 1989: 25). The ethnographic analysis shows that the blessing for the *mikrolet* venture, together with establishing the need to rehabilitate the graves, makes explicit a network of relations with the ancestors that goes beyond a simple counter-gift. Rather, it combines both short-term and long-term retributions that bring about an increasing integration of kinsfolk – including those who are now in their graves – that extends time. Existing tensions with the memory of the resistance era, as well as multiple forms of solidarity among those who took part in that struggle, are all part of this process. In this chapter, I have argued that, taken as an ethnographic category, hope among the Fataluku underlies this expansion of both temporalities and social networks of which ancestors are not only an integral part but also play a key role (see also Barnes and Trindade, Chapter 8) – namely, ancestors mediate tensions among kind, integrating short-term and long-term cycles of exchange. Their continuous presence transforms each small project of prosperity into a larger event in time and place.

References

Bloch, M. and Parry, J. (1989) *Money and the morality of exchange*, Cambridge: Cambridge University Press.

Bovensiepen, J. (2016) 'Visions of prosperity and conspiracy in Timor-Leste', *Focaal: Journal of Global and Historical Anthropology*, vol. 75, pp. 75–88. doi.org/10.3167/fcl.2016.750106.

Crapanzano, V. (2003) 'Reflections on hope as a category of social and psychological analysis', *Cultural Anthropology*, vol. 18, no. 1, pp. 3–32. doi.org/10.1525/can.2003.18.1.3.

Fox, J. J. (2000) 'Tracing the path, recounting the past: Historical perspectives on Timor', in Fox, J. J. and Dionisio Babo Soares, D. (eds) *Out of the ashes: Destruction and reconstruction of East Timor*, Canberra: ANU E Press, pp. 1–29.

Hirsch, E. and Stewart, C. (2005) 'Introduction: Ethnographies of historicity', *History and Anthropology*, vol. 16, no. 3, pp. 261–274. doi.org/10.1080/02757200500219289.

Jornal da República (2008) *Decreto-Lei* 28/2008 [Journal of the Republic (2008) Decree-Law 28/2008], Série 1, Nº 35, 13 August. Available at: mj.gov.tl/jornal/lawsTL/RDTL-Law/RDTL-Decree-Laws/Decree%20Law%2028-2008.pdf [English version].

Kammen, D. (2009) 'Fragments of utopia: Popular yearnings in East Timor', *Journal of Southeast Asian Studies*, vol. 40, no. 2, pp. 385–408. doi.org/10.1017/S0022463409000216.

Keane, W. (2002) 'Money is no object: Materiality, desire and modernity in an Indonesian Society', in Myers, F. R. (ed.) *The empire of things: Regimes of value and material culture*, Santa Fé: School for Advanced Research Press, pp. 65–90.

McWilliam, A. (2009) 'The spiritual commons: Some immaterial aspects of community economies in eastern Indonesia', *The Australian Journal of Anthropology*, vol. 20, no. 20, pp. 163–177. doi.org/10.1111/j.1757-6547.2009.00024.x.

McWilliam, A. (2011) 'Exchange and resilience in Timor-Leste', *Journal of the Royal Anthropological Institute*, vol. 17, no. 4, pp. 745–763. doi.org/10.1111/j.1467-9655.2011.01717.x.

McWilliam, A. (2012) 'New Fataluku diasporas and landscapes of remittance and return', *Local-Global: Identity, Security, Community*, vol. 11, pp. 72–85. Available at: mams.rmit.edu.au/9b3ykdptkndf.pdf.

McWilliam, A. (2015) 'Rural-urban inequalities and migration in Timor-Leste', in Ingram, S., Kent, L. and McWilliam, A. (eds) *A new era? Timor-Leste after the UN*, Canberra: ANU Press, pp. 225–234. doi.org/10.22459/NE.09.2015.15.

Nixon, R. (2012) *Justice and governance in East Timor: Indigenous approaches and the 'New Subsistence State'*, London and New York: Routledge.

Sarró, R. (2015) 'Hope, margin, example: The Kimbanguist diaspora in Lisbon', in Garnett, J. and Hausner, S. L. (eds) *Religion in diaspora: Cultures of citizenship*, London: Palgrave Macmillan, pp. 226–244. doi.org/10.1057/9781137400307_12.

Schefold, R. (2001) 'Three sources of ritual blessings in traditional Indonesian societies', *Bijdragen tot de Taal-, Land- en Volkenkunde*, vol. 157, no. 2, pp. 359–381. doi.org/10.1163/22134379-90003812.

Scheiner, C. (2017) 'Timor-Leste's oil wealth: Financing government, building for development and providing for its people' (Presentation to the Conference marking 25 Years of the International Platform of Jurists for East Timor), *La'o Hamutuk*. Available at: www.laohamutuk.org/econ/briefing/ScheinerIPJET29May2017en.pdf [accessed March 2018].

Traube, E. G. (2011) 'Planting the Flag', in McWilliam, A. and Traube, E. G. (eds) *Land and life in Timor-Leste: Ethnographic essays*, Canberra: ANU Press, pp. 117–140. doi.org/10.26530/OAPEN_459352.

Viegas, S. M. and Feijó, R. G. (2016) 'Memórias contestadas: monumentos funerários em Lospalos' [Contested memories: Funerary monuments in Lospalos], in Smith, S., Mendes, N. C., da Silva, A. B., Ximenes, A. da Costa and Fernandes, C. (eds) *Timor-Leste: The local, the regional, the global. Proceedings from the Timor-Leste Studies Association Conference*, Melbourne: Swinburne University Press, pp. 85–89.

Viegas, S. M. and Feijó, R. G. (2018) 'Moving the dead and building the nation: Martyrs in Timor-Leste'. in Havik, P. J., Mapril, J. and Saraiva, C. (eds) *Death on the move: Managing narratives, silences and constraints in a transnational perspective*, Newcastle upon Tyne: Cambridge Scholars Publishing, pp. 245–262.

10

Negotiating 'darkness' and 'light': Meshworks of fluidity and fire in Baucau[1]

Lisa Palmer

While Timor-Leste's cosmologies and western philosophy may seem worlds apart, in this chapter I draw on the work of Karen Barad (2003), Tim Ingold (2011, 2015) and Marilyn Strathern (1996) to explore approaches to the materiality of different 'resources' in Timor-Leste. By interrogating particular cosmological understandings of water, stone and metal, my aim is to shed light on locally differential attitudes towards modernist development practices – in this case, a cement mine and factory. My argument unfolds by triangulating a discussion of cosmology, landscape and ancestral relations to make connections with, and build a narrative account of, a number of ritual prescriptions and proscriptions involving metals. In this discussion, I focus on the movement and flows of relations that are associated with, and are potentially cut off by, various agencies entangled with metallurgical matter. I ask what all this means for the authorisation of the ongoing activities involved in the creation and use of metals and other hardened objects. By the chapter's end, I draw

1   I would like to acknowledge the extremely fruitful discussions about and/or comments on earlier drafts of this paper provided by Katarina Schneider, Balthasar Kehi, Andrew McWilliam, David Hicks, Ann Hill and Sandra Blakely. I would also like to acknowledge the helpful insights contributed by all of the participants at the Canterbury workshop and, in particular, this collection's editor Judith Bovensiepen. All errors and omissions are mine.

these insights into a discussion about visions for the future in Timor-Leste framed by particular Timorese approaches to place, the mutual constitution of human and more-than-human agencies, and industrial resource extraction.

Meshworks

As a starting point, I will briefly explore how, as with western scientific understandings, indigenous Timorese understandings of materiality are articulated through a focus on causal interactions – what in science is known as measurement, and which in Barad's (2003: 824) agential realist account concerns the 'local separability of different "component parts" of the phenomenon, one of which ("the cause") expresses itself in effecting and marking the other ("the effect")'. Barad is interested in the ways that:

> discursive practices are not human-based activities but rather specific material (re)configurings of the world through which local determinations of boundaries, properties, and meanings are differentially enacted. And matter is not a fixed essence; rather, matter is substance in its intra-active becoming – not a thing but a doing, a congealing of agency. And performativity is not understood as iterative citationality … but rather iterative intra-activity. (Barad 2003: 828)

Of such performativity, Ingold (2015: 85) has written that the world is 'immersed in sentience', wherein places:

> are like knots, and the threads from which they are tied are lines of wayfaring. A house, for example, is a place where the lines of its residents are tightly knotted together. But these lines are no more contained within the house than are threads contained within a knot. Rather, they trail beyond it, only to become caught up with other lines in other places, as are threads in other knots. Together they make up what I have called the *meshwork.* (Ingold 2011: 149)

Within these meshworks of place (and matter), it is movement that enables the dynamic reconfiguring of the intra-active components of phenomena, and it is the resultant material-discursive 'congealing' of what Ingold calls 'knots' or Barad calls 'substances' that gives meaning and order to our worlds.

Previously, I have drawn on the work of Ingold to examine the fluidities of a meshwork created by more-than-human agencies activated through water (Palmer 2015). By tracing the spiritual ecology of a karst hydrosocial system in the Baucau and Viqueque districts of Timor-Leste, I explored the agential, symbolic and material connective capacities of water, as well as the intricate connections between society and nature created by the flow of water. By bringing together material on water, kinship, affinity, ritual and narrative, I was able to explore the ritual ecological practices, contexts and scales through which the use, negotiation over and sharing of water occur. This enabled me to show the complex functioning and social, cultural, economic and environmental interdependencies of hydrological societies in this eastern region of Timor-Leste.

My concern in this chapter is with more hardened things – chiefly, rock and, more specifically, metals extracted from the minerals in rock by the use of fire. Janowski (2015) has written that in the highlands of Borneo, *lalud*, or 'power' and 'life force', coheres or 'knots' in stone where it may reside as a substance and/or be associated with a distinct spirit within the stone. Similarly, in Timor, rather than considering hardened objects such as rocks[2] as flows through a meshwork, it seems appropriate to think about them as dense concentrations of congealed agency, as flows that have knotted together in movement to manifest a hardness – and often a brilliance – understood as cohering (spiritual) power (cf. Janowski 2015). Here, I examine the power and role of the human agency that becomes embedded in these 'objects'. A process that Blakely has described elsewhere as the 'the intellectual and symbolic mastery of the nature–culture transition' (Blakely 2006: 158). With my lens trained on local ecologies of spirit, I am interested in the particular ways in which human agency is activated by interweaving with the more-than-human – flowing, cohering and growing in the knots embedded in a broader meshwork. I am particularly interested in the process of holding apart and bringing together these different types of matter, as well as in the local struggle to maintain a semblance of control over the process. For analytical insight, I turn to Strathern's (1996) notion of 'cutting the network'. She asks us to consider the ways and circumstances in which networks of relations are, by necessity, cut; for example, they may be severed in order to enable more limited ownership of property or to create space for relational

---

2   In Timor, I could extend this analysis to include the properties of hardwoods, such as ironwood, or even bone and shell, which also have particular powers when fashioned by humans; it could be argued that wood, shell and bone each have their own fiery principle.

recalibration. Such 'cuts', Strathern argues, enact stops, which can be permanent or only temporary pauses or blockages in the flow of relations, enabling the rerouting of arrangements in new ways. Considering, for example, marriage exchange relations, Strathern (1996) argues that the possibility of enacting 'cuts' in relations is as important as the relationally enabling effects of the exchange itself. In this chapter, I am concerned with the ways in which particular 'cuts' in relations (or relational networks, as Strathern puts it) may also be dangerously transgressive, interrupting the broader relational architecture of flows and knots.

Fiery objects

Taking up Strathern's notion of 'cutting the network', my object of analysis in this chapter is fire – more particularly, it is the fiery elements of metals that are liquefied and then worked, material forms woven through with particular properties and meanings. From an interpretation of my own ethnographic data from the region, I argue that the form and materiality of metals involves a 'cut' in relational flows, and as such also reveals quite a bit about the ambiguous relationality between human and more-than-human agencies during times of social change (cf. Miller 1994: 417). Within the frame of local lifeworlds, I argue that metals are objects with powerfully generative (and potentially destructive) capacities. Taking as my starting point the transformation of rocks to metals, I argue that this is a process that, cosmologically speaking, constitutes the same kind of double movement found in the transformation of regional house-based social relations: one of 'recomposition and differentiation, anchorage and flow, source and issue' – in this case, between fluids and solids (McKinnon 1991: 280; cf. Schneider 2012; Strathern 1996). Although these transformations offer 'pathways that extend growth into the future' (McKinnon 1991: 282), I argue that such processes, especially in relation to metals, can also be understood as dangerously containing relations. For this reason, metals need to be treated as transgressive substances – ones that can even potentially stop the flow of life.

Rocks and metals continually appear, often confoundingly so, as actors in my ethnographic data. In Timor, rocks often manifest as sacred megaliths, while metals liquefied by fire are worked into swords, breast discs or other jewellery. These objects are frequently associated with powerful ancestors and kept in or near particular sacred houses as sacra. But there are also many stories that refer to the use – as well as prohibitions and constraints on the use – of more mundane metals and rocks. Nails, fishing hooks, farm machinery, weapons, small stones and even the metal pipes in karst landscapes may all have a particular agency in certain times and places, which is understood as at once powerful, enabling and dangerous. Below, I will explore the reasons for these periodic and seemingly random prohibitions in relation to metals, and argue that, in contrast to water, which embodies relational flows, and stone, which condenses non-human agency, metal, as a result of human intervention involving the reconstitution of forms, is understood as condensing and potentially enclosing *both* human and non-human power and agency. As a result of their human-fashioned transformations (from solid to liquid to solid), metal 'substances' become 'stops' that are simultaneously alluring, powerful and dangerously transgressive of relations between the ancestral and the living worlds (the worlds of darkness and light). In order to provide a context for this exploration, I will first introduce a series of local responses to a large-scale development intervention in the Baucau subdistrict in the northeast of the country.

Risking transgression

In mid-2014, the 'barren' drylands of Caisidu and nearby areas in the district of Baucau were embroiled in simmering tensions over the proposed development of a cement mine and factory. While the local village heads were said to have given their support in favour of the development, the two clans with acknowledged traditional authority over the Caisidu region had not been engaged and consulted. The relations of these clans with others in the community who supported the development were rapidly deteriorating, resulting in high sensitivity and threats of violence.

Others from outside Caisidu welcomed the vision of regional economic development but were concerned about the risks of the venture. It was said that the ritual leaders from all of the villages needed to be brought together to discuss the matter. However, while these leaders could attempt to *koalia* ('ask for ancestral permission'), there was no guarantee that they could ameliorate the consequences of digging up the karst. Before actions could proceed, it was said that local negotiations needed to take place between the 'world of light' and progress, on one side, and the 'dark' and powerful world of the ancestral beings who continue their fluid movements through the landscape, on the other.

Announced in late 2013, the US$450 million proposal included plans to mine the local karst for the next 50 to 100 years. Brokered by politicians and bureaucrats at the national level, the foreign venture promised economic development and hundreds of local jobs. The local village heads, the political leaders of seven of the villages in the subdistrict, were said to have expressed their support for the development, but at that point the proposal was only at the exploration stage. Even before the social, cultural and environmental assessments of the proposal had been carried out, community relations were not proceeding well; apprehension was beginning to spread throughout the community. A local ritual leader recalled a time in the 1960s when a small area of karst was quarried to build the Baucau airport; seawater had begun to rise up through the soil, after which time the project had been abandoned. Others also remarked that the removal of rock from the coastal areas around Caisidu would result in the sea rising up to swallow all of the agricultural land. Some were concerned about movement of the *talibere* ('python') and the proper flow of the region's hydrosocial cycle. Others from the inland areas feared that such quarrying would simply cause the underground waters connected to the *talibere* (in this case, the eels known as *marui masara*) to dry up. Yet, even among those expressing concerns, there was an openness to inquire into the possibilities of mining, itself framed by the possibilities for such an action to receive sanction from the world of darkness, the ongoing source of all life. It was hoped such development would bring prosperity to the region, enabling people in the newly independent country to travel further forward 'into the light' with jobs and associated social benefits. Nonetheless, even if ancestral permission was sought and received, there remained a lingering doubt about the outcomes for the land and its people over the longer term.

The agency of metals

In his book *Stone*, Jeffrey Cohen (2015) examines the ambiguous collaboration between humans and lithic matter throughout time, focusing in particular on medieval approaches to rocks, stone and gems. His argument is that we need to understand lithic histories not as 'frozen in stone', but rather as both fluid *and* unstable processes constituted by continual metamorphosis and agency. Stones, configured as earth's embrace of water, are fascinating 'because they are engendered through long processes and trigger wondrous effects as they move through the world' (Cohen 2015: 15; cf. Tilley 2004; Janowski 2015). He insists:

> that medieval writers thought about materiality in ways worth investigating for the challenge they pose to those who would disenchant the world … where enchantment functions [as] a way of thinking that contests dreary and destructive modes of reducing matter to raw materials, diminishing objects to uses. (Cohen 2015: 10)

Similarly, in relation to metals, their transgressive and risky qualities, the prescriptions for and prohibitions against their use, are documented in literature from the ancient Greeks to accounts of metallurgy and ritual in recent Africa (cf. Blakely 2006, 2012; Barndon 2012; Haaland et al. 2002). Below, I will examine the ways in which stone, reconfigured as metal, has challenged – and continues to challenge – the collaboration between humans and lithic matter in the Baucau/Viqueque region of Timor-Leste.

Many local spring narratives across the region recount the danger of introducing fishing hooks into the ancestral realm (Hicks 2007, 2016; Palmer 2015). In many of these narratives, a shark or a crocodile (who is actually an ancestral ruler of the subterranean world) is inadvertently hooked by a fisherman, who must then descend undersea to extract the hook and save the ruler's life. All the while, the fisherman conceals the true properties of the offending object, the hook (deftly substituting it with a vegetative substance, such as a small sharp stick or thorn, when it is eventually extracted). Later, when the subterranean ruler makes return gifts of thanks to the human world above, these gifts emerge through springs as vegetative substances such as gourds and vines. Only later, after the sun has risen, do these gifts transform into wealth, including ornamental gold discs, swords and often buffalo.

Another example of caution over the use of metals involves the use of metal machinery in agriculture. In some areas, horses and buffalo are still preferred to puddle wet rice fields, and there are strict prohibitions against iron machinery such as ploughs, tractors or threshing machines entering the fields. The fields in question are usually those that were first 'opened' by the ancestors in the distant past, and that today remain central to ongoing ritual exchanges with ancestral spirits as clan groups seek agricultural and human fertility. In other cases, machinery may be allowed to work such fields, but only once the permission of the ancestors has been requested and granted at rituals carried out at the clan's sacred house. Likewise, many of these sacred houses have prohibitions on the use of iron nails and other metals in their structures (across Timor, a sacred house is ideally woven and knotted together, and in many places only wooden nails may be used). Meanwhile, some clan groupings prohibit the construction of new, modern concrete- and steel-enforced houses until their associated sacred houses have been rebuilt (many sacred houses are only now being reconstructed after the widespread destruction of the Indonesian era). In karst limestone landscapes found across the region, elders continually advise that the placement of metal pipes underground will result in a cessation of groundwater flow or in another calamity. Moreover, pregnant women travelling through places known to be frequented by powerful nature spirits, such as springs or caves, are advised to place a sharp object – for example, an iron nail – in their hair in order to ward off the unwanted attention of malevolent spirits. Indeed, people are cautioned to avoid powerful places such as springs and burial sites in the midday heat. This is when the sun's radiance is at its most powerful, agitating life into the spirits below.

Elsewhere in the regional literature, this agency attributed to metals is said to involve its apotropaic power to avert evil influences or spirits (Strathern and Stewart 2002: 70). When I inquired about this in Timor, people simply said that such metals were not used by the ancestors; furthermore, and perhaps as a result, ancestral beings and nature spirits were in general averse to metals. I want to suggest here, however, that this agency attributed to metals also concerns something more about their (human-enabled) properties and their power.

While it is clear from my previous work that water in the region enables the flow and connection of diffuse spiritual agency through all bodies and things, it is also clear that this agency is transformed into life itself by the radiance of fire, often represented as the power of the sun. A major 'historical' tale from the western coastal region of Baucau tells of a famous colonial-era figure, a man called Joao Lere, whose magical powers gave him the capacity to manipulate fire with his giant bellows (which are still present in this landscape, revered as twinned megaliths called Mamau Toha). At some point, he asserted his intention to use the fire generated by these bellows to break up the earth, which would cause the sea to rise up and divide the island in two. This anti-colonial act aimed to banish the Portuguese from the eastern quarter of the island (Palmer 2015). Meanwhile, in a coastal cave with freshwater pools near the site of this (failed) transgression, innumerable pythons are said to live (also connected to the narrative of Joao Lere's power).

In the Baucau region, the python, often known as *talibere* (or 'the great rope'), is the main protagonist who creates and ensures the ongoing functioning of the hydrosocial cycle. The python's body both contains and connects water (blood), rock (bone) and fire (an oily radiance), an essential mixture responsible for the renewal of life cycles (agricultural and human fertility) (cf. Strathern and Stewart 2002). In the narrative of Joao Lere, a man who also mixed water and fire, Lere is clearly a human counterpart to that which is found in the 'natural' world in the form of pythons (and, indeed, the narrative maintains that he transformed into one upon his death; see Palmer 2015).

Pythons are animals that, once brought to the light of the surface world, may also manifest as gold, one of the only metals to occur naturally in its native form. Yet if pythons are linked to gold and underpin the proper functioning of the hydrosocial cycle, it is also significant to note here that gold is somewhat different to other metals. It is in many ways a metal already complete in its radiance, as it is often found in nugget form and does not necessarily need to be worked by fire. Most other metals cohere as minerals in rock and are primarily extracted (and activated) by the workings of fire and human agency – a process that I suggest makes working with metals not only potentially powerful, dangerous and enabling, but also radically transformative (cf. Blakely 2006). Just as fire is instrumental in converting land into productive swidden gardens (or pasture), it is also the transformational substance for creating smelted metals. According to local oral histories, when this knowledge of metalwork arrived in the region, it was accompanied by radical social change, enabling a renewed process of ritual exchange between intermarrying clans (Palmer 2015). Metal tools would also transform agricultural productivity. If gold in nature is linked to the python and to spiritual potency (*lulik*) – that is, if it has its own agency – it is also clearly an agency that is embedded in the land (cf. Bovensiepen 2015; Wardlow 2004). Yet, when such rocky potencies are activated and liquefied by fire and transformed into metals, this agency is also radically transformed and harnessed for use by humans (cf. McIntosh 2004).

The alchemist's fire

The social anthropologist David Hicks (2007: 50–51) has argued that in narrative tales collected in Timor and the wider eastern archipelago, the fishing hook acts as a form of dynamic agency and as a mediator between human and ancestral worlds, which involves social transformations of profound importance. According to Hicks, the hook is an object that mediates changes of ontological and sociological significance. Focusing on its visual appearance and tactile nature, he suggests that its instrumental role is to convey the notion of 'snagging divinity', suggesting a parity – and even periodic superiority – of humans over the divine in some contexts and circumstances. Drawing on the early work of Marcel Mauss, Hicks argues that these encounters demonstrate that in the cosmic exchange of existence, humans must replenish and care for the gods and vice versa. This correlates with the fact that in Timorese ancestral religions, aspects of the divine/spirit world are also immanent in the physical world, requiring constant vigilance and communicative awareness (Hicks 2004).

I want to build on Hicks' work to suggest that a further – and not necessarily incompatible – link can be made between the hook and other ontologically related metals (understood as a particularly powerful congealing of agency) and their relation to the exercise of human agency. This insight is relevant to the mythic narratives of fishermen compelled to hide the true properties of a fishing hook from an ancestor snagged in subterranean water. It also helps to explain why people might feel the need to ask ancestors for specific permission to build a new, modern (and permanent) concrete- and steel-enforced house, or to use tractors in particular fields.

My hypothesis is that cultural narratives of the human world involve a concern for the physical and metaphysical transgression of reintroducing metals, or other similar objects of spiritual agency manipulated and cohered by humans, into a primordial ancestral world of diffuse watery spiritual power. The smelting and smithing of metals enables humans to fashion and tame the congealed substances or knots of agential power that cohere ('naturally') in minerals. As such, the *lulik* or spiritual potencies of rock – of the earth itself – are now able to be harnessed by humans via the human manipulation of fire, providing an additional source of power (which at the same time always remains potentially dangerous and excessive). Humans are themselves brought into this world by the alchemy of fire and water ('hot' male and 'cool' female properties) and traditionally birthed and warmed for 40 days by household hearths in a process euphemistically termed *tur ahi* – 'sitting on the fire'. In death, humans need first to be ritually cooled by complicated and extended funerary rites, which realign cosmic forces and prepare the deceased for their journey back into the subterranean or 'dark' world. In life, humans also require forms of heating and cooling to render their bodies into a healthy and non-threatening state. For example, when used in war, metal weapons (and their users) need to be taken to particular springs at the conclusion of a battle to be ritually cooled, reducing their accumulated heat (including from the blood of enemies) and their 'congealed' potency. For this reason, in times past, periods of warfare were ritually demarcated and controlled so that this dangerously hot enmity would not harm the warriors' own communities (McWilliam 2007: 80).

Like eighteenth-century European alchemists (see Chang 2012), Timorese ritual specialists understand both metals and water to have combustible qualities: both are intimately connected to fire, which differentially enlivens them. This is why in many spring-associated narratives and ritual practices, it is sacra such as swords (*surik*) and alloy discs (*belak*) that control and draw forth water (Palmer 2015). Here, metal's inherent fiery principle or combustible qualities are harnessed in the service of human beings. Whereas rocks and pythons are 'natural' mixtures of water, earth and fire, worked metals signify processes through which, as the world moves from darkness to light, humans have activated and tamed fire and associated objects.[3]

Yet even as it is domesticated, the ever-present threat of wildfire remains. Many regional narrative myths detail the destructive 'escape' of fire subsequent to its domestication (Palmer 2015). I contend that in the material cultural system that I have studied in Baucau and Viqueque, there is clearly an acknowledgement that such working of 'spirit substances' into human-made knots of metal may be too dangerous and transgressive. The process of working 'rock' with fire risks cutting (i.e. disrupting or destroying) the careful arrangements and flows of fire and water, dark and light, whose normally ordered and generative movements are essential to the flow of life itself. In Baucau, blacksmiths continue to carry out

---

3   Given the circular nature of the movement from darkness to light, this transgressive power of metals is likely also associated with the time before the separation when all 'beings' and relations were one.

collective annual ceremonies and offerings at the river or sea to cleanse their bodies and their implements of the accumulated heat and potency of metals. At these times, ash from the blacksmiths' fires is thrown in the water so that it may return to its place of otherwordly origin. Meanwhile, a goat is sacrificed, and an augury is carried out on its liver to foretell the blacksmiths' prospects for the coming year.

By working with and fashioning metal, humans can be understood as 'working life' and 'cohering power' – 'taming' it, 'channelling' it and 'knotting' it. This accumulation of human agency and energy, mixed with more-than-human agency and cohered by working with fire, tames the diffuse *lulik* (or spiritual power) of the underworld and gives it a new coherence, power and permanence – a type of agency that the ancestors of the dark world did not have access to. Although such *lulik* and non-*lulik* agencies must be ordinarily held apart, periodic transgressions (such as life cycle and fertility rites) are also necessary for life to progress. At some level, metals solidify this transgression ('cutting the flow'); this is what makes them both powerful and disruptive. In contrast to life cycle or agricultural rituals, metals are more fixed, and the fact that they have been fashioned via human agency mixing in with *lulik* agencies requires careful attention to the ways in which the flow of life might be threatened. In summary, in the entanglements of cosmology, landscape, ancestral relations and fiery materiality, it is both the ongoing flow of relations and the condensing (or anchorage) of relations in objects that matters – this is what Ingold terms the 'meshwork'. As has been shown in this chapter, metals threaten such processes by solidifying the transgression, and potentially but not necessarily disrupting and destroying the flow of life. To counter this threat, attention must be carefully directed to both the separation and the coming together of phenomena – hence the hypervigilance in relation to many of the periodic and seemingly random prohibitions on metals in Timor-Leste.

Conclusion

What do such metaphysics and material practice mean for future visions of extractive resource development in Timor-Leste? I have provided a story of agencies that need both to come together and be held apart. As Barad (2003: 829) argues, there is a great deal of work to be done in thinking 'about the kind of understandings that are needed to come to terms with how specific intra-actions matter'. She writes:

[p]articular possibilities for acting exist at every moment, and these changing possibilities entail a responsibility to intervene in the world's becoming, to contest and rework what matters and what is excluded from mattering. (Barad 2003: 827)

Variegated local visions for the future associated with extractive resource development projects in Timor-Leste can be gleaned through close attention to the relational frameworks by which 'things' come to matter. In these cosmological understandings, oscillating differences (separation) *and* a greater unity (a coming together) are central to ensuring that proper communications are enabled between the worlds of darkness and light. It is the relations between the parts in this whole that require continual calibration, and this is done most powerfully via the human 'tending' of affective more-than-human relations. Extractive resource development is one way of enabling the power and possibilities of the world of light to be further activated. Yet while refashioning (excavating) these knots of congealed agency may offer hope for a brighter future, enacting such 'cuts' in the flow of relations is understood to be a very risky business. Yet, whether it is marking the end of a marriage alliance, the end of enmity and discord or the end of a period of ritual veneration, 'cuts' are also necessary ways of marking the possibilities for new beginnings.

From this chapter, it is apparent that in order to 'authorise' the practices that matter in Timor, attention must be paid to how to recompose, reconfigure and transform – yet still enable – the flow in life's meshwork of threads and knots. Metals, as an epitome of human agency, need to be used with caution lest their transgressive potential disrupt the flow of life. I have argued that rocks and metals can be understood as 'fiery objects' that, in consort with broader regional cosmologies, provide both anchorage (in the ancestral world) but also a new mobility (even a severance of relations) woven through with the power of possibility. The same metaphysics applies to large-scale disturbances of the karst landscape of Baucau, which is considered the conduit for the flow of life in the region's hydrosocial cycle (Palmer 2015). In such local readings for cause and effect, assessments of 'environmental feedback' are carried out via the embrace of continual caution and uncertainty, underpinned by the knowledge that while we may not be prisoners to the parameters of our individuated bodies, nor even to space and time, we remain prisoners to the laws of the larger universe.

The work of affective geographies reminds us that humans are always woven into a wider ecology of things. In Timor-Leste's state-centric and crowded cacophony of high modernist aspiration, 'tradition' is currently considered little more than background noise (cf. Meitzner Yoder 2015). As has been shown in this chapter, people's ritual relationships with rocks and metals have long enabled a slow dance with time and more-than-human agencies (including the potent energies of water and fire). Yet as the new nation-state increasingly embraces late modernity and fast-tracks old-fashioned industrialisation, this ambiguous relationality between human and more-than-human agencies will be tested to its limits.

References

Barad, K. (2003) 'Posthumanist performativity: Toward an understanding of how matter comes to matter', *Signs: Journal of Women in Culture and Society*, vol. 28, no. 3, pp. 801–831. doi.org/10.1086/345321.

Barndon, R. (2012) 'Technology and morality – Rituals in iron working among the Fipa and Pangwa peoples in Southwestern Tanzania', *Archeological Papers of the American Anthropological Association*, vol. 21, no. 1, pp. 37–48. doi.org/10.1111/j.1551-8248.2012.01036.x.

Blakely, S. (2006) *Myth, ritual and metallurgy in Ancient Greece and recent Africa*, Cambridge: Cambridge University Press.

Blakely, S. (2012) 'Daimones in the Thracian Sea: Mysteries, iron, and metaphor', *Archiv für Religionsgeschichte*, vol. 14, no. 1, pp. 155–182.

Bovensiepen, J. (2015) *The land of gold: Cultural revival and post-conflict reconstruction in Independent Timor-Leste*, Ithaca: Cornell University Press, Southeast Asia Program Publications.

Chang, H. (2012) *Is water H_2O? Evidence, realism and pluralism*, Dortrecht: Springer. doi.org/10.1007/978-94-007-3932-1.

Cohen, J. J. (2015) *Stone: An ecology of the inhuman*, Minneapolis: University of Minnesota Press. doi.org/10.5749/minnesota/9780816692576.001.0001.

Haaland, G., Haaland, R., and Rijal, S. (2002). 'The social life of iron: A cross-cultural study of technological, symbolic, and social aspects of iron making', *Anthropos*, vol. 97, no. 1, pp. 35–54.

Hicks, D. (2004) *Tetum ghosts and kin: Fertility and gender in East Timor*, 2nd edition, Long Grove: Waveland Press.

Hicks, D. (2007) 'Younger brother and the fishing hook on Timor: Reassessing Mauss on hierarchy and divinity', *Journal of the Royal Anthropological Institute*, vol. 13, no. 1, pp. 39–56. doi.org/10.1111/j.1467-9655.2007.00412.x.

Hicks, D. (2016) 'Impaling spirit: Three categories of ontological domain in eastern Indonesia', in Arnhem, K. and Sprenger, G. (eds) *Animism in Southeast Asia*, London: Routledge, pp. 257–278.

Ingold, T. (2011) *Being alive: Essays on movement, knowledge and description*, London: Routledge.

Ingold, T. (2015) *The life of lines*, London: Routledge.

Janowski, M. (2015) 'Life in stone: Megaliths in the highlands of Borneo and beyond', Paper presented at the 8th EuroSEAS Conference, Vienna, 11–14 August.

McIntosh, I. (2004) 'The iron furnace of Birrinydji', in Rumsey, A. and Weiner, J. (eds) *Mining and Indigenous lifeworlds in Australia and Papua New Guinea*, 2nd printing, Wantage, Oxon, UK: Sean Kingston Publishing, pp. 12–30.

McKinnon, S. (1991) *From a shattered sun: Hierarchy, Gender and alliance in the Tanimbar Islands*, Madison: University of Wisconsin Press.

McWilliam, A. (2007) 'Meto disputes and peacemaking: Cultural notes on conflict and its resolution', *The Asia Pacific Journal of Anthropology*, vol. 8, no. 1, pp. 75–92. doi.org/10.1080/14442210601161740.

Meitzner Yoder, L. S. (2015) 'The development eraser: Fantastical schemes, aspirational distractions and high modern mega-events in the Oecusse enclave, Timor-Leste', *Journal of Political Ecology*, vol. 22, pp. 299–321. doi.org/10.2458/v22i1.21110.

Miller, D. (1994) 'Artefacts and the meanings of things', in Ingold, T. (ed.) *Companion encyclopedia in anthropology*, London: Routledge, pp. 396–419.

Palmer, L. (2015) *Water politics and spiritual ecology: Custom, environmental governance and development*, London: Routledge. doi.org/10.4324/97813 15883250.

Schneider, K. (2012) *Saltwater sociality: A Melanesian island ethnography*, Oxford and New York: Berghahn Books.

Strathern, A. and Stewart, P. (2002) *The python's back: Pathways of comparison between Indonesia and Melanesia*, Connecticut and London: Bergin and Garvey.

Strathern, M. (1996) 'Cutting the network', *Journal of the Royal Anthropological Institute*, vol. 2, no. 3, pp. 517–535. doi.org/10.2307/3034901.

Tilley, C. (2004) *The materiality of stone: Explorations on landscape phenomenology*, Oxford: Berg.

Wardlow, H. (2004) 'The Mount Kare python: Huli myths and gendered fantasies of agency', in Rumsey, A. and Weiner, J. (eds) *Mining and Indigenous lifeworlds in Australia and Papua New Guinea*, 2nd printing, Wantage, Oxon, UK: Sean Kingston Publishing, pp. 31–67.

11

Misreading the night: The shadows and light of a solar technology[1]

Chris Shepherd

When Timor-Leste won independence, former resistance-leader-turned-statesman, Xanana Gusmão, stated: 'our dream was to be self-governing, but now our dream is to develop, to become a developed nation' (RDTL 2002: 3). Since then, Timor-Leste's development industry has advanced a torrent of new ideas of what constitutes 'development'. It has brought to the Timorese people a dizzying mix of fantasies and propositions, sifting out the problems in 'tradition' and 'culture' that are perceived to present obstacles to development, and urging one or another form of intervention as 'solutions'. At the opposite end of the spectrum to fanciful, state-driven, high-modernity schemes (Meitzner Yoder 2015) has arisen a panoply of practical, small-scale non-governmental organisation (NGO)–led proposals to improve village and household services. Of these, solar technology has been favoured, not least for lighting rural areas beyond the reach of grid power. This chapter traces one such initiative in which an international NGO (INGO) contracted a national NGO to distribute solar lamps in the district enclave of Oecusse to replace 'suboptimal', mainly kerosene-based, lighting. Since I assessed the impacts of the program, the solar lamps are explored through my personal experience of evaluation and reporting. Through an analysis of the politics of

---

1   I thank Judith Bovensiepen, Alex Grainger and Ann Wigglesworth for their suggestions on a draft version of this chapter. I have refrained from citing reports or webpages to protect anonymity.

knowledge, I show how the process of understanding the local experience of 'old' light and 'new' light was influenced by the NGOs in question. In particular, I explore my encounter with an institution that was reluctant to acknowledge the discrepancies between the 'real impacts' and what had initially been held out as the anticipated impacts of the solar lamps.

The mismatch between development's idealised futures and what happens in reality has been an enduring theme in the anthropology of development and 'post-development' literature (for example, Ferguson 1990; Sachs 1992). In the edgy world of performance-dependent funding, development institutions survive by strategically dealing with mismatches, seeking control over information and interpretations to avert criticism. Building on the idea that development has a 'front stage' and a 'backstage' (see Goffman 1959), which includes or excludes various audiences and perspectives through the generation of 'public' and 'hidden transcripts' (Scott 1992), I argue that the symbolic investment in imagined futures is so great that these futures continue to be propped up over time, even in the face of contradictory evidence. Institutions conceal their backstage 'shadow side' just as they strive to fashion a public, authoritative, expertise-based 'consensual community of knowers' to cloak their interventions in positive values (Mosse 2005).

Project evaluation undertaken by external consultants occupies a unique position in relation to these private–public dynamics. Not only do consultants have access to confidential knowledge, they also comprehend that their reporting influences broader perceptions, legitimacy and funding. In shaping project knowledge, evaluators must decide what to conceal (shadows) and what to reveal (light): they may highlight or ignore ambiguity in the data; raise or suppress counter-interpretations; acknowledge or overlook bungles; and report or ignore malpractice (see Ferguson 1997). In doing so, they navigate the boundary between the 'vision of the future' and what is empirically observed 'on the ground'. In some cases, however, explicit or tacit trade-offs between consultants and organisations ensure that consultancies remain favourable. In other cases, organisations conceal certain situations from evaluators, impress upon them the privacy of information or edit their documents (Crush 1995).

Bringing the 'anthropology of light' (Bille and Sorensen 2007) to bear on the 'new ethnography of aid' (Mosse 2005), the following account of project evaluation shows how my assessment of the solar-lamp initiative was compromised by a 'promised future' of what improved light would mean for beneficiaries. I became implicated in the shadows of both aforementioned institutions (the NGO and the INGO) when I began to modify research methods, raise doubts over received wisdom and draw attention to questions of ethics. I was equally enrolled in the 'promotional light' – namely, the auspicious internet-based, public relations (PR) campaign of the INGO. At stake was an 'imaginary of light': a culturally specific set of representations, images, signs and metaphors, with hierarchical values placed on the darkness and lightness of pasts, presents and futures (cf. Mahmud 1999). The imaginary of light had assembled a vision of 'the beneficiary' as benefiting in set ways, of the NGOs as transparent, philanthropic actors and of the solar lamps as life-changing technology; implicit, too, was the association of darkness with the underdeveloped past and present, and light with progress and modernity (see Kammen, Chapter 1; and Palmer, Chapter 10) Behind the investment in what is presented below as a misreading of the Oecusse lightscape, we see yet another expression of the general determination of development organisations of all types to secure their reputations and funding sources.

The vision of the Radiant Nights program

Grace Foundation (GF) was founded in 2010 by two individuals who came to believe that the simplest and best technologies for the so-called developing world were not reaching isolated people. Working with local partner organisations, GF's proposal was to introduce water filters, rolling drum water transporters and drip-irrigation systems to places that were the most remote and to people most in need. The organisation's technology of choice, however, was a kind of solar lantern called d.lights; just as these had been brought to Indonesia, the Philippines and India, they were also tried on Timor-Leste's Ataúro island and in Oecusse. The initiative was called Radiant Nights.

Radiant Nights was not all technology in the material sense. The ideas that travelled with the technology were equally important. The intervention adapted common development imaginaries of poverty to the harsh living conditions of Timor-Leste, where people depended on subsistence agriculture and fishing. Specifically, the targeted recipients were said to suffer from 'energy poverty', the rationale for which began with the absence of grid power. In Oecusse, the grid radiated out unevenly for several kilometres from the district capital, Pante Makassar, beyond which 60,000 people used kerosene lamps, candles, battery flashlights, firelight and moonlight. For want of better lighting, women were said to cook in relative darkness, certain livelihood activities were restricted to the daytime, children could not study properly at night and income-generating activities were hampered. The common kerosene lamps were described as especially problematic because they shed a dim light, blew out in the wind, caused house fires, emitted toxic smoke and taxed the scant economic resources of rural people.

Radiant Nights foresaw a growing collective of beneficiaries no longer reliant on dim, costly, dangerous, unhealthy and antiquated kerosene, candle or other lighting. Instead, they would receive bright, cheap, safe, salubrious, efficient, modern d.lights. The lamps would facilitate all the activities that development specialists presumed poor people without much light should be doing more of at night, and by better light: studying and learning; cooking and weaving; fishing and farming. The positive impacts of brighter light would include more money, more education, more security, more happiness and better health. This 'public transcript' of a gloomy present and a brighter future was already in place when d.lights were first shipped in. Local partner organisations repeated the imaginary, and the same ideas were conveyed to prospective beneficiaries in information sessions when distribution commenced. Notions of what a brighter future would mean, one could say, had been inscribed onto the technology.

The imaginary of Radiant Nights was consolidated over successive evaluations and impact assessments. Posted on GF's webpage, reports made concrete what had already been held out as a brighter d.light future. A before-and-after survey structure allowed for the contrast of baseline and follow-up figures. General progress narratives gave way to precise data and statistics. Bar graphs, pie charts and histograms lent visual clarity and exactitude to what had been promises and potentials. The reduction in kerosene-based and other lighting was specified to a tenth of a decimal point, and increases in average times spent attending to livestock or studying at night were calculated to the minute. The apparently unequivocal evidence based on such figures was boosted by photographs depicting the various uses of d.lights and the indubitable testimony of local people. 'Off-the-shelf' development narratives were also readily deployed to confirm the benefits of d.lights. Narrative logic was sometimes oxymoronic; for instance, d.lights were said to redress gender inequality as it was supposed that women were burdened by a greater share of the nightly household labour. Equally important to the imaginary were narratives and metaphors that underlined the altruistic character of GF, its donors and local partner organisations. Indeed, publicising that their high subsidies had reduced d.light prices to a quarter of the market value reinforced this humanitarian idea.

Becoming a technology impact evaluator

GF gave funding and guidance for assessors or 'fellows' to undertake evaluations of the initiative. Among other things, an interest in solar technology led me to accept GF's consultancy offer. The reports of four previous assessors, an established survey method and the optimism surrounding the initiative became my inheritance when I arrived at GF's head office in Singapore in May 2013, as the fifth GF assessor to be sent to Timor-Leste. I was introduced to those I would be reporting to and to the artefacts I would be examining: the disk-like S-1 (*lampu kabuar*), the cylindrical S-10 (*lampu a'as*) and the durable S-250 (*lampu bo'ot*). My tasks were to conduct surveys (with the local partner's support), write a series of public blogs and a final technology impact report (to be posted on GF's website), check that distribution and pricing were fair, and find out why d.lights had turned up across the border in Indonesian West Timor, where no such program existed.

A few days later, I was in Oecusse meeting GF's partner organisation, Sustainability Now And Forevermore (henceforth SNAF), the dozen staff of which ran programs in health and adult literacy. GF's partnership with SNAF had begun in late 2010 and, since then, 6,000 d.lights had entered the enclave. GF also covered the wages of two SNAF staff. As stipulated by contract, SNAF was permitted a mark-up of around 15 per cent to its own targeted groups, and slightly more for individuals purchasing a limited number of lamps directly from the office. According to the SNAF director, the subsidised sale price of d.lights was as it should be (between US$6 and US$14 for the three models), but 'some naughty people' had come to the office, claiming to represent a group, had purchased many boxes of d.lights and sold them on at higher prices. Evidently, approximately a hundred d.lights had crossed the border to Indonesia at Melihat (near Passabe).

SNAF showed no enthusiasm for my technology assessment. The director suggested that his staff do the surveys so I could relax on the beach. Insisting on doing the surveys myself, and reminding him of the arrangement that transport would be made available, the director eventually agreed to lend me his personal motorbike. This, however, was the extent of SNAF support: no details about how many d.lights had gone where were available; my request to tag along with staff in the routine distribution of d.lights could not be met because d.lights were apparently out of stock; and a staff member could not be spared to help me with the surveys. So I took to exploring Oecusse's four subdistricts and 18 (or so) villages on my own. From the main routes that connected Pante Makassar to Sakatu (the eastern border with Indonesia), Citrana (western border), Oesilo (southern border) and Passabe (southwestern border), I followed tracks at random. When spotting the bright red d.lights recharging in the sun, I would seek out the owners for surveying.

I soon noticed major discrepancies in pricing. The lamps had been fetching twice, treble or quadruple their subsidy price inside Oecusse and, I would later find, up to tenfold their subsidy price on the Indonesian side of the border. In Oecusse, I made extensive enquiries in order to understand the channels and modes of lamp distribution from the SNAF office to a range of lowland and highland villages. I sought information on how lamps had been directly purchased from the SNAF office by traders or by UN workers, and at what price; which SNAF staff might have been implicated in private mark-ups, how much these mark-ups were, and when and where transactions took place; how lamps might have entered into formal or informal trading chains, and the degree to which successive sales inflated prices; and whether, how and for how much the director, independently of SNAF, had been selling d.lights through his family networks. I also sought to determine how previous evaluators might have been 'kept in the dark'; for example, if they might have been deliberately directed to places where subsidies had been respected (and not elsewhere). I provoked 'admissions' from SNAF staff as to how they or others might have been involved in unofficial d.light sales, and for how long certain distribution models might have been operating since the inception of Radiant Nights.

By combining direct testimony and personal observations, and then categorising and enumerating known instances of d.light sales and purchases, I assembled a perspective on how and when d.lights had been distributed by which actors, and at what prices. I also extrapolated from what I took to be a sufficient number of cases, to generalise about patterns of distribution. However, not everything could be quantified or was empirically straightforward. I considered the fact that SNAF, for example, was not a homogenous entity, that SNAF management and staff might be 'in collusion' on one front but 'in conflict' on another. It was not clear, moreover, exactly where to draw the line between 'unintentional mismanagement' and what some would interpret as 'wilful abuse of contract', as independent trading chains, not SNAF's sales, appeared to be elevating d.light prices to their highest levels; nor could I be certain who was responsible for taking d.lights across the border into Indonesia. This fact-finding effort led me to conclude that some elements within SNAF had been selling d.lights at various sites at inflated prices, even to UN workers, and that SNAF and other actors had turned subsidies into profits.

The director of SNAF, meanwhile, became incensed when he heard of my pricing probe. He called me to his office and confronted me. Nervously, I only acknowledged the possibility that certain SNAF staff might have been raising the price of d.lights behind his back, and that he would need to consider new accountability measures prior to the next delivery of lamps, which, I assured him, would soon be dispatched. The director recovered his composure—and me mine—and from then on attitudes changed: a staff member was ready to help with surveys; boxes of d.lights appeared from behind a locked door; and a 'socialisation session' was arranged for my viewing.

Surveys and publicity

I resumed the surveying with a SNAF staff member. The tried-and-tested method sought information on the constitution of households (number, age, gender), household expenses, lighting methods and costs, and whether and why the various methods were valued, either positively or negatively. The survey also sought information on night-time activities—who performed them, for how long, using which kind of light and user perceptions of the effectiveness of each. It asked how happy respondents were before and after d.lights, and to rate that happiness on a scale of 1 to 10. I modified the survey by adding a raft of questions on income and assets.

While the internal, 'backstage' correspondence with GF concerned the complex methods of distribution (to indict or exonerate SNAF, as the case may be), the information derived from the surveys (and the conversations that surrounded them) sufficed to build a 'front stage' of public blogs that appeared on GF's website for PR purposes. I succeeded in showing how much beneficiaries preferred the brighter light of d.lights over every other light, and I quantified the savings derived from an elimination of or reduction in regular outlay for kerosene, torch batteries and candles. The possession of two or three d.lights, I emphasised, was enough to do away with kerosene and other lighting-related purchases.

My blogs reported mini–case studies, such as one of a certain upland subsistence farmer named Domingas. Although I had been moved by the abject conditions of Domingas' bare existence, I was hardly aware at the time of the gap that opened up between my experience and feelings, on the one hand, and the detachment and calculation that went into my portrait of her, on the other. I made hers a story of forced relocation, personal misfortune, limited agricultural land and a solitary chicken to her name. After her husband had died at home (due to an untreated infection) leaving her alone with two children, she had to make do with an annual income of US$100. Online went a photograph of a painfully thin, unkempt Domingas posing with a d.light in her hand. I described how d.lights had made an appreciable difference to Domingas' life, permitting her an annual saving of US$50. 'Rice, not kerosene, was now her single largest expense', and Domingas was happy because 'she didn't have to sit in the dark anymore'.

Another of my blogs covered the lowland household of the Ulans, a newly-wed couple that, thanks to a micro-credit scheme, had opened three roadside businesses: a grocery store, a garage and a carpentry workshop. Within a few years, their annual income had shot up from almost nothing to a couple of thousand dollars. The blog related to an international audience a story of successful entrepreneurship in which d.lights had played a pivotal role: the acquisition of three in 2010 had set the Ulans back a mere US$30, but had saved them US$400 a year in 'old' lighting costs. I proposed that d.lights had been a driving force behind this young family's upward mobility, as well as their very transition from a near-subsistence household, as it was then, to a semi-subsistence household, as it was now.

These stories were not 'untrue'. And yet I took for granted that they were contrived, front-stage compositions designed to maximise the perceived value of d.lights through the construction of 'promotion subjects'. I would spend the mornings in Oecusse's sole café crafting the sketches, interweaving development, poverty and happiness logics with anecdotes and testimony. The sketches showed that what had once been held out as the 'promised future' of d.lights had materialised. The grounding of these stories in a careful selection of 'the facts' made them credible. However, nobody but me could have known that, of all possible cases, I had highlighted the cases of Domingas and the Ulans because they most graphically illustrated the messages I intended to transmit. Also relegated to the backstage was information about the real cost of d.lights, doubts over reported household expenses and incomes, and impacts on local kerosene traders. That the Ulans were about to upgrade to a solar system with a fixed roof-top panel was not quite an accidental oversight. My all-positive, reductive accounts betrayed the complexity of Timorese livelihoods and the actual role of d.lights therein.

Some of the blogs made their way to ETAN (East Timor & Indonesia Action Network) and other online fora. I drew vain satisfaction from being on the inside celebrating development as opposed to the outside critiquing it. I could not see how anthropological critiques of development applied to the case at hand (Hobart 1993; Meitzner Yoder 2015). I had no concerns about the contrived nature of the d.light stories because in my mind the end justified the means. The real-life 'use value' of the d.lights, after all, was many times greater than the 'purchase value', as I observed through experiment when I unsuccessfully tried to acquire d.lights from their owners at US$100 apiece.

A change of method

As my enthusiasm for d.lights grew, my confidence in the survey method crumbled. I felt frustrated by the routine nature of surveying, I questioned the accuracy of responses and was disconcerted by their predictability. The surveys did support what would have been obvious without surveys; namely, that the people preferred d.lights and saved money through a lesser reliance on 'old' lighting. But beyond that I doubted the surveys could provide 'data' reflecting Timorese experience. It seemed, rather, that they mirrored the development industry's need for disposable PR-oriented information through a method that lent itself to quantification.

On page two of the survey sheet, for example, came the question about activities – exactly which ones did d.lights light up? There were five boxes to fill in with activities, below which came two rows of boxes in which to jot down how many people in the household performed these activities and how long they spent doing them. My question 'what activities do you use d.lights for?' usually returned a blank stare. So, I would prompt my interlocutors: 'Cooking?'; 'Eating?'; 'Washing dishes?'; 'Children's study?'. As for how long they performed these activities each night, my guess was as good as theirs. So the surveys proceeded from one prompted activity to the next as I tried to come up with original prompts.

Needless to say, reflecting on activities, accounting for time and rating happiness were foreign to the respondents. I was worried by the poverty of the data and their eventual, and expected, translation into precise figures of how, when and for how long d.lights were employed. I wondered why d.lights could not be studied as ethnographers would study a spear or a hoe, by following it for some time and watching how the technology is woven into social life. Realising that surveys were more suited to understanding the social life of surveys than the social life of d.lights, I resolved to switch from day shift to night shift. To avoid sitting in huts night after night, I would venture out on a series of night rides, stopping at every d.light I encountered, recording its specific use and making conversation with the owners.

So it happened that on Saturday, 15 June 2013, at 6.45 pm, I left Pante Makassar, riding west into the night along the coast towards Citrana. Just beyond the end of the power grid in Lifau, I chatted to a couple of men who were corralling the pigs with the aid of one S-250. Further along the road, I surprised a family under a d.light-lit verandah who, when asked what they were doing, professed to be 'only sitting'. Beyond the river, I met five people walking along the road with their d.light, who said they were going 'nowhere'. Rounding a curve in the road, I skidded to a halt at one d.light and four girls, who ran off screaming when I dug into my bag for my camera – 'research method needs further refinement', I jotted down in my notebook. Arriving at a village at 7.35 pm, I was advised not to stay out any longer for *ninjas* were about. *Ninjas*, I discovered, were tall figures, dressed all in black with big boots; they stole things and took children's heads, placing them under bridges. After observing d.light use in the village, I motored on towards Citrana in the pitch black, stopping only to photograph one man and two children on the beach scanning the rock pools for trapped fish with their d.light. The man issued a stern warning about *ninjas*. I rode on until the latent, shadowy presence of *ninjas* became too spooky.

I kept up the excursions for the next couple of weeks. I saw d.lights being used for all manner of activities – cooking, eating, weaving, fishing, threshing, shucking, washing, playing cards, looking for something (a cup), going somewhere, getting something or running away from someone. D.lights were also being used for shedding a lamp-light on my own activities, such as to determine who it was calling out at the gate, to complete a remaining survey, or to have my puncture mended in the dead of night. But still, my observations were limited to 'use'. One morning, I came across the words of Tim Ingold (2000: 253), who noted that we have become so intrigued by *seeing* that we have 'lost touch with the experience of light'. I resolved to glimpse beyond the pragmatic *seeing* or *using* d.light beneficiary to the one whose sensibility was imbued with light, shade, colour, glare or tint.

That night was windy and faintly starlit. The rice fields that caught my eye stretched across a plain between black mountains and grey sea. D.lights appeared as constellations of stars, by whose steady glow I navigated my way from the roadside, where I had parked, across an ocean of stubble. Stumbling along, I drew ever closer to the islands of light, of which one became my destination. Soon I was able to discern children's laughter, men's threshing banter, women's gaiety around the open fire, the scent of steaming maize and the drone of a threshing machine. All was suffused in soft light. My next blog read like this:

> D.lights were suspended, perched or sitting in their places around the encampment … This sheltered lightscape was a place of work, fun, conversation and cooking; children, too many to tell, tested that borderland between the light, bright and safe, and the lurking obscurity. The light illuminated men, who fed rice stalks to a grunting machine, and women who stoked the fire and stirred a pot. Shreds of husks blew away downwind, flickering like meteorites; upwind a small child slept on a tarpaulin, blanketed in blue. In the shadows, a woman, her back turned, breastfed; one curious toddler peered out at a stranger from behind her mother's legs; just beyond the circle of light, glowing eyes, perhaps a cat's, reminded us that we could be seen but we could not see them. Yet they could not enter because this defining light was ours, not theirs.

Definitely, d.lights were being used for all sorts of activities. But equally importantly, I added in the blog, d.lights illuminated words, stories, laughter, tears, feelings, touch and furtive glances. They lent colour and clarity to exchanges, expressions and gestures. D.lights were helping to bring people together in socially meaningful and affective ways, to strengthen their bonds, enjoy each other's company, share cigarettes and reinforce their culturally shaped mode of being so they could better be that way at night under brighter light (see Bille and Sorensen 2007).

More than just practical lighting actants, d.lights could be read as subtle ontic modifiers of night-time being. D.lights even illuminated 'non-use'. Children tended to sleep beside a burning d.light all night long, and another one would often be left lighting up the verandah after the grown-ups had turned in. D.light, perhaps, was the all-night light that made people feel safe – safe from prowlers, killers, spirits, ghosts, spooks, witches and *ninjas*. D.light was the only light that could realistically – dare one say economically – be left on *to'o dadeer* (until dawn), as most survey respondents had put it when asked how long they used their d.lights each night. Night-time observation put *to'o dadeer* into context.

Misreading light and GF's editorial erasure

Night research exposed oversights, inaccuracies and even fallacies that had been maintained through the daytime survey. One fallacy, in particular, stood out. A major selling point for Radiant Nights had been that children could now do their homework after the sun went down. Previous surveys, as well as my own, had borne out the fact that d.lights were driving a revolution in children's nocturnal study habits. Over the course of my night rides, however, I saw no kids studying. So where were all the diligent Oecusse kids doing their homework?

It became clear that this dedicated night-time village study did not take place under any kind of light, not even in broad daylight. Kids had no reason to study and no materials to study with. Why, then, did surveys tell us one thing and observation another? The survey's 'study' prompt was partly responsible. But behind the prompt, it seemed to me, lay development imaginaries and policy ideas constantly reiterated by the state and NGOs. What d.light recipients had not picked up through generalised policy dissemination, they had learned through 'socialisation sessions' that accompanied d.light acquisition. By the time people were responding to surveys, they already had a strong sense that children's evening study was highly valued and that saying 'yes' to study was the 'correct' answer – correct in the sense of imitating nation-building ideas of education and progress; to state otherwise, they knew, might have invited disapproval (see Shepherd 2004). 'What has failed us', read a draft blog:

> is not so much the d.lights than the survey method itself. D.lights are therefore just part of the answer to a multifaceted problem, whose resolution must encompass improvements in school infrastructure, teacher professionalism, the availability of study materials and changes in village values.

The same draft blog continued that when the survey method produced fallacies 'there is much to be learned about ourselves and how the development industry shapes knowledge'. GF was troubled by the content of that blog. A coordinator contacted me suggesting that the children of Oecusse had perhaps put their books aside for the holidays.

GF would not have wanted to reveal to its benefactors how it shaped knowledge. Nor would it be inclined to recognise a more complex 'problem configuration', for that did not fit with the promotion of technologies that claimed exclusive rights over 'the solution' – the technology had to be a heroic actant. As both a 'vision of the future' and, subsequently, a demonstrated 'fact', GF had invested heavily in the proposition that d.lights alone would have and had had far-reaching impacts on children's study and, by extension, education and life chances; statistics, graphs, charts and testimony were all advanced as solid evidence. Could it be admitted that this had been a misinterpretation? That equivocal draft blog never found its way onto GF's website.

GF directed me to write the final technology impact assessment. Obligingly, I assembled the same bar graphs and pie charts as other evaluators had done, based on survey data that could not possibly have been accurate and that conferred a misleading authority on the otherwise mostly fair claims concerning the advantages of d.lights. I was told to present information on SNAF's sale of d.lights as an internal document ('Part B'), which I did. No public mention was ever made of GF's termination of partnership with SNAF. (That termination of partnership following my departure from Oecusse may or may not have resulted from my internal reporting.) By the time the technology impact assessment could be viewed online, all my praise for the initiative had been highlighted in bold font, but the inadequacies of the survey method and the program's negligible impacts on education had been erased from the executive summary.

Conclusion

'Our' developer-visions of the future of 'developees' are inevitably expressed as 'their needs', even 'their wants', as if there were some universal rendition thereof (Shepherd 2004: 237). In practice, these needs and wants might be fully or partly fictitious projections, which then become 're-translated' and 'inscribed' in all manner of ways over the course of 'implementation', when they intersect with real local visions, practices and the contingencies of appropriation. The vision of the future inherent in Radiant Nights had many ramifications inside Timor: initiatives were operationalised, partner organisations enrolled, boxes unloaded, technology circulated and d.lights appropriated. Meanwhile, expert opinion was mobilised in the form of foreign evaluators to assess 'impacts' by way of an institutionalised survey method. That method served to confirm the originally anticipated outcomes, correlating expected impacts with actual impacts, and results were channelled into PR.

I then appeared as an evaluator, adopted and expanded the same method, and took to the optimisation of PR. The empirical method showed up all sorts of technology effects, which concerned 'use', but went far beyond it, covering a multitude of practical and affective engagements with the technology. However, the more empirical night-method, as well as a critical approach, showed up discrepancies – discrepancies between the real and purported modes of technology distribution, the real and purported suitability of the survey method, and the real and purported impacts. Then, the backstage was poised to absorb, deflect and conceal the mismatches. This backstage was mobilised precisely because 'the future' had been narrativised in a particular, vested way. The point is not simply that 'the future' failed to materialise as it was supposed to; rather, it is that the tension between the 'unrealised future' and 'reality' materialised all sorts of effects in the here and now in Timor-Leste and beyond, not least of which were the negotiations surrounding my impact assessment.

I may not have been a typical evaluator. Nevertheless, the case puts the spotlight on the otherwise hidden knowledge filters that produce the front and back stages that are activated in an ongoing relationship with future visions. These stages, I believe, structure all development theatres with an acute awareness of how particular initiatives have pictured and promoted a given future; the stages are deployed precisely to manipulate the perceptions of various audiences about 'the future' as it has been projected, anticipated or promised, at some time in the past, to legitimise and resource an intervention. Evaluators, for their part, are drawn into this impression management that casts shadows and light, even though their reporting generally poses as 'neutral'; neutrality itself is a front-stage artifice designed to deny the existence of the hidden transcripts of vested interests, personal desires and so on. None of this is new (see Ferguson 1997; Mosse 2005). If there is anything new to this chapter, it is the proximity of the author to the case at hand: a narrative about an evaluation experience has been formed by a critical ethnographer of development (me) who has had direct access to the subjective world of an evaluator (mine).

As I went about exposing the backstage of the less powerful SNAF and mostly fortifying the front stage of GF, I was doing my own stage work. This centred on matters of power and the web of relationships that I had to work within, as well as touching on various ethical conundrums (Visweswaran 1994). In writing this chapter, too, I remain bound to power relations and risks inherent in representation, particularly when legality is at issue. To be clear, I am not saying that the organisation called SNAF was 'corrupt'. (What one thinks privately is often a different matter.) The antagonistic, simplistic notions of 'corruption' and 'good governance' are context-dependent and interpretatively flexible in ways that defy the normative boundaries imposed by foreign developmentalism. The slippery slope of temptation, the life circumstances of development staff, the 'ordinary commercial impulses' of traders, and the balance of communalism, professional commitments, family obligations and self-interest of management itself, are some factors that contextualise the imported, good-versus-bad moral framework of the development industry.

To relate this personal tale of 'consultancy' to consultancy in general, I would argue that consultant evaluators can only assess 'real impacts' within institutional frameworks of knowledge management, the primary concern of which is to prevent 'visions of the future' from unravelling in a contingent local-development arena where interventions never proceed according to design. Put otherwise, evaluators embark on an orchestrated process of gathering information and representing situations that defend visions, converting 'projected needs' of subject peoples into a kind of institutional capital based on rehearsed demonstrations of positive impacts (Mosse 2005; Shepherd 2004). In my evaluation, I resisted the script at times, but, for the most part, I played the role. Perhaps there was nothing unusual about my 'consultancy experience' after all, except for the fact that I have now written a chapter on it.

In the act of illuminating one set of shadows – the NGO shadows of dubitable modes of distribution, of questionable impacts and of unsatisfactory methods – I have created another set of shadows since, by definition, a chapter such as this can only be a 'public transcript'. Were readers, for example, privy to previous drafts of this chapter or to the editorial deliberations concerning publishable content and appropriate style, they would uncover layers of hidden transcripts in these too. And more hidden transcripts and shadows lie behind the writing of this chapter as well as my experiences in Oecusse in Dili. As academics, researchers or development specialists (and, of course, development beneficiaries too), we are all moving between back and front stages, often uncomfortably aware of our back stage and, ideally, carefully managing the front. This chapter is no less a contrived front-stage performance than the PR portraits of the solar technology recipients in Oecusse – the conventions differ, but the shadows and light are the same.

References

Bille, M. and Sorensen, T. F. (2007) 'An anthropology of luminosity: The agency of light', *Journal of Material Culture*, vol. 12, no. 3, pp. 263–284. doi.org/10.1177/1359183507081894.

Crush, J. (ed.) (1995) *Power of development*, London: Routledge.

Ferguson, J. (1990) *The anti-politics machine: Development, depoliticization and bureaucratic power in Lesotho*, Cambridge: Cambridge University Press.

Ferguson, J. (1997) 'Anthropology and its evil twin: "Development" in the constitution of a discipline', in Cooper, F. and Packard, R. M. (eds) *International development and the social sciences. Essays on the history and politics of knowledge*, Berkeley: University of California Press, pp. 150–175.

Goffman, E. (1959) *The presentation of self in everyday life*, Garden City: Doubleday Anchor Books.

Hobart, M. (ed.) (1993) *An anthropological critique of development: The growth of ignorance*, London: Routledge.

Ingold, T. (2000) *The perception of the environment: Essays on livelihood, dwelling and skill*, London: Routledge. doi.org/10.4324/9780203466025.

Mahmud, T. (1999) 'Postcolonial imaginaries: Alternative development or alternatives to development?', *Transnational Law and Contemporary Problems*, vol. 9, no. 25, pp. 25–34. Available at: digitalcommons.law.seattleu.edu/cgi/viewcontent.cgi?referer=www.google.com/&httpsredir=1&article=1353&context=faculty.

Meitzner Yoder, L. S. (2015) 'The development eraser: Fantastical schemes, aspirational distractions and high modern mega-events in the Oecusse Enclave, Timor-Leste', *Journal of Political Ecology*, vol. 22, pp. 299–321. Available at: jpe.library.arizona.edu/volume_22/Yoder2015.pdf. doi.org/10.2458/v22i1.21110.

Mosse, D. (2005) *Cultivating development: An ethnography of aid policy and practice*, London and Ann Arbor, MI: Pluto Press.

RDTL (Democratic Republic of Timor-Leste) (2002) *Komisaun planu: Timor Lorosa'e 2020: Ita nia nasaun, ita nia futuru*, Dili.

Sachs, W. (ed.) (1992) *The development dictionary: A guide to knowledge and power*, London and New Jersey: Zed.

Scott, J. C. (1992) *Domination and the Arts of Resistance: Hidden Transcripts*, New Haven: Yale University Press.

Shepherd, C. (2004) 'Agricultural hybridity and the "pathology" of traditional ways: The translation of desire and need in postcolonial development', *Journal of Latin American and Caribbean Anthropology*, vol. 9, no. 2, pp. 235–266. doi.org/10.1525/jlca.2004.9.2.235.

Visweswaran, K. (1994) *Fictions of feminist ethnography*, Minneapolis: University of Minnesota Press.

12

Christianity and *kultura*: Visions and pastoral projects[1]

Kelly Silva

The revival of customary practices, known as *kultura, adat* or *usos e costumes* is considered one of the main effects of Timor-Leste's restoration of independence, according to various ethnographic studies (e.g. Barnes 2010; Bovensiepen 2015; McWilliam et al. 2014; Silva 2013; Silva and Simião 2012). It is also a common argument among agents of the Catholic Church. For them, however, such a revival generates not only epistemic anxiety (as it does for researchers) but considerable political worry. This phenomenon is seen as a threat to the hegemony of Catholic Christianity in a country that is, in relative terms, the largest Catholic country in Southeast Asia.

This chapter explores the relationship between *kultura* and Catholicism, addressing discourses and political projects that respond to the revival of *kultura* in Timor-Leste, and examining the perception of some East Timorese priests that Catholicism is being weakened by this revival.[2] From the priests' perspectives, the relations between *kultura* and Christianity are

1   This article is an outcome of research supported by the Brazilian National Council for Scientific and Technological Development (CNPq) by means of grant nos 307043/2012-6, 457845/2014-7 and 310991/2015-3. I have also benefited from a sabbatical year at The Australian National University under the School of Culture, Language and History.
2   In Silva (2013), I discuss – with regard to marriage negotiations in Dili – how *kultura* has encompassed Christianity.

associated with conversion to Christianity. They expect that conversion to Christianity implies discontinuity – a break with practices and beliefs in local spiritual agents (cf. Keane 2007). I examine how my interlocutors try to explain the continuity of Timorese people's commitments to these institutions and their agents. In other words, how they try to make sense of the way in which adherence to Christianity is not effecting (nor, for some, should it effect) discontinuity or rupture. Furthermore, I explore how Catholic clergy attribute the revival of *kultura* to what they see as a *superficial, formalist, passive* and *low-quality* adherence to Catholicism by some Timorese people. Given this fact, some of my interlocutors present projects for purification and monopolisation of faith (Latour 1994) to confront the 'spiritual ecologies' (Palmer 2015), which characterise the mystic practices of most people.[3] Nevertheless, not all clergy in Timor-Leste agree with these attempts to rid Catholicism of the remnants of customary practices; there is no overall consensus on the appropriate relationship between *kultura* and Catholicism. There are ranks within the Church that defend the coexistence between *kultura* and Christianity, arguing in favour of the need for inculturation.

I identify among my interlocutors three distinct projects that shape the relationship between *kultura* and Christianity and motivate interactions of clergy with their parishioners: the first, a project for a tactical use of *kultura* as a transitory means for the introduction and strengthening of Christianity; the second, a project that supports an enduring coexistence and mutual reinforcement of *kultura* and of Christianity, with some selectivity; and the third, a project that seeks the extinction of *kultura*, because of its supposed incompatibility with Christianity.

Such projects cast light on the diverse arrangements the relations between *kultura* and Christianity may take in the future; these projects thus entail visions of what the future of religious life in Timor-Leste should look like. Further, they also express the different trends of cultural change in the

---

3   As carved out by Latour (1994: 16), purification consists of processes of separation and imposition of exclusive ontological frontiers and limits of power among the various experiences, beings and domains that compose social life. By means of these processes of separation, these agencies are either inscribed to certain typical-ideal places for their existence or configurations considered to be legitimate are projected onto them. In this context, one highlights that purification processes are political instruments that produce multiple power effects. Oppositions such as nature and culture, religion and popular beliefs, traditional and modern, politics and science, justice and power, human and non-human, civilised and non-civilised are examples of this separation process.

country.[4] It seems that if the project supporting the mutual enforcement of *kultura* and Christianity will end up being the predominant one, we will see the consolidation of *kultura* and Catholicism as separate yet equally important domains of agency, following the same trend existing in regions of Indonesia (Howell 2001). On the other hand, if the tactical use of *kultura* to strengthen Christianity was to gain prominence, Christianity would be likely to encompass *kultura* in the future. Finally, the project aiming to extinguish *kultura* points to a historical development in which people would internalise an alienated consciousness about their past, present and future, similar to that which Robbins (2004) identified in the Urapmin population (of Papua New Guinea's West Sepik province) in the past decade. This is because such a project is framed by the expectation of rupture with a previous order that is considered morally inferior, while still remaining present in people's modes of social reproduction. Of course, we do not have any means of predicting the future. However, as Bovensiepen (Chapter 6) highlights, such disparate visions of the future affect people's actions and choices in the present.

As in other colonial frontiers, the words custom, *adat*, *kultura* or *usos e costumes* (Bourchier 2007; Davidson and Henley 2008; Mamdani 1998; Roque 2011) were introduced and consolidated in Timor-Leste as contrasting and inter-ethnic categories with floating meanings (Silva and Simião 2017). Most often, these signifiers are used to refer to the practices or values that are perceived to be indigenous or those that are simply different from others deemed foreign. East Timorese people use these categories when they are interested in marking their distinction from others, whether positively or negatively, as do foreign or local agents as self-attributed 'civilising' missionaries, whether religious or civil. From the perspective of some clergy, *kultura* is also a signifier that evokes reminiscences of pagan and earlier religious practices (cf. Keane 2007), which, it is hoped, will be abandoned as soon as possible so that people understand and truly practise Catholicism. Moreover, it is also important to recognise that *kultura* is a category of governance, mobilised by different actors with various political objectives (Silva 2014).

Against this background, the chapter is organised in two main sections. The first explores discourses of the Church's agents concerning the nature of conversion and the adherence of East Timorese people to Christianity.

---

4   Throughout the chapter, I use *kultura* (with a 'k') as an emic category, whereas *culture* (with a 'c') is an etical, analytical concept.

Arguments about the lack of proper understanding of Christianity and the nature of religious experiences among Timor-Leste people are developed in particular subsections the first part is made up of. In the second section, I analyse three pastoral projects concerning the relationship between *kultura* and Catholic Christianity. In the concluding remarks, I consider potential future relationships between Christianity and *kultura* in Timor-Leste, briefly considering some trends in Indonesia and Oceania.

Before I proceed, let me make explicit some methodological and theoretical mediations that have organised the production and analysis of the information discussed below. First, my understanding of pastoral project is oriented by Foucault's (2008: 155–174) term 'pastoral power'; namely, the action of guiding people in their ordinary lives by caring for them. Foucault developed the term 'pastoral power' to describe a form of governmentality typical of religious power first placed in the Near East among Hebrews. He maintains it has evolved from ancient times to contemporary days all over the world, largely by means of Christian religious institutions, but not exclusively. The primary objective of pastoral projects is to bring people closer to God by living a Christian life. To that end, the clergy act as mediators; pastoral power is mobile and it legitimises itself by proclaiming it is doing good.

My interest in the relationship between Christianity and *kultura* developed from a desire to understand practices of marriage exchanges in contemporary Dili. This chapter is based on five interviews I conducted with Timorese priests working in Dili, as well as on interviews published in other sources such as books, the newspaper *A voz da Cultura* (*Voice of culture*) and the newsletter *Revista Seara*. The data discussed was the result of fieldwork carried out in Dili from 2008 to 2013.

Conversion in doubt: Quantity versus quality and the re-evangelising project

The Catholic Church is frequently mentioned as a key influence in Timor-Leste's colonial history in several important respects: the alliance between Church and state and their role in producing 'civilised people'; the role of Dominican missionaries in maintaining Portuguese sovereignty over Timor in the sixteenth and seventeenth centuries; and the Catholic Church's hegemony in the provision of school education in the period of

Estado Novo (the New State)[5] in Portugal (Fernandes 2014). Curiously, however, statistics indicate that only 28 per cent of the population could be considered nominally Christian in the 1970s (Durand 2004: 69).

This situation changed radically during the Indonesian occupation. *Pancasila* (the five tenets of Indonesian state ideology) and the role the Catholic Church acquired in defending human rights were catalysts for the fact that 89 per cent of Timorese people were registered as Catholic (Durand 2004) by the end of the 1990s. The Timorese resistance strategically referred to the increased numbers of Catholics as a reason for why the territory's independence from Indonesia was necessary, where the majority of the population is nominally Islamic.

Reflecting on this period, one of my interlocutors affirmed that, during the Indonesian occupation, the number of people baptised by the Church was more important than the quality of the conversion. To avoid the conversion of Timorese people to Islam – as *Pancasila* obliged the adherence of all Indonesian citizens to a monotheist religion – the Catholic Church promoted mass baptisms. According to him, before 1975, missionaries only baptised those people who were properly prepared in rigid re-education processes. As a consequence, the conversions had a distinct quality. After 1975, the Church began to baptise and administer its sacraments in a less controlled manner. The people who requested the sacraments were not subject to rigorous preparation or, perhaps, had no preparation at all. The effects of this policy, he affirmed, are felt today. The conversion of people to Christianity is more *formal* and *superficial* than *factual,* in his terms.

The Catholic Church became more demanding in the post-independence period. As a condition for receiving certain sacraments, today the Church requires that the person has already received the sacraments that precede the one requested. The Catholic Church also expects the parents and/ or descendants of the prospective adherent to have already received the sacraments for which their children were eligible. For example, for someone to marry in Church, they must prove that they were baptised and confirmed into the Catholic Church, that their parents were married or their children baptised. Nevertheless, there were still considerable

---

5   The New State was a term Antonio Salazar used to describe his government when he was appointed Portugal's prime minister in 1932, the beginning of decades of authoritarian rule.

difficulties in deepening people's Christian religious practice. According to this interlocutor, Timorese people only invest in the Catholic God a tiny portion of the energy that they invest in *kultura*.

Another category that is frequently mobilised to give meaning to how the East Timorese experience Christianity is *dualism*. Some sources understood people to be living between two different worlds: the Christian world and the local one. In the words of one of the priests, 'by day they are Christian, at night they conduct *kultura,* and they like this. Then they come to Church, confess that they did *kultura* and feel pardoned'.

Many couples live together and have children before receiving the Church's sacrament of marriage and only arrange their wedding – with the Catholic mass it entails – when they attain the financial resources necessary to conduct the *kultura*-based marriage exchanges. That fact is often presented as an indicator of their *lack of understanding* or the *superficiality* of their conversion to Christianity. It is suggested that people marry in Church more often because of an attachment to social convention than because of a belief in the sacrament. All the priests I talked to believed that, among Timorese people, attention to *kultura* takes precedence over Christian obligations.

In fact, my conversations with young couples and their families about the dynamics of marriages today confirm *kultura*'s precedence. For them, responding to the expectations of *kultura* – as expressed in the exchange of goods – is more important than a church ceremony. This is because disrespect for *kultura* raises the threat of punishment; however, disrespect for the Christian God does not.

The problem of the lack of understanding

My interlocutors explained the inexistent rupture or discontinuity between local beliefs and Christian ones among Timorese as a *lack of understanding*, either of Christianity or of *kultura*. The alleged lack of understanding is said to be responsible for the subordination of Christianity to *kultura*. In a critical tone, one of my interlocutors affirmed that most people use Christian institutions to support the reproduction of *kultura* and not the opposite. The great challenge for the Church, in the postcolonial context, would be to invert this logic radically.[6]

---

6   Lack of understanding is a category of accusation that seeks to promote moral exclusion, as Boarccaech (2013) indicated in his work among Catholic Christians and adherents to the Assembly of God in Ataúro.

As mentioned above, the allegations of a lack of understanding do not exclusively concern Christianity but also *kultura*. The diversity of practices considered to be *kultura* in Timor-Leste, as well as the absence of a written record of these practices, are said to facilitate this easy transition between local and Christian institutions. People do not experience their coexistence as a contradiction because, according to one interlocutor, they do not have a deep understanding of what is implied by either one of them.

The absence of a unified position from the Catholic Church on local mystical practices was also mentioned as a reason why Timorese people have not broken from their *kultura*. The absence of a unified position is considered to be a product of the diversity and fragmentation of *kultura* on a national scale. As my sources suggested, the lack of an official Church position contributes to a situation in which phenomena that – from an outside perspective – could be considered contradictory are not experienced that way in local daily life. An example is the presence of Catholic priests at inauguration ceremonies for sacred houses or for sepulchres in the backyards of Dili houses. Members of the Catholic Church participating in events dedicated to the cult of local mystical entities is seen to confuse people, making it difficult for them to interpret and experience Christian conversion as a break from *kultura*.

During the Dili fieldwork, I participated in events named as *kultura* in which priests were present. I even witnessed a case in which a priest acted as a *lia-nain* (ritual speaker) to negotiate his niece's marriage exchanges, communicating to the *fetosaa* (wife-takers or the husband's family) what the bride's family expected as gifts. Positions such as these are at times justified to corroborate the project that Christianity be seen as part of *kultura,* not something that is in opposition to or separated from it. I will return to this question later.

Cultural policies

One of my interlocutors perceived the state's appreciation of *kultura* as preventing true Christian conversion of Timorese people. The country's constitution attributes a positive value to *kultura* and public policies that provide financial support and special acknowledgement from the state exist to reconstruct sacred houses (Fidalgo Castro 2015). These facts are interpreted by some Catholic priests as weakening the Catholic Church in Timor-Leste since they place *kultura* and the Church on an equal footing.

In this context, the policies of a laic state – backed by the socialist Fretilin party during its time in government – is frequently quoted as a political challenge to the Church. The conflict between the Church and the Fretilin Government in 2005, concerning the policy to make religious education optional in schools, is mentioned as an example of public policies aimed at weakening the Catholic Church. Others presented the conflict as showing a lack of respect for the role of the Catholic Church leadership in the resistance to Indonesian occupation (Silva 2008). One of my interlocutors associated Fretilin's projects with the Cuban Government's actions in that country after the revolution. It revived the local culture to weaken the Church. Note that for this interlocutor, *kultura* and Christianity were like oil and water: they should not be mixed.

The political and economic interests of older people involved in ritual exchanges are also mentioned as reasons for the absence of rupture between *kultura* and Christianity. Given that *kultura* entails the circulation of goods and money, the older people of the families who, according to custom, should receive these resources, work to reproduce *kultura* because it benefits them.

The religious experience in question: Aesthetic performance or interiority?

What are perceived as East Timorese mentalities are also mobilised to make sense of the way people experience Christian life. The Catholic priests I interviewed for this chapter suggested that, according to East Timorese converts, you would become a Christian simply by affirming that you were one. The newly converted parishioners were not interested in gaining a rational understanding of Christianity or to assume an exclusive commitment to its precepts.

In early 2013, the then Bishop of Dili, Dom Ricardo, travelled to Liquiçá district to prepare young people for confirmation. To evaluate the youths' understanding of the sacrament they would receive, the Bishop chose five teenagers and asked them about the dogmas that would be confirmed. None of those chosen were able to respond correctly. Disappointed, the Bishop cancelled the ceremony and ordered all of them to return to the preparatory course. My interlocutor presented the event as an example of the superficiality of East Timorese people's adherence to Christianity.

In his comparative work about Christianity in Ataúro, Boarccaech (2013) discussed a fact that cast light on features that characterise certain East Timorese people's adherence to Catholicism. To select a religious education teacher in the subdistrict of Ataúro in 2009, the Catholic Church issued a test to measure the candidates' biblical knowledge. Most of them were catechists and masters of the Eucharist. However, the test grades showed that none had sufficient knowledge of the Bible to be able to teach religion.

The five Timorese priests – my interlocutors – suggested that, for most people in their country, being Christian only implied taking part in events of the Christian liturgy, such as the mass, praying the rosary and walking in processions. People were neither concerned about rupture with *kultura* nor with any changes in worldview. The priests saw these facts as a challenge to overcome, to lead people to achieve a more active and aware engagement with Christianity. This diagnosis has engendered projects such as that presented in the book *50 anos da paróquia Sagrado Coração de Becora* (*Fifty years of the Sacred Heart of Becora Parish*) (Silva et al. 2015), a systematic history of the parish and its future plans. The book states that the Church's main challenge is to attract Christians to its regular activities, so they are more active in the institution and thus deepen their faith. The book presents the reactivation of the parish's pastoral council as an essential strategy for making the lay members more engaged with the Church and Christianity. It explains:

> The pastoral council allows those who are baptised to know more and love Jesus Christ more, living according to the Gospel, in words and deeds. The meetings … in the parish are important for them to find their identity and for the quality of their actions. (Silva et al. 2015: 84)

Despite the narratives discussed herein, it is possible for us to interpret the quality of Timorese people's commitment to Christianity in a more positive and less ethnocentric way. As Keane (2007) recalls, the way people conceptualise, experience and reproduce their relation with mystic, supernatural entities and/or other domains of existence (phenomena phased as religion by certain western epistemology) is always a cultural construction. The expectation that religious practice is based on faith, in which external actions are a product of internal and sincere dispositions cannot be universalised. This particular idea, according to Keane, is a Calvinist construction. The understanding that religion concerns a set of subjective beliefs, and not material forms and rituals, was established and consolidated during the Protestant Reformation (ibid.: 67). Protestantism promoted the subordination of external expressions of faith to internal belief (ibid.: 75). Apparently, such subordination and expectation are also shared among the Catholic priests I interviewed.

To explain the way Timorese people experience Christian religiosity, one of my interlocutors affirmed that many people live as Christians based on the ideas that guide their relations with local spiritual agents. There is a sort of projection of meanings and expectations from the realm of *kultura* to the realm of Christianity. In another publication, I hypothesised that religious experiences in Timor-Leste may be thought of as aesthetic management and contemplation, 'given the compulsory nature of its materialisation, highly regulated in the form of rituals where words, relics, sacrifices, and gifts have agency, especially in the *Lulik* [sacred] universe' (Silva and Sousa 2015: 7–8).

The impact of *kultura* and my interlocutors' political anxieties formed the context for their demands, which were framed by expectations of deep changes in the way their compatriots experience their religion. From *superficial* and *formal* experience, they believed it should become *deep* and present in actions in daily life, shaping individuals' internal dispositions. According to the priests I interviewed, religion and culture should be two separate domains, echoing Latour's (1994: 16) description of modernity's drive towards 'purification', according to which material and spiritual spheres need to be neatly separated from one another. There was a need to make the Christian God the sole object of worship, to whom faith and power are attributed. Finally, instead of centring on ritual performance, the religious experience should be based on faith. Therefore, more important than converting people to Christianity through baptism, the pastoral tactic of the Church in the post-independence context has been to 'evangelise the baptised'.

Pastoral practices for re-evangelicalising: Policies for the relationship between *kultura* and Christianity

The non-rupture with *kultura* observed among East Timorese people who adhere to Christianity is a source of frustration for the Catholic Church clergy. This frustration has given rise to different pastoral praxis, aimed at enabling East Timorese people to achieve *true* conversion. Until now, my field studies have identified three ideal types of pastoral projects concerning the relationship of *kultura* and Christianity. Project One: making a tactical use of *kultura* in order to strengthen Christian conducts. Project Two: foster the enduring coexistence and mutual reinforcement of *kultura* and Christianity, with some selectivity. Project Three: banning *kultura* because of its supposed incompatibility with Christianity. In this section, I analyse practices and discourses that illustrate each of these three projects. As ideal types, these projects do not exist in a pure form. Moreover, the ideologies that define them, as well as their effects, may overlap.

The respect and appreciation for what the Catholic Church identified as *kultura* in the mid-1960s, at the conclusion of Vatican Council II, should be a guide for the different pastoral practices of this institution throughout the world. This project was cited by two of my interlocutors who belong to religious orders that have historically used local social reproduction practices to support the introduction of Christian knowledge and behaviour. According to them, it is possible to find the principles of Christianity in most societies, and these existing beliefs should be used to promote the conversion of people. These two sources respectively belong to the Jesuits and Divine Word Missionaries (SVD [*Societas Verbi Divini*]). Both clerical orders are known for making good use of local institutions to introduce Christianity.

In 2012, Father Adriano Ola published an example of the pastoral practice through which elements of the local mystic repertoire are used to introduce Christian conducts or particular visions of the Catholic Church in Timor-Leste. The article 'Fila ba Isin Lolon' ('The return to the body') – in number 14 of the *Revista Seara*, in a section entitled Pastoral Affairs – calls for Catholics to pay attention to their bodies because the body is the home of the holy spirit (Ola 2012). The text's central argument consists of emphasising control over the body, particularly of sexuality, to avoid contracting HIV/AIDS. It is a pedagogical narrative designed to inculcate in readers control over sexuality so that sexual relations are restricted to marriage and monogamous relationships. In this context, HIV/AIDS is presented as a punishment from God for men and women who allegedly do not respect their bodies because they have sex before marriage or are not monogamous. As indicated above, most people are not celibate as it is quite common for couples to live together and have children before marriage in Church. Given this, a major aspect of the proposed conduct is unusual for most people.

The narrative tactic Ola uses to sustain his argument is as important as the argument itself. The article is divided into four sections, which are framed to produce homologies between the Catholic Church and the sacred houses, and analogies between Christianity and *kultura*. In the first section, entitled *Timor nia uma lisan* (*Traditional Houses of Timor*), the author argues that the Catholic Church is the shelter – the support structure for traditional houses. Based on evocations of complementary dualism that characterise the ritual poetry in Eastern Indonesia and Timor-Leste (Fox 1988), Ola suggests that nothing in the world is isolated and absolute – everything needs an opposite to generate balance. What the priest appears to be saying is that the Catholic Church and the *uma lisan* are complementary. It is the relationship between them that generates equilibrium.

In the next section, *Uma kreda* (*The Church*), Ola suggests that each Christian embodies the Church itself. The Church lives in each one of us and Christ is presented as the head of the *matebian* (deceased relatives). He also writes that baptised people should base their faith on the resurrection of Christ. If there is no faith in Christ's and our own resurrection, life loses meaning.

In the third section, entitled *Isin lolon, uma kreda no tradisaun Timor* (*Body, Church and Timorese Tradition*), Ola argues that *lisan* (tradition) serves to fertilise and reproduce the world, in all its senses. The function of the prayers that the *lia-nain* make to their ancestors is the same as the prayers that baptised people make to God; all are conducted to promote the fertilisation and reproduction of life. In this section, he uses as a metaphor the action of sowing. The ritual practices, Christian or pagan, have the objective of sowing to guarantee reproduction and fertility.

In the fourth section, entitled *Problema Ne'ebe ita hasoru* (*The Problem that We Encounter*), Ola presents the contemporary world immersed in crisis. This crisis is generated by the lack of attention to the body as the temple of the Church and of God. He then presents HIV/AIDS as a consequence of people's lack of respect for their bodies, portraying it as a curse, a spell or a punishment from God.

Finally, Ola concludes by affirming that *lisan* and Christianity serve the same ends: *lisan* helps people to connect with each other and to find balance, as does the Church and Christianity. Thus, a homologous conclusion is: just as a consequence of not observing *kultura* is disease and even death, disrespect for Christian precepts generates punishments, such as HIV/AIDS.

We observe that the author uses both local and Christian cultural references to make the facts he is reporting intelligible to the reader. Ola mobilises Christianity and elements of local cosmologies to establish mutual clarifications, although he emphasises the elucidation of Christian elements and the suggestion that HIV/AIDS is God's punishment. At first, the author uses complementary dualism to suggest that the relationship between Christianity and *kultura* (which he calls *lisan*) is not exclusionary. He affirms that these institutions, though within a hierarchy, are complementary. Ola suggests that the Church encompasses *lisan,* reinforcing the idea in the following section where he indicates that Jesus is the chief, the head of the *matebian*. Therefore, he does not deny the existence of the *matebian* but only suggests that Jesus is above them – commanding them, as the Church hosts all the *uma lisan*. He then argues that the functions of the prayers made in a church and by the *lia-nain* are the same: part of the quest for fertilisation and reproduction. Ola later resorts to the rationale that interprets illness as the mystical agents imposing punishment – present in the local networks of causality – to give meaning to the appearance of HIV/AIDS. The subtext of the article is this: active sexuality before or outside of marriage is disrespectful to the body. True Christians should restrict their sex life to marriage and should remain celibate until they marry in Church.

A second project, which can be understood as a radical version of the first, proposes the continuing coexistence between *kultura* and Christianity. This is not just a temporary and tactical use of *kultura* for pedagogical purposes. This is an explicit intention for Christianity to encompass and encapsulate *kultura* to keep *kultura* alive, to reproduce it because it is considered a source of identity. Therefore, the Catholic Church should immerse itself in the local culture ('to inculturate'). Father Matheus, the rector of the Balide parish in 2008, raised this vision in an interview with the newspaper *A voz da Cultura*.

In the interview, entitled 'As normas da cultura não são contraditórias com a doutrina de Jesus' ['The norms of culture do not contradict the doctrine of Jesus'], published on 5 May 2008, Father Matheus suggested that *kultura* and Catholicism are both monotheistic and allow for the recognition of a single higher God (*Maromak*) (Afonso 2008). To support this argument, the priest proposed that *kultura* allows people to be in contact with the spiritual world. Nevertheless, *kultura* does not reveal to people who their supreme ancestors are. It is the Church that does that; the Church reveals that *Maromak* is the highest of the spirits through the revelations of Jesus Christ.

According to Father Matheus, many local religious practices are found in the Bible. He used the example of animal sacrifice. The priest argued that it originates with Abraham as a teaching of God. The priest presented inculturation as the Church's most important pastoral practice, initiated by the incarnation of God in the form of Jesus Christ. Father Matheus described the ontological transformation of God into Man – through His incarnation in Jesus Christ[7] – as the greatest sign of the need for the Church's inculturation. He interpreted the incarnation of God in the form of man as an inculturation of God.

Father Matheus affirmed that the mission of inculturation is to show that all *kulturas* have a positive value and that they have good, positive messages/learnings. *Kultura* would improve if it evolves, taking Jesus Christ into consideration. To do so, some adjustments may be necessary, such as the recognition that *Maromak* is the supreme ancestor.

According to Father Matheus, some of Jesus's teachings imply the need for an adjustment in *kultura*. The priest highlighted that this does not mean losing *kultura*. For example, the custom of giving food to the dead must stop because the dead, as spirits, do not have bodies that need to eat. To avoid contradictions emerging between *kultura* and Christianity, the priest also suggested that people should seek greater knowledge about *kultura* and about Jesus Christ. He said that one cannot stop practising *kultura* because *Maromak* is the foundation for the ancestors. For Father Matheus, *kultura* is a pathway to attain *Maromak* and should be maintained because it lies at the base of peoples' identity.

Other Timorese priests defended an opposite pastoral tactic. They suggested that for people to convert *truly* to Catholicism, it is necessary to eliminate from its liturgy any reference to local religious practices or entities. Also, the presence of local musical instruments or religious songs must not be permitted. In a certain way, such a project resonates expectations and practices shared among most of Christian missionary agents prior to Vatican Council II acting in the Portuguese Timor (Bovensiepen and Rosa 2016). For them, local beliefs in *lulik* powers were

7   I owe this insight to Daniel Simião.

incompatible with Christian values and liturgy. Nevertheless, one of my interlocutors indicated that this position is very difficult to maintain due to the very engagement of the Timorese clergy with local institutions and beliefs.

Most of the Catholic priests I spoke to criticised a position of intolerance or unwillingness to negotiate or understand *kultura*. They said that this lack of knowledge or intolerance present in some of the local clergy was formerly promoted by conservative priests sent to Timor-Leste during Portuguese colonialism. The distant relationship some of the local clergies had with communities resulted from the conservative character of the Catholic Church in Portugal, which acted as the main ideological apparatus of the colonial state. Moreover, my interlocutors suggested that priests have greater or lesser tolerance of local institutions depending on the religious orders to which they belong. Those with clerical orders that have a history of working with techniques of inculturation would mostly be sympathetic to dialogue with *kultura*.

In this context, references to Protestants frequently emerge. Many of my interlocutors propose that Protestants are much more severe and demanding with their converts, compared with the greater tolerance of the Catholic Church to local practices. In fact, the work of Boarccaech (2013) confirms this hypothesis for the case of Ataúro.

In addition to the Catholic Church's greater tolerance or respect for the local religious practices and knowledge, the greater adherence of the Catholic Christians to *kultura* might be explained, at least partially, as a product of how the clergy engage with local communities. In many rural villages, the presence of a priest is rare. At most, he visits a village once a week, or when he is called to give the sacraments; he then leaves, due to pastoral choices or institutional commitments elsewhere. In contrast, the Protestant pastors are much more present. Many of them live permanently in the villages, thus allowing closer and more demanding pastoral oversight. Moreover, I observed that my younger interlocutors had a greater willingness to accept *kultura* than the older ones.

Conclusion: The future of Christianity in Timor-Leste

There was some agreement between my clergy interlocutors, despite the differences framing their pastoral projects and praxis. All of them referred to *kultura* and Christianity as exclusive moral realms and considered most East Timorese people's adherence to the latter as shallow. In other words, at the time of my research, all of them recognised the fact that Christianity did not encompass *kultura* and that religion and *kultura* were different domains of action. Although they shared assumptions, they also pointed to diverse ideal arrangements for the relationship between these two moral orders. To conclude, I discuss some comparative examples from Indonesia and Melanesia in order to think critically about the disparate pastoral visions about the future of the relationship between religion and *kultura* discussed in this chapter.

In the introduction, I suggested that the project supporting the mutual enforcement of *kultura* and Christianity may nourish an understanding of culture that considers religion a realm of action separate from *kultura*. On the one hand, such an arrangement evokes the image of culture as a mosaic, made up of the sum of diverse domains of action that do not overlap, similar to that which Howell (2001) identified among the Lio on the island of Flores and other people in Indonesia.

On the other hand, the current encompassment of Christianity by *kultura*, criticised by my interlocutors and discussed throughout the chapter, recalls a common way of making sense of such a relationship in parts of Melanesia. According to Tonkinson (1982), Christianity is part of *kastom* (custom) in Vanuatu, for instance. The two are not thought of as exclusive domains of action since Christianity (religion) is contained in *kastom*. Conversely to the image of a mosaic, *kastom* and religion relate one another as an alloy, as an amalgam. Opposing that, many of the clergy in Timor-Leste work for Christianity to encompass *kultura*, using the latter in a tactical way. Father Adriano Ola's article in *Revista Seara* is an example of that praxis.

However, the understanding that conversion involves a rupture with a previous and supposedly inferior moral order is very much present in the higher Catholic clergy and among other Christian denominations. For many people, the coexistence of *kultura* and Christianity must be overcome. Such an objective is pursued by derogatory discourses about local ways of life and beliefs that nourish negative representations and a troubled self-awareness for East Timorese people. Whatever the future arrangements between *kultura* and religion will be, the projects and practices this chapter explores have already played a role in shaping them.

References

Afonso, Matheus (2008). 'The norms of culture is not contradict with doctrine of Jesus [*sic*]', Interview by Father Matheus in *A voz da Cultura*, 5 May, p. 6.

Barnes, S. (2010) 'Nation-building and the "resurgence of custom"', in Grenfell, D., Walsh, M., Soares, J., Anselmie, S., Sloman, A., Stead, V. and Trembath, A. (eds) *Nation-building across the urban and rural in Timor-Leste*, Conference Report, Melbourne University: RMIT, pp. 12–14. Available at: cultura.gov.tl/sites/default/files/Conference_report_English_web_combined.pdf.

Boarccaech, A. (2013) *A diferença entre os iguais* [The difference amongst the equals], São Paulo: Editora Porto das Ideias.

Bourchier, D. (2007) 'The romance of *adat* in the Indonesian political imagination and current revival', in Davidson, J. S. and Henley, D. (eds) *The revival of tradition in Indonesian politics: The deployment of adat from colonialism to indigenism*, London: Routledge, pp. 113–129. doi.org/10.4324/9780203965498.

Bovensiepen, J. (2015) *The land of gold: Cultural revival and post-conflict reconstruction in independent Timor-Leste*, Ithaca: Cornell University Press, Southeast Asia Program Publications.

Bovensiepen, J. and Rosa, F. D. (2016) 'Transformations of the sacred in East Timor', *Comparative Studies in Society and History*, vol. 58, no. 3, pp. 664–693. doi.org/10.1017/s0010417516000311.

Davidson, J. S. and Henley, D. (2008) 'In the name of *adat*: Regional perspectives on reform, tradition, and democracy in Indonesia', *Modern Asian Studies*, vol. 42, no. 4, pp. 815–852. doi.org/10.1017/s0026749x07003083.

Durand, F. (2004) *Catholicisme et protestantisme dans l'île de Timor: 1556–2003* [Catholicism and Protantism in Timor Island: 1556–2003], Toulouse, Bangkok: IRESC.

Fernandes, A. J. M. (2014) 'Em searas do Timor Português: Um estudo sobre as práticas de mediação da Diocese de Díli no período colonial (1949–1973)' [The Seara newsletter of Portuguese Timor: A study on Dili Diocese mediation practices in colonial times (1949–1973)], Dissertação de Mestrado [Master's dissertation], Universidade de Brasília.

Fidalgo Castro, A. (2015) 'Objetos incómodos: El lugar de las "uma-lulik" en el Estado-Nación de Timor-Leste' [Uncomfortable objects: The place of the 'uma-lulik' in the Timor-Leste state building], *Cadernos de Arte e Antropologia*, vol. 4, no. 1. Available at: cadernosaa.revues.org/849. doi.org/10.4000/cadernosaa.849.

Foucault, M. (2008) *Segurança, território, população* [Security, territory, population], São Paulo: Martins Fontes.

Fox, J. (1988) 'Introduction', in Fox, J. (ed.) *To speak in pairs: Essays on the ritual languages of Eastern Indonesia*, New York: Cambridge University Press. doi.org/10.1017/CBO9780511551369.001.

Howell, S. (2001) 'Recontextualizing tradition: "Religion", "state" and "tradition" as coexisting modes of sociality among the northern Lio of Indonesia', in Liep, J. (ed.) *Locating cultural creativity*, London: Pluto Press, pp. 144–158. doi.org/10.2307/j.ctt18fs9q6.15.

Keane, W. (2007) *Christian moderns. Freedom and fetish in the mission encounter*, Berkeley: University of California Press.

Latour, B. (1994) *Jamais fomos modernos* [*We have never been modern*], Rio de Janeiro: Editora 34.

Mamdani, M. (1998) *Ciudadano Y súbdito: África contemporánea y el legado del colonialismo tardio* [Citizen and subject: Contemporary Africa and the legacy of late colonialism], Madri: Siglo XXI Editores.

McWilliam, A., Palmer, L. and Shepherd, C. (2014) 'Lulik encounters and cultural frictions in East Timor: Past and present', *The Australian Journal of Anthropology*, vol. 25, no. 3, pp. 304–320. doi.org/10.1111/taja.12101.

Ola, A. (2012) 'Fila ba Isin Lolon', *Revista Seara* 14.

Palmer, L. (2015) *Water politics and spiritual ecology: Custom, environmental governance and development*, London: Routledge. doi.org/10.4324/9781315883250.

Robbins, J. (2004) *Becoming sinners: Christianity and moral torment in a Papua New Guinea society*, Berkeley: University of California Press.

Roque, R. (2011) 'Etnografias coloniais, tecnologias miméticas: A administração colonial e os usos e costumes em Timor-Leste no final do século XIX' [Colonial ethnographies, mimetic technologies: Colonial administration and customs in late nineteenth century Timor-Leste], in Silva, K. and Sousa, L. (eds) *Ita maun alin: O livro do irmão mais novo. Afinidades antropológicas em torno de Timor-Leste* [The younger brother's book. Anthropological affinities around Timor-Leste], Lisboa: Edições Colibri, pp. 155–168.

Silva, A. et al. (2015) *Tinan 50 parokia Sagrado Coração de Jesus Becora* [50 Years of Sagrado Coração de Jesus Becora Parish. From a missionary church to a people's church], Husi igreja Missionário ba Igreja Povu Nian: Dili, Offcet Sylvia Dili.

Silva, K. (2008) 'The Bible as constitution or the constitution as Bible? Nation-state building projects in East Timor', *Horizontes Antropológicos*, vol. 4, pp. 1–16.

Silva, K. (2013) 'Negotiating tradition and nation: Mediations and mediators in the making of urban Timor-Leste', *The Asia Pacific Journal of Anthropology*, vol. 14, no. 5, pp. 455–470. doi.org/10.1080/14442213.2013.821155.

Silva, K. (2014) 'O governo da e pela *kultura*: Complexos locais de governança na formação do Estado em Timor-Leste' [The government of and through *kultura*: Local clusters of governance in Timor-Leste state building], *Revista Crítica de Ciências Sociais*, vol. 104, pp. 123–150. doi.org/10.4000/rccs.5727.

Silva, K. and Simião, D. (2012) 'Coping with "traditions": The analysis of East-Timorese nation building from the perspective of a certain anthropology made in Brazil', *Vibrant*, vol. 9, no. 1, pp. 361–381. doi.org/10.1590/S1809-43412012000100013.

Silva, K. and Simião, D. (2017) 'Negotiating culture and gender expectations in Timor-Leste: Ambiguities in post-colonial governance strategies', in Niner, S. (ed.) *Women and the politics of gender in post-conflict Timor-Leste: Between heaven and earth*, Oxford: Routledge. doi.org/10.4324/9781315657387.

Silva, K. and Sousa, L. (2015) 'Art, agency and power effects in East Timor: Provocations', *Cadernos de Arte e Antropologia*, vol. 4, no. 1, pp. 3–16. Available at: cadernosaa.revues.org/829. doi.org/10.4000/cadernosaa.829.

Tonkinson, R. (1982) 'Kastom in Melanesia: Introduction', *Mankind*, vol. 13, no. 4, 302–305. doi.org/10.1111/j.1835-9310.1982.tb00995.x.

Afterword: A study in contrasts

Andrew McWilliam

I thank Judith Bovensiepen for her invitation to present a closing reflection to this new collection of critical perspectives on contemporary developments in Timor-Leste – now 16 years beyond the historic celebrations of independence in 2002. Today, with the turbulent early years of government seemingly settled in a unity of political purpose and bounteous oil revenues fuelling an ambitious infrastructure program, it is timely to reflect on the impact and implications of these initiatives for the future prosperity of the nation.

In her introduction to the volume, Judith highlights the widespread importance of hope in Timor-Leste society as an underlying and productive commitment to the future and a force for future wellbeing. The resilience of hope and its powerful capacity to sustain life under conditions of hardship was no more eloquently displayed than in the drawn-out Timorese struggle for independence that ultimately prevailed against all odds and ushered in an unprecedented opportunity for societal renewal. For really the first time in the modern history of the region, the people of Timor-Leste found themselves in a position to determine their own future(s) and on their own terms. The unprecedented baby boom that accompanied independence was a peacetime dividend that served to reinforce, in dramatic terms, a fervent belief in the benefits to come.

Nearly two decades later, Timor-Leste citizens remain enthusiastically engaged with processes of post-conflict recovery and the broader challenges of nation-building, but any notion of a collective vision of the future is much more fragmented and widely contested. In the diversely democratic, post-independence landscape of contemporary Timor-Leste, visions of the future among Timorese households reflect a shifting array of personal and shared aspirations directed to sometimes very different material ends, with all working purposefully to shape their own versions of a post-conflict future and better quality of life.

The present volume offers an extended commentary on the range and limits of these visions for the nation in the making. It considers the extent to which the hard-won hopes of independence may yet be fulfilled under the prevailing economic and social trajectories. Given the weight of expectations attaching to these optimistic prospects, the likelihood is that many will be disappointed, and even resentful, when the much-desired and often-promised fruits of independence fail to materialise.

Certainly, there is a persistent scepticism voiced by many observers about the likelihood of success under the current approach to fast-tracked oil resource–based development transformations. Indeed, the failure of exaggerated development claims to fulfil their promise is in many respects a recurrent historical pattern in Timor-Leste. Douglas Kammen's opening chapter reviewing the experiences of former governing regimes of the territory underlines this point. The Portuguese colonial regime's persistently thwarted plans and projects for advancement in order to establish the colony as a financially viable possession is a salutatory lesson. So too is Kammen's critique of the failure of occupying Indonesia to integrate the former colony into a shared territorial unity, and the well-intentioned if misguided regulatory stewardship of successive interim United Nations programs. His examples highlight the risks and pitfalls of trying to engineer prosperity from above in Timor-Leste.

One striking difference, which may make all the difference, is that now the question of who will guide the imaginative future of Timor-Leste devolves to the Timorese themselves and their own elected representatives, rather than those governing on behalf of external powers, however well-intentioned. Timorese resentments over critical commentaries casting doubt on their chances of contemporary success lead to comparisons with the independence struggle and the demonstrated Timorese capacity to prevail against unlikely odds. It is also perhaps not surprising that the terms on which these debates and differences are conceptualised and prosecuted find expression in distinctive cultural and symbolic ways. Two recurring and overlapping thematic distinctions are particularly prominent and inform many of the contributing perspectives in the volume. The distinctions reflect the contrast between (1) regulatory power and ritual authority, and (2) a related distinction around the luminous qualities of lightness and darkness applied to specific knowledge domains and morally inflected fields of action. Both are semantically rich cultural fields with complex symbolic associations and inferences that apply across Timor-Leste. In multiple ways, they are contemporary iterations of what anthropologist James Fox (1980: 333) has previously described in terms of dynamic shared categories of social reproduction expressed as 'metaphors for living encoded in pervasive binary form'.

Regulatory power and ritual authority

One of the sharpest distinctions drawn in the volume is that between the ambitious state-based (*estado*) visions of development (*dezenvolvementu*), underwritten by the still-bounteous revenues from offshore oil resources; versus the quieter, albeit insistent, revivalist practices based around Timorese custom and tradition (*lisan/adat*). The latter in so many ways continues to underpin household and intergenerational wellbeing across the country – the 'good life' (*tempo rai-diak*), as Trindade and Barnes refer to it. Thematically, this distinction expresses a dynamic tension between the regulatory power of the state and the ritual authority of custom. In the contemporary context of Timor-Leste, this can also been seen as a tension between oil and ancestors; between a futuristic imaginary of hyper-modernity versus another more grounded agenda that derives persuasive force from the vital engagement with the agency of ancestors in the present. The tension is variously and insightfully addressed by many of the contributing authors, who demonstrate with a restrained critical appreciation that these two orientations are for the most part divergent fields where much of the population is actively excluded and marginalised in the implementation of government development projects, despite much rhetoric and speechmaking to the contrary. The phrase, 'Development whether you like it or not' (*Hakarak ka lakohi*) neatly encapsulates this relation (see Bovensiepen, Chapter 6).

Laura Meitzner Yoder's critical appreciation of the Oecusse-based ZEESM (*Zonas Especiais de Economia Social de Mercado de Timor-Leste*, or Special Economic Zone of Social Market Economy of Timor-Leste) project also highlights this tension. The ZEESM vision is one that explicitly rejects the past as a source of inspiration and seeks to 'supersede the present' as something wholly new and transformational. Conversely, local Oecusse perspectives cherish the past as an idealised time. The 'past informs the present (and future), providing a framework within which decisions are made and life makes sense', Yoder writes. Her characterisation of the importance of the ancestral past and its relevance to present and future practice resonates strongly with chapters by Viegas, and Trindade and Barnes, where local understandings of the present and future possibilities are inevitably and intimately framed in precisely this way. The most senior Naueti elder of Daralari for example, tells Susana Barnes that 'we should govern ourselves, according to our own customs … That is what we wanted then [1975] and what we want now'. In a similar fashion, Susana de Matos Viegas demonstrates how Fataluku ancestors are integral participants in events of the living and form part of the social collectivity that anticipates future wellbeing. These are not views that seek to reject or supersede the past. On the contrary, they find strength and comfort in its customary embrace and continuing authority.

The growing weight of criticism voiced against what are seen as policy excesses and the heavy financial commitment by government to Timor-Leste megaprojects highlights the emerging division between active participation in the policy process and its commensurate rewards, and those who remain passive onlookers or marginal participants in the whole endeavour. Lavish expenditure and preferential tendering enriches the institutions of state power, business elites and coteries of politically connected clients (Roll, Chapter 7; and Neves, Chapter 3), while disenfranchising the poor and politically marginal. The new reality confirms Douglas Kammen's perceptive point, at least in the context of the various megaprojects, that 'one cannot help but notice that Timorese [people] are almost entirely absent'. These are 'plans without people' and, on the face of it, exemplary models of exactly the high modernist, technical schemes characterised by James Scott (1998) in his critique of the state and its various schemes that prove to be disastrous failures for its citizens.

On the lightness and darkness of being

A second recurring distinction expressed by many of the authors in the volume is the metaphorical contrast between light and dark. Judith Bovensiepen introduces the volume with this distinction, referencing the enthusiastic description of the Tasi Mane infrastructure project by the subdistrict administrator of Betano, who thought these efforts would lead Timor-Leste 'out of darkness and into light'. The allusion references a frequently expressed characterisation of the future in Timor-Leste and one with a long pedigree. Closely tied to allied notions of progress and liberation from ignorance and dogma of the past, it offers a vision of the world that is open to transformation from within (Cascardi 1992: 6). In this respect, the popular sense of progress into the light from darkness arguably has its conceptual origins in the European enlightenment and the self-justifying imperative to spread the assimilationist, civilising mission of western society to far-flung, benighted, colonial dependencies such as Portuguese Timor.

Here the notion of progress and advancement, from darkness into light, is also intimately associated with Catholicism and a relinquishing of the perceived fetishised superstitions of tradition.[1] In Portuguese Timor, the 'civilised' indigenous Timorese (*çivilizados*) denoted individuals who were regarded as culturally modern, which in practice referred to the privileged, urban-dwelling Timorese who had converted to Catholicism; those who had 'seen the shining light' of God's love and teachings as they abandoned the 'morally compromised', traditional customs (*usos e costumes*) of ancestor worship and blood sacrifice. As Webb Keane puts it, 'People first experienced what they understood to be modernity as having a Christian face. Conceptually the idea of modernity seems to have been shaped in a dialectical relationship to a moral understanding of progress and agency' (2007: 47).

In practice, and despite the avowed objectives of the Portuguese civilising mission, the ability of indigenous Timorese (by definition, *nao-çivilizado*) to achieve the status of *çivilizado (*or *assimilado*) was heavily circumscribed and, for most people, unattainable. According to a 1950s source, for example, just 1.8 per cent of the population of Portuguese Timor had managed to achieve this privileged status, but the category included the Portuguese themselves and other non-indigenous populations. It meant that nearly 98 per cent of indigenous Timorese remained outside the enlightened status of the progressive and desirable urban and Catholic modernity (Weatherbee 1966). Today the force of these earlier racial distinctions and discriminations have weakened significantly in the context of postcolonial independence but resonances between town (*cidade*) and country (*povu*), and between the (great) *maun bo'ot* and the (lowly) *ema ki'ik* undoubtedly persist.

---

1   Namely, 'the pagan's inappropriate ascription of agency to non-human subjects' (Keane 2007: 677).

Chris Shepherd in his analysis of certain development practices offers a play on the modernist vision of moving from darkness to light, through his critique of a technical assistance project distributing solar lights into Timorese rural communities. The mismatch between glowing reports of success of the program (known as Radiant Nights) and the rather different realities of practice echoes a broader anthropology of development critique on the failure of expectations of modernity. It also highlights what Shepherd argues is the complex shadow effect of interventions that so often reflect the desires and hopes of the providers of aid and technology rather than the presumed recipients.

Ironically, the cultural values and symbolism associated with darkness and light in terms of metaphorical expressions of indigenous Timorese values and beliefs are, in many ways, the reverse of the presumed trajectory of modernity. Lisa Palmer, in her chapter on the distinction that people of Baucau make between the bright/light world of the living and the dark, powerful world of the ancestors, references the dynamic, ascribed qualities of metallurgy, agency and the materiality of relationships between the living and the dead, and between human and non-human realms. Darkness in this cultural construction is a deeply valued source of authority, protection and blessing, one that provides meaning and direction to the world of the living through reciprocal obligation and sacrificial communication. This is not an orientation motivated by a desire to recreate the past in the present, but rather, as Trindade and Barnes say, people draw on the past to negotiate the future. In this sense, custom or tradition always operates as a contemporary response to the challenges of the present in order to anticipate a better future. In other words, it is the productive combination of darkness and light that ensures a prosperous future, not a rejection of the former in favour of the latter.

Beyond the resource curse

The aspirational vision of the state championed in the *Timor-Leste Strategic Development Plan 2011–2030* includes two especially ambitious objectives. First, it declares a goal for Timor-Leste to become an upper-income country with a healthy, well-educated population by 2030; and second, it seeks to secure the foundations of a sustainable and vibrant economy through the development of the petroleum sector. The latter objective is seen explicitly as a vital prerequisite for the broader goal and a recognition that, for the near future at least, Timor-Leste's economic fortunes will rest on its capacity to further develop and build upon oil- and gas-based revenues to underwrite state budgets and investment. The present government is pursuing this development course and remains seemingly steadfast in its commitment to multimillion-dollar investments in infrastructure projects, like those of Tasi Mane and ZEESM, to fulfil their aspirational visions.

This approach is problematic, however, because it invites precisely the litany of economic and developmental problems generated by the now familiar and distorting effects of the resource curse. Authors in the present volume illustrate this aspect in compelling detail (see Neves, Almeida, Meitzner Yoder and Bovensiepen), and the result of a singular focus on oil and gas is that it leaves precious little space or consideration of alternative approaches to Timorese livelihood futures. In fact, the non-oil sectors of Timor-Leste's economy, particularly agriculture in its broadest sense, upon which most of the population still depend, have suffered under the seductive attractions of lucrative oil revenues. All of the productive primary industries, including food crops, fisheries and forestry production have been marginalised and underfunded since independence. By way of example, within the US\$1.7 billion national budget for Timor-Leste in 2014, a very modest US\$36 million, or just 2 per cent of the budget, was allocated to the agriculture portfolio, which also includes forestry and fisheries development. From another perspective, imports of subsidised Vietnamese rice, now well over 100,000 metric tonnes per annum, have effectively undercut and out-competed local producers, thereby creating a major deterrent to increased domestic production and undermining any prospects of food sovereignty in the future (Young 2013).[2] Even the coffee subsector, which has been the leading non-oil export commodity for many years (currently valued at US\$17.8 million per year), holds out little prospects for expansion or significantly increased yields (OEC n.d.).

One might conclude that policymakers in Timor-Leste have largely given up on agriculture as a prospective alternative pathway to prosperity, or at least as a major contributor to the economic future of the country. The reality is that despite the declining levels of oil and gas production and the absence of any significant new production fields and platforms under development, Timor-Leste remains overwhelmingly dependent on

---

2   Even as economic studies such as Young (2013) highlight the cost-effectiveness of imported rice versus domestic production.

its oil revenues at 76 per cent of gross domestic product (GDP). This compares with just 4.7 per cent of GDP derived from productive parts of the economy, largely limited to agriculture and local manufacturing (Scheiner 2015: 75). Moreover, this situation is unlikely to change anytime soon, because the current arrangements are providing windfall gains to well-positioned vested interests and beneficiaries of the bounteous flow of petro-dollars. This is also the point of Guteriano Neves when he concludes that:

> A vision of the future of Timor-Leste based on oil is a vision that will decidedly benefit the elites. If we are to envision a future that includes and benefits everyone, it will have to be one without oil.

But it might also be one where the relative contribution of oil revenues is dramatically reduced.[3] Either way, the challenge of moving beyond the resource curse and building a vibrant, diverse and inclusive economy for the benefit of all remains an elusive one that looms increasingly large as time goes by.

So, in the spirit of offering a prospective contribution to the shape of this alternative economic landscape beyond the resource curse, I will close by highlighting one prospective new development sector within Timor-Leste. This is the rapid expansion of international labour migration opportunities for young workers and the subsequent growing return flow of cash remittances to grateful Timor-Leste households and communities.

For some years now, the Government of Timor-Leste has been actively supporting a number of formal bilateral agreements with regional neighbours (Malaysia, South Korea and Australia). These alliances have focused on temporary in-country employment arrangements that have enabled participants to generate lucrative savings through limited-term overseas work contracts (see Thu and Silva 2013; Wigglesworth and Fonseca 2016). While offering significant personal benefits for those involved and generating some US$11.2 million in 2017 (Curtain 2018), these programs were overshadowed by the highly popular and spontaneous informal labour migration to Western Europe, and especially the United Kingdom. This latter pathway has attracted thousands of young, mostly male, participants from different areas of Timor-Leste, travelling on Portuguese passports and embracing low-skilled but comparatively

---

3   The 2018 bilateral agreement between Timor-Leste and Australia to settle the maritime boundary in the Timor Sea paves the way for the much-delayed exploitation of the Greater Sunrise oil and gas fields and with it a major new source of petro-dollars in the longer term.

lucrative work in the service towns and factories of England and Northern Ireland (McWilliam 2012, 2015). Estimates that up to 16,000 young Timorese may have taken this option over recent years are based on data sourced from the Portuguese Embassy in Dili (Staff of the Census Team, pers. comm., 2015).[4]

In a study of the impact of Timorese labour migration to the United Kingdom (Reis et al. 2016), the authors reported data on overseas fund transfers into Timor-Leste. They looked specifically at cash transfers via Western Union and Moneygram facilities for the calendar year 2015. Western Union in particular is the preferred channel for delivering cash remittances into Dili by UK-based Timorese migrants. According to the report, a total of nearly US$25 million (US$24,933,632) was remitted in 2015, and of this amount fully 75 per cent of the funds derived from the United Kingdom (US$18,700,227). In comparative terms, these transfers are greater that the total export value of the Timor-Leste coffee crop and the tourism industry. It means that informal labour migration may well now provide the most significant source of non-oil revenue for the country. I note that these figures are also likely to capture only a portion of the total remitted funds from UK employment, given that many returning and visiting labour migrants often carry with them substantial amounts of undeclared cash for distribution to relatives and family in Timor.[5]

Although the macro-economic impact of these cash remittances remains comparatively modest, the growth of the remittance economy in Timor-Leste is having powerful transformative effects for those households benefiting from regular infusions of cash (McWilliam 2012; Shuaib 2008).[6] These developments point to new opportunities for young people in Timor-Leste to imagine rather different futures for themselves than those of earlier generations; futures that go well beyond the distorting impacts of the resource curse and point to new and viable livelihood pathways to prosperity. I see these developments as grounds for optimism, offering the prospect that Timor-Leste will yet achieve the rewards of the 'good life', the *rai tempo diak*, that its citizens have long sought and surely deserve.

---

4   The 2015 National Census recorded a total of 5,345 Timor-Leste citizens living in what they classified as 'Other European Countries (excluding Portugal)', the vast majority of whom are likely to reside in Britain.
5   A widespread practice undertaken to avoid paying the high commissions charged by Western Union and as a kind of courier service for friends in the UK who wish to send money back to their own relatives.
6   The implications of the recent Brexit vote notwithstanding. Just how formal separation from the European Union affects Timorese work opportunities in Britain remains a work in progress.

References

Cascardi, A. J. (1992) *The subject of modernity*, Cambridge: Cambridge University Press. doi.org/10.1017/CBO9780511597428.

Curtain, R. (2018) 'Remittances biggest export earner for Timor-Leste after oil', *Devpolicy Blog*. Available at: www.devpolicy.org/remittances-biggest-export-earner-for-timor-leste-after-oil-20180322/ [accessed 15 July 2018].

Fox, J. J. (ed.) (1980) *The flow of life: Essays on eastern Indonesia*, Harvard: Harvard University Press. doi.org/10.4159/harvard.9780674331907.

Keane, W. (2007) *Christian moderns: Freedom and fetish in the mission encounter*, Berkeley: University of California Press.

McWilliam, A. R. (2012) 'New Fataluku diasporas and landscapes of remittance and return', *Global, Local: Identity, Security, Community*, vol. 11, pp. 72–85.

McWilliam, A. R. (2015) 'Time and the other for transnational Timorese migrants: Changing patterns of engagement', paper presented at the American Anthropological Association Annual Meeting, 18–22 November, Denver, Colorado.

OEC (The Observatory of Economic Complexity) (n.d.) 'Timor-Leste', *OEC*. Available at: atlas.media.mit.edu/en/profile/country/tls/#Exports [accessed 12 December 2017].

Reis J. S, Cabral, L. D. and Valentim, J. V. (2016) *Impaktu Traballador Iha Ingleterra no Norte Irlandia be Prosperiedade Familia iha Munisipiu Lautem*, Final report, Asia Foundation, Jakarta, with support of PLG (Policy Leaders Group) and Australian Aid.

Scheiner, C. (2015) 'Can the Petroleum Fund exorcise the resource curse from Timor-Leste?', in Ingram S, Kent, L. and McWilliam, A. R. (eds) *A new era? Timor Leste after the UN*, Canberra: ANU Press, pp. 73–101. doi.org/10.22459/NE.09.2015.06.

Scott, J. C. (1998) *Seeing like a state: How certain schemes to improve the human condition have failed*, Yale: Yale University Press.

Shuaib, F. (2008) *East Timor country report*, Canberra: Department of Foreign Affairs and Trade.

Thu, P. M. and Silva, I. M. da (2013) *The Australian seasonal workers program: Timor-Leste's case*, SSGM In Brief 2013/13, Canberra: State, Society & Governance in Melanesia, ANU. Available at: ips.cap.anu.edu.au/ssgm.

Weatherbee, D. (1966) 'Portuguese Timor: An Indonesian dilemma', *Asian Survey*, vol. 6, issue 2, pp. 683–695. doi.org/10.2307/2642194.

Wigglesworth, A. and Fonseca, Z. (2016) 'Experiences of young Timorese as migrant workers in Korea'. Paper presented at the 2016 Australasian Aid Conference, Canberra.

Young, P. (2013) *Impacts of rice imports on rive production in Timor-Leste*, Commissioned study for the Seeds of Life program, Dili: Ministry of Agriculture and Fisheries, Timor-Leste.

www.ingramcontent.com/pod-product-compliance
Lightning Source LLC
Chambersburg PA
CBHW040150270326
41926CB00063B/4625